EDITIONS SR

Volume 19

Memory and Hope
Strands of Canadian Baptist History

David T. Priestley, Editor

Published for the Canadian Corporation for Studies in
Religion / Corporation Canadienne des Sciences Religieuses
by Wilfrid Laurier University Press

1996

Canadian Cataloguing in Publication Data

Main entry under title:

Memory and hope

(Editions SR ; 19)
Includes bibliographical references and index.
ISBN 0-88920-267-2

1. Baptists – Canada – History.   I. Priestley,
David T. (David Thomas), 1936-   . II. Canadian
Corporation for Studies in Religion.   III. Series.

BX6251.M45 1996   286'.171   C95-933122-0

Cover design by Leslie Macredie

Printed in Canada

Memory and Hope: Strands of Canadian Baptist History has been produced
from a manuscript supplied in camera-ready form by the author.

Order from:
WILFRID LAURIER UNIVERSITY PRESS
Waterloo, Ontario, Canada   N2L 3C5

Table of Contents

Part Three: People and Their Contributions

Illustrations

Maps

Tables

Contributors

G. Richard Blackaby, minister, Friendship Baptist Church, Headingley, Manitoba; currently, president, Canadian Southern Baptist Seminary, Cochrane, Alberta.

Judith Colwell, archivist/librarian, Canadian Baptist Archives, McMaster Divinity College, Hamilton, Ontario.

David R. Elliott, guest lecturer in religious studies, University of Victoria, Victoria, British Columbia; currently, Francis Xavier University, Antigonish, Nova Scotia.

Walter E. Ellis, minister, Fairview Baptist Church, Vancouver, British Columbia, and part-time lecturer in political science, Trinity Western University, Langley, British Columbia; currently, retired in Victoria, British Columbia.

William Gillespie, private scholar; minister of Priory Park Baptist Church, Guelph, Ontario (1978-86).

Philip G. A. Griffin-Allwood, minister, Lawrencetown United Baptist Church, Lawrencetown, Nova Scotia.

Barry D. Morrison, minister, Westmount Baptist Church, Montreal, Quebec.

Mark Parent, minister, First Moncton United Baptist Church, Moncton, New Brunswick; currently minister, Tereaux United Baptist Church, Canning, Nova Scotia, and visiting lecturer at Mount Allison University, Halifax.

Ernest K. Pasiciel, professor of history, Providence Bible College and Theological Seminary, Otterburne, Manitoba.

David T. Priestley, professor of historical theology, Edmonton Baptist Seminary, Edmonton, Alberta.

Harry A. Renfree, retired executive minister and pastor, Canadian Baptist Federation, Victoria, British Columbia.

J. Brian Scott, international development consultant (CIDA) and part-time instructor in religious studies, University of Ottawa and Carleton University, Ottawa, Ontario.

Paul R. Wilson, doctoral candidate, University of Western Ontario, London, Ontario.

Jarold K. Zeman, professor of church history, Acadia Divinity College, Wolfville, Nova Scotia; currently, director of the Acadia Centre of Baptist and Anabaptist Studies, Wolfville, Nova Scotia.

Abbreviations

ABHMS	American Baptist Home Mission Society
ABHS	American Baptist Historical Society
ABMU	American Baptist Missionary Union (earlier, American Baptist Foreign Mission Society)
ABQ	*American Baptist Quarterly*
AUA	Acadia University Archives, Vaughan Memorial Library, Wolfville, Nova Scotia
BCOQ	Baptist Convention of Ontario and Quebec
BGC	Baptist General Conference (USA)
BGCC	Baptist General Conference of Canada
BHAC	Baptist Heritage in Atlantic Canada (documentary series)
BUWC	Baptist Union of Western Canada
BYB	*Baptist Year Book* (earlier, *Canadian Baptist Register*)
CB	*The Canadian Baptist*
CBA	Canadian Baptist Archives, McMaster Divinity College, Hamilton, Ontario
CBF	Canadian Baptist Federation/Federation of Canadian Baptists
CBR	*Canadian Baptist Register*
CCSB	Canadian Convention of Southern Baptists
EFC	Evangelical Fellowship of Canada
FEBC	Fellowship of Evangelical Baptist Churches in Canada
NABA	North American Baptist Archives, North American Baptist Seminary, Sioux Falls, South Dakota
NABC	North American Baptist Conference
NAC	National Archives of Canada
SBC	Southern Baptist Convention (USA)
UBCAP	United Baptist Convention of the Atlantic Provinces (earlier, UBC of the Maritime Provinces)
UFBC	Union of French Baptist Churches/Union d'Églises Baptistes Françaises au Canada

Introduction

Strands of One Cord

David T. Priestley

Baptists have shared in the multifaceted development of the Protestant churches in Canada. Although their tradition originated in 17th-century English Puritanism, their beginnings here are solidly within the larger movement of North American evangelicalism. Their first Canadian congregations appeared temporarily among the Maritime "planters" in the 1760s who brought with them the ethos and issues of the New England Great Awakening. Nova Scotia revivals in the 1770s and 1780s generated permanent Baptist churches among Congregational and Presbyterian New Lights, by the same process that had formed "Separate" Baptist churches in New England in the 1750s. In Central Canada, Baptists were among the religiously diverse United Empire Loyalists who migrated into what remained of British North America after 1783.

Beyond their specifically religious contributions, the single major "constitutional" impact Baptists have had on Canadian life came in the area of education. In 1841, in the face of exclusively Anglican or Presbyterian schools in the colony, they founded the first Nova Scotia college without confessional tests for students or faculty (now Acadia University). Later, they were integral in the movement to secularize the clergy reserves in Central Canada, funds that in 1854 provided the beginnings for public education in Ontario. If they since have been in the public eye only rarely, they shared the evangelical agenda for Canada and pursued it vigorously with Congregationalists, Methodists, and Presbyterians throughout the 19th century and into the 20th.

Interdenominational cooperation involved Baptists in all the social and theological changes that have affected Canadian churches since 1800. Evangelical ecumenism blunted their ecclesiological distinctives. Theological imitation influenced them toward late-19th-century liberalism. Evangelical passion for social reform engaged some in early 20th-century Social Gospel activism. The fundamentalist controversies of the 1920s divided Baptists into separate bodies in both central and western Canada; in the Maritimes, these strains came to a head, though not to separation, only after World War II when the force of liberal evangelicalism was diminishing.[1]

1

The North American-United Kingdom evangelical milieu for these currents among Baptists in Canada was diversified further by continental Baptists and others of pietistic and biblicistic orientation (Germans, Scandinavians, Ukrainians, Czechoslovaks, Hungarians) who began to immigrate in the late 19th century. Half a century earlier, freed and fugitive slaves from the United States had begun black congregations in Atlantic and central Canada. Twentieth-century immigration from the Caribbean, Southeast Asia, and Latin America continues to multiply the racial and ethnic strands among Canadian Baptists.

Susceptibility to American example and appeals for American advice have been constant, often inconspicuous, though sometimes overt. North-south migration to settle, to study, to teach, to evangelize, and to serve congregations has sustained a constant current of American Baptist and evangelical thought and practice among Baptists here. These colonial origins have been tempered constantly by confessional literature from England and Scotland and by transatlantic immigration.

The influence of the United Church of Canada (UCC) and its antecedent bodies also has been continuous and varied, once the polemical relations of the early 19th century were superseded by the ecumenicity of evangelicalism and the joint struggle for religious pluralism in Canada. Cooperation stopped short of merger, however, when the Baptist Convention of Ontario and Quebec in 1907 formally refused the invitation to cooperate in the talks out of which the United Church arose in 1925. Nevertheless, the Baptists shared a hymnal with the UCC from 1936-73 and jointly produced church school curriculum from 1938-65. Thus, many strands of life and doctrine are entwined into the cord that constitutes "Baptists" in Canada.

Organizationally, also, Baptists are distinguished in several strands. More than ten "denominations" share a common history and preserve a distinct past. The Canadian Baptist Federation (CBF) unites four regional bodies in by far the largest strand: the United Baptist Convention of the Atlantic Provinces (UBCAP), the Baptist Convention of Ontario and Quebec (BCOQ), the Union of French Baptist Churches (UFBC), and the Baptist Union of Western Canada (BUWC). The CBF roots are farthest back in Canadian history, roots which are American, English, and Scottish, making them the "oldline" senior tradition.

Three bodies are offshoots of CBF unions from which congregations and individuals separated in the wake of the modernist-fundamentalist controversies of the 1920s: the Association of Regular Baptist Churches in Ontario (ARBC), the Canadian Convention of Southern Baptists (CCSB), and the Fellowship of Evangelical Baptist Churches in Canada (FEBC). The latter two pursue vigorous church-planting policies across the country.

Two small groups maintain theological distinctions that arose in the 17th century: the Free Will Baptists (FWB) and the Seventh-Day Baptists

(SDB). Canadian congregations of the former persuasion have existed since the 18th century; the latter appeared in Canada only in 1978.

Three fellowships persist from ethnic origins among German, Scandinavian, and Ukrainian immigrants respectively. The North American Baptist Conference (NABC) and the Baptist General Conference in Canada (BGCC) have full denominational structures; and in the urban and suburban communities where their churches minister, the ethnic roots are no longer relevant. The Ukrainian Evangelical Baptist Convention of Canada (and the Union of Slavic Churches of Evangelical Christians and Slavic Baptists of Canada) remain a strongly ethnic fellowship; most of their churches are dually aligned with one of the other Baptist bodies. Uncounted congregations originating as ethnic churches have assimilated into the Anglophone unions.

A count of unaffiliated Baptist churches and independent baptistic "community" churches is impossible, though the total might be significant relative to those in unions and conventions. While this fragmentation complicates the story, the denomination is considerably more unified in Canada than in the United States with its some twenty separate conventions. Distinct though the strands of history, ethnicity, region, theology, and structure may be, they entwine in a single cord of broad confessional and practical agreement.

The historical essays gathered in this volume examine both the unity and the diversity of this confessional cord. The study of Canadian Baptist history has experienced a national flowering in the past twenty years.[2] One catalyst has been Jarold K. Zeman, professor of church history, Acadia Divinity College, Wolfville, Nova Scotia (1968-91). He planned two Baptist Heritage Conferences at Acadia Divinity College and edited the papers for publication; he participated in three similar events sponsored by other schools.[3] In classroom, correspondence, and conversation, he has encouraged students and colleagues to explore, document, and interpret this heritage. Scholars and general interest readers alike are beneficiaries of the productivity his enthusiasm has generated; of particular value is *Baptists in Canada 1760-1990: A Bibliography of Selected Printed Resources in English.*[4] From another perspective, George A. Rawlyk at Queen's University applied his skills and insights as a historian to study Canada's larger religious heritage and as teacher and editor to encourage research far beyond the limits of one denomination's history.[5]

The studies presented here were read first at the 1990 Baptist Heritage Conference in Edmonton. They discuss individuals, institutions, and issues which have stirred Baptists in "the hard part of North America" for two centuries. They present recurrent concerns in education, overseas mission, domestic church planting, and social responsibility. They examine how they relate to one another and the whole Church. They describe how, professing to follow the authority of the word of God and to cultivate an experience of the grace of God, these kinds of Christians in our nation have proclaimed and responded to that experienced word in different ways.

These essays bring into focus elements of Baptist history in central and western Canada; other papers that address the Atlantic Baptist story are published elsewhere.[6] As noted above, the history of Canada's Baptist churches and their agencies is not simple or unilinear. The following essays fit at different points into that narrative of diversity and unity. The information, insights, and ideas they offer enlarge and refine the picture of Canada's Baptists; many aspects will doubtless find parallels in other confessional bodies. They illustrate the diversity of ideas, movements, and personalities that have shaped and resulted from a once-distinctive confessional movement. They also favourably represent the current state of denominational historical studies.

Fittingly representing his recent influence, Jarold K. Zeman's keynote address gives his call and suggestions for the task of research and dissemination at local, regional, and national levels (chap. 1). He sees history as the task of the congregation and pastor no less than of the professional; remembering and preserving is essential for healthy continuance. There is nothing parochial or sectarian about this appeal; it asks all Christians to cultivate a memory and thereby sustain an identity.

The perception is widespread even among Baptists that, apart from the questions of who is to be baptized and how much water is necessary, they are a theologically indifferent ecclesial movement. These chapters challenge that misapprehension. The two chapters of Part 1 address *ideas* that continue to concern Baptists in Canada—confessionalism and eucharistic theology and larger theological currents shape the movements and persons introduced in succeeding chapters.

Since the 17th century, Baptists have been assiduous composers of theological confessions.[7] Colonial Baptists had assumed that congregational identity and cooperation in other ministries grows out of theological agreement. William Gillespie surveys the Ontario tradition (borrowed from New York and New England) that included a "compendium of doctrine" as one of the first articles in association constitutions (chap. 2). He argues that for reasons of administrative centralization and ecumenical cooperation a policy shift about such compendia took place in the BCOQ after WWII; "religious liberty" came to be prized over confessional or theological definition. The poignancy of this description is that it appears to confirm the theological charges made in the twenties out of which the FEBC later took shape.[8]

Immersion only after voluntary confession of faith has been the consistent hallmark of the movement. Understanding and celebration of the second Christian sacrament has been less stable. The Lord's Supper underwent considerable reduction among Baptists during the 19th century. Barry

D. Morrison thinks that a simplistic Protestant reaction against Roman Catholicism has destroyed 20th-century Baptist memory of the classic Calvinist and Puritan sacramental theology found in the earliest confessional and polemical writings of the movement (chap. 3). Using *Baptism, Eucharist, and Ministry* as a springboard, the chapter challenges Baptists also to rethink this aspect of their faith and order. To aid that reconsideration he analyzes the writings of John Smyth, the Separatist minister out of whose Amsterdam congregation the first Baptist church appeared in 1611.

The strands that combine in the Baptist family of churches are also structural (Part 2). Among the *movements* that have contributed to their diversity in Canada are immigration, theology, and society. Ethnicity has been a criterion by which congregations have gathered and associated regionally. Two essays describe the effort and effect of Baptist evangelism and church planting among Germans who immigrated to western Canada from 1880 to 1960. David T. Priestley traces the birth of congregations and the rise of institutions in Alberta that persist today as the largest of the province's five Baptist unions (chap. 4). In cooperation with the "German Baptist Convention" formed earlier in the United States and with financial aid from both Canadian and American Baptists, churches were organized on the prairies and in the cities of the province. They soon formed an association and later founded a college and a seminary. Ethnicity and evangelicalism combine in a story of assimilation and distinctiveness.

Ernest K. Pasiciel uses H. Richard Niebuhr's categories to take a broad sociological look at these immigrant Baptists and finds that they change significantly between 1883 and 1974 (chap. 5). Ethnic isolation diminishes; socioeconomic status rises; geographical concentrations shift westward; women and youth are given greater public roles. The net result is that NABs have become "virtually indistinguishable" among evangelicals.

Ethnicity combined with theology in another time and place. The Scots who organized the "Particular Covenanted Baptist Church of Canada" (1840s) are more peripheral to the larger Ontario Baptist story than are the Germans in Alberta; but a memory of these few whose strict Calvinism seems peculiar even to most who share the name "Baptist" today is worthy of preservation. Paul R. Wilson relates the fruit of his investigations into "old school" Baptists in Elgin County, Ontario (chap. 6). Theology made evangelism problematic for them after the first generation (1818ff.) though in politics and education they played significant roles in their townships. Their loyalty to a distinctive theology and self-understanding makes their future doubtful.

In Canada's prairies and western mountains, theological controversies resembling those in Ontario split the BUWC in 1927. G. Richard Blackaby traces how the initially fragmented conservatives, particularly in

British Columbia and Alberta, sought to organize cooperative agencies and find resources to maintain their "baptistness" (chap. 7). Some found a focal point in the literature, programs, and missions of the Southern Baptist Sunday School Board. Political manoeuverings within the Southern Baptist Convention in consultation with other Baptist unions in North America resulted in the formation of a "truly Canadian" Convention of Southern Baptists in 1984. Precipitated by theology, this small movement arose to serve the purposes of orthodoxy and fellowship.[9]

Baptists relate not only among themselves but also with other Christian churches. Walter E. Ellis, political scientist and theologian, surveyed the mobility of Baptists in western Canada in the 1980s to determine how important denominational identity is to the average church member (chap. 8). Membership transfers in and out of the responding congregations reveal ambiguous commitments to evangelicalism, ecumenism, Baptist confessionalism, and personal origins. He finds these statistics generate little hope about denominational futures but support his partisan proposal.

Some like to accuse Baptists of being a people with little sense of Church beyond the local congregation; even when they find ways to relate among themselves, they are supposed to just as promptly find ways to dissociate. Contrariwise, Philip G. A. Griffin-Allwood surveys Baptist impulses toward denominational cooperation from the early 19th century through the formation of the Canadian Baptist Federation in 1944 (chap. 9). Far from being a "fissiparous folk," it would appear that Canadian Baptists more often have responded to the magnetism of cooperation.

Harry A. Renfree even perceives potential for tightening of the strands as he surveys the Baptist story in Canada (chap. 10). Distilling impressions from his national history of the denomination,[10] he observes that the constant impulse to alliance among churches and associations has recently found expression in "doctrinal restoration." Furthermore, growing interunion cooperation suggests that Baptists are moving toward a recognition of their common heritage rather than reinforcing their past differences.

History is more than biography writ large. Nonetheless, *people* weave ideas into action and entwine them in movements. Four essays describe Canadian Baptists who represent diversity and agreement in thought and mission.[11]

Baptists played a central role in the modern missionary movement. Initially, Canadians served under the American Baptist Foreign Mission Society (ABMU). Until a Canadian mission agency was organized in 1873, local associations might have underwritten as much as full support for missionaries from their churches; but the administration was left to the American society. Judith Colwell tells of the first Canadian-born missionary (chap. 11). Samuel Stearns Day served in India from 1836-53 and subsequently promoted mission needs for the ABMU until 1859; he illustrates the family and health difficulties, the administrative hardships, the humanity, and the spiritual struggles of a pioneer in international mission.

David R. Elliott sketches the lives of three Canadian fundamentalists—William Aberhart, L. E. Maxwell, and T. T. Shields—who were reputedly Baptists (chap. 12). He sees them as ecclesiastical mavericks, converted within and influenced by theological currents independent of any confessional tradition. Consequently, their links with the Baptist movement were convenient rather than convinced.

The most notable of these three for his impact on the Baptist movement in Canada doubtless is T. T. Shields. While the Toronto minister is remembered, he is variously understood. Looking carefully at the Toronto fundamentalist's theology, Mark Parent perceives a shift in his thought (chap. 13). From a rather orthodox trinitarian and Chalcedonian Christology, this analysis suggests that Shields moved to a somewhat monophysitic and docetic view of the person of Jesus Christ that allowed an ill-advised veneration of the Scriptures. This essay raises intriguing questions about the reciprocal influences of theology and context.

J. Brian Scott introduces two western Canadian Baptists at the opposite end of the theological spectrum from fundamentalism (chap. 14). D. R. Sharpe and A. A. Shaw were advocates of a "social Christianity" deeply indebted to the theological reflections of the American German Baptist Walter Rauschenbusch. Incidentally, they illustrate the persistent American connection of Canadian Baptists—men born in Canada, educated in Canada and the United States, who served pastorates and/or taught in both countries. More importantly, they represent the generation that shaped T. C. Douglas, the views that antagonized Shields and Maxwell, and the concerns addressed erratically by Aberhard.

Shaw's addresses to the BUWC in 1908 and Sharpe's 1920 report to the Baptist Convention of Saskatchewan on the social mission of the Church exemplify the social passion and comprehensive vision of evangelical liberalism. In the long run, the energies of these and likeminded men tended to transcend denominational limits; their sphere of influence became civic and educational, rather than strictly ecclesiastical. While a recent conservative resurgence among old-line Baptists may be discerned, these benevolent and reformist ideals persist. Branches that formed in the early 20th century bore a bitter fruit of severed doctrine, ethics, and fellowship; but their roots in 19th-century evangelical activism promise a sweeter produce as this century ends.

So many strands of influence and organization, of ideas, movements, and people—is it foolish to think them one cord? The common name testifies to a common memory; and much in their way of thinking is held in common. So in the shared memory, there is hope.

Historically, Baptists have understood the shape of the Christian life somewhat differently than do the older churches whose heirs they are. The resulting Baptist tradition has had sociological and institutional effects which others now cultivate in an ecclesial life modified by the Baptist witness.

"Baptistification" may be a problem for "catholic" Christians.[12] It has not been all that easy for Baptists themselves. They constantly are confronted with (though many choose to ignore) the question: in what ways is the Baptist way a distinctive way—not for the sake of mere distinctiveness, but for the sake of offering a "peculiar" obedience to the Lord of the Church without denying the true obedience of Christians "denominated differently"? Several answers may be inferred from the essays collected here.

Nonetheless, Baptists in Canada seem convinced they have a future to be shared with the nation and the Church. Obviously, whatever future they have must be built on the past—the Church's past, the Canadian past, the Baptist past. So as the diverse Baptists explore the different threads of their varied past, they should be enabled to enter the future with a clearer self-understanding. Psychiatrists help individuals to escape from a past that binds and to affirm a past that has the seeds of health. Historians can help people collectively also to discover what may hinder obedience and what may help to recover, clarify, and advance the vision the ancestors understood was God's.

This collection of essays both illustrates and contributes to such hope. In response to an invitation from North American Baptist College, Edmonton, Alberta, presenters came from across Canada and from all but one of the national Baptist bodies (an absence only fortuitous) in May 1990. As part of the school's year-long celebration of its fifty years of Christian higher education, we listened to one another and talked together; we disagreed and dreamed.

Though in initiative this volume is one school's production, in reality it is both the accomplishment of all and an offering to all. In telling one confession's story, it illuminates the larger story of religion in Canada. Specifically for ourselves, it represents the hope that Canada's Baptists may continue to uncover one common heritage amidst the diversity of how each union and congregation strives to be Baptist as well as Christian. In finding ourselves, we may well find ourselves together. In discovering our heritage, we may well find our future. In memory, there is hope.

Notes

[1] See Robert S. Wilson, "Atlantic Baptists Confront the Turbulent Sixties," in *A Fragile Stability: Definition and Redefinition of Maritime Baptist Identity*, ed. David T. Priestley, Baptist Heritage in Atlantic Canada (BHAC), 15 (Hantsport, NS: Lancelot Press, 1995), 149-69.

[2] D. G. Bell, "All Things New: The Transformation of Maritime Baptist Historiography," *Nova Scotia Historical Review* 4, no. 2 (1984), 69-81; and David T. Priestley, "Canadian Baptist Historiography," in *Faith, Life, and Witness: The Papers of the Study and Research Division of the Baptist World Alliance—1986-1990*, ed. William H. Brackney with Ruby J. Burke (Birmingham, AL: Samford University Press, 1990), 76-92.

[3] Two Acadia conferences were held—in 1979 and 1987; McMaster Divinity College hosted two—in 1982 and 1984; North American Baptist College/Edmonton Baptist Seminary planned the 1990 meeting represented in this volume; Central Baptist Seminary and Ontario Theological Seminary jointly sponsored another in Toronto in 1993. The research presented at these conferences has been published in a variety of volumes: Jarold K. Zeman, ed., *Baptists in Canada: Search for Identity amidst Diversity* (Burlington, ON: G. R. Welch, 1980); Barry M. Moody, ed., *Repent and Believe: The Baptist Experience in Maritime Canada*, BHAC, 2 (Hantsport, NS: Lancelot Press, 1980); *Baptist History and Heritage* 15, no. 2 (1980); *Foundations* 23, no. 1 (1980); *Ontario History*, 70 (1978); R. F. Bullen, ed., *Expect a Difference* (Mississauga, ON: Baptist Federation of Canada, 1979); Murray J. S. Ford, ed., *Canadian Baptist History and Polity* (Hamilton, ON: McMaster Divinity College, 1982); Paul R. Dekar and Murray J. S. Ford, eds., *Celebrating the Canadian Baptist Heritage* (Hamilton, ON: McMaster Divinity College, 1984); Jarold K. Zeman, ed., *Costly Vision: The Baptist Pilgrimage in Canada* (Burlington, ON: G. R. Welch, 1988); Robert S. Wilson, ed., *An Abiding Conviction: Maritime Baptists and Their World*, BHAC, 8 (Hantsport, NS: Lancelot Press, 1988); George A. Rawlyk, ed., *Canadian Baptists and Christian Higher Education* (Kingston-Montreal: McGill-Queen's University Press, 1988); Priestley, ed., *Fragile Stability*.

[4] Philip G. A. Griffin-Allwood, George A. Rawlyk, and Jarold K. Zeman, eds., BHAC, 10 (Hantsport, NS: Lancelot Press, 1989). The series "Baptist Heritage in Atlantic Canada" (BHAC), cosponsored by Acadia Divinity College and the Baptist Historical Committee of the UBCAP, is another fruit of Zeman's vision and enterprise.

[5] Rawlyk edited two volumes in the BHAC series: *New Light Letters and Spiritual Songs*, BHAC, 5 (1983), and *The Sermons of Henry Alline*, BHAC, 7 (1986); shared in editing the *Baptists in Canada* bibliography; and explored maritime religious history in *Ravished by the Spirit: Religious Revivals, Baptists, and Henry Alline* (Kingston-Montreal: McGill-Queen's University Press, 1984); *Wrapped up in God: A Study of Several Canadian Revivals and Revivalists* (Burlington, ON: G. R. Welch, 1988); *Champions of the Truth: Fundamentalism, Modernism, and the Maritime Baptists* (Kingston-Montreal: McGill-Queen's University Press, 1990); *The Canada Fire: Radical Evangelicalism in British North America, 1775-1812* (Kingston-Montreal: McGill-Queen's University Press, 1994); and ed., *Canadian Baptists and Christian Higher Education.*

[6] Priestley, ed., *Fragile Stability*, combines five papers from the 1990 Heritage Conference with four from the 1993 Toronto sessions; another presentation constituted the basis for the introductory essay for Grant Gordon, *From Slavery to Freedom: The Life of David George, Pioneer Black Baptist Minister*, BHAC, 14 (Hantsport, NS: Lancelot Press, 1992). Yet another research report flowered into a full-scale book: Paul R. Dekar, *For the Healing of the Nations: Baptist Peacemakers* (Macon, GA: Smith & Helwys, 1993). Regrettably, an impressive essay on "Baptists, Nativism, and World War I" could not be prepared for inclusion here.

[7] See W. L. Lumpkin, ed., *Baptist Confessions of Faith*, rev. ed. (Valley Forge, PA: Judson Press, 1969); and William H. Brackney, ed., *Baptist Life and Thought: 1600-1980, A Source Book* (Valley Forge, PA: Judson Press, 1983).

[8] See from the first Acadia conference, Clark H. Pinnock, "The Modernist Impulse at McMaster University, 1887-1927," in *Baptists in Canada*, ed. Zeman, 193-207.

[9] The story of one region of the much larger FEBC that arose from the same theological springs is well told by J. S. H. Bonham, *FEBCAST [FEBC of Alberta, Saskatchewan, and the Territories]: Our Lord, Our Roots, Our Vision* (Three Hills, AB: EMF Press, [1980]).

[10] Harry A. Renfree, *Heritage and Horizon: The Baptist Story in Canada* (Mississauga, ON: Canadian Baptist Federation, 1988).

[11] See also Gordon, *From Slavery to Freedom.*

[12] Martin E. Marty, "Baptistification Takes Over," *Christianity Today* 27, no. 13 (2 September 1983): 33-36.

Chapter 1

Building a Future on the Past

Jarold K. Zeman

On 25 March 1852, John Mockett Cramp, the prolific Baptist educator, historian, and apologist, delivered a lecture in Wolfville, Nova Scotia, on the topic, "The Future of the Baptists and Their Duty to Prepare for It."[1] After seven years in Montreal, Cramp had assumed the presidency of Acadia College in the previous year. The meeting in Wolfville was convened to consider the raising of an endowment fund of £10,000 for the expansion of the school.

In the published text of his lecture, Cramp cited current examples of "the revival of evangelical religion, the new Reformation," in various parts of the world and concluded:

> Believing that the Baptist denomination exhibits the nearest approach to the ideal of primitive Christianity, we entertain the conviction that it will become the centre to which the religious movements that have been now alluded to, will converge.... May we not hope for a large accession to our numbers? And will not that accession be manifestly traceable to our acknowledged harmony with the word of God, and our thorough and consistent protest against the Papacy?

With unwavering confidence, he exclaimed: "There is A FUTURE for the Baptists...in the new Reformation. It is their duty to observe the signs, and to prepare for coming developments."[2]

Almost a century and a half later and in a vastly different context, Canadian Baptists face the same question with an even greater sense of urgency: Is there a future for Baptists in Canada? What kind of future? As historians and as persons interested in the Baptist heritage, we seek to decipher some clues for tomorrow from the past pilgrimage of the people called Baptists.[3]

When one surveys the 230 years of Baptist history in Canada, one cannot escape the impression that there were, from time to time, short periods which had lasting impact on the subsequent life of the churches and the denomination. Such brief spans of accelerated development might be compared to the turbulent rapids in the flow of a river or to the turning points in a road. Usually, they encompassed a decade, or slightly more, and seem to have occurred about once in every generation.

11

The limitations of space make necessary the selection of only a few examples of such "watersheds," or "decades of destiny," in Canadian Baptist history: three from the Maritime region in the 19th century, and two from central Canada in the present century. Because of insufficient access to sources of information about other Baptist bodies, the choice had to be confined to the oldest and largest stream of the Canadian Baptist tradition, namely the churches which are now affiliated with the Canadian Baptist Federation. However, the same methodological approach may be applied to the study of the other streams in the Canadian Baptist heritage.

Major Watersheds in the Maritime Baptist History during the 19th Century

In the first decade of the 19th century, a major portion of the Allinite tradition of New Light revivalism, with its indifferent attitude to church ordinances and polity, underwent a gradual transition to the Calvinist (Regular) Baptist theological orientation and church order. Infant baptism was no longer recognized as a valid option, and admission to communion was limited to immersed believers. In spite of a temporary loss of four congregations, the clear stand taken by the Nova Scotia Baptist Association in 1809 "settled a disturbing issue and in the end helped to promote, rather than hinder, denominational growth."[4] Even more important was the ensuing clarification of identity for the majority of Baptist churches. Several small dissenting groups, opposed to the Calvinistic stance, maintained their separate existence.

From the mid-1830s to the mid-1840s, the Regular Baptists reached a new stage in the process of maturation. The decade may well be perceived as the second major watershed. The areas affected were education, denominational organization, and missionary enterprise at home and abroad.

In Wolfville, Horton Academy (1829) was expanded into Queen's College (1838) and later renamed Acadia College. The Baptists in New Brunswick opened their Seminary (high school) in Fredericton in 1836. During the same decade, an informal network of black Baptist congregations in the Halifax area and beyond began to evolve into the future African Baptist Association. In 1845, Richard Burpee and his wife left for Burma as the first Baptist missionaries from the Maritimes. The constitution of the (Regular) Baptist Convention of the three provinces was delayed till 1846. Meanwhile, the New Brunswick Christian Conference was formed in 1834; and the Nova Scotia Free Christian Conference, two years later.[5]

The third major turning point in the Baptist road cannot be pinpointed as easily as the first two. During the second half of the 19th century, Maritime Baptists experienced their golden age of evangelistic outreach and church planting. In two generations, from the formation of the Regular Baptist Convention in 1846 to the Union with the Free Baptists in 1905-1906, the membership in the Regular Baptist churches increased from 14,000 to 52,000, a growth of 270 percent. There was comparable growth in the other Baptist groups.

The evangelistic zeal during that period appears to have been sparked, at least for some leaders, by the revival on the campus of Acadia College in the spring of 1855. Isaiah Wallace, pastor, itinerant evangelist, and church planter for fifty years, must be mentioned as perhaps the best exemplar of the rich harvest related to the 1855 revival. In his *Autobiography and Revival Reminiscences*, he confessed: "Whatever of success may have attended my life's work in the Lord's service...is traceable in some degree, at least, to that gracious renewing of 1855."[6]

The impact of the revival at Acadia is confirmed by several other leaders, among them John Mockett Cramp. In spite of the different piety to which he had been accustomed in his native England, he attributed, near the end of his life (1881), the growth and vitality of the Maritime Baptist churches primarily to the recurrent revivals during the two decades following the event on the Acadia campus in 1855.[7]

In such local revivals, outdoor baptisms by immersion became powerful acts of witness with profound impact on whole communities. Large crowds gathered to watch the ritual, often conducted in frigid water at the seashore or through a hole cut in the ice on rivers during the winter months.[8]

The second half of the 19th century was a time of spiritual vitality and fruitful evangelistic outreach for Maritime Baptists. When the United Baptist Convention of the Maritime Provinces was formed in 1905-1906, its membership was just under 65,000. In the 1911 census of Canada, Baptists accounted for 23.3 percent of the population in New Brunswick, the largest Protestant denomination in the province. In Nova Scotia, their numbers were lower (17.0%) but still second only to the Presbyterians (23.3%) among the Protestant churches.[9]

By contrast, the 20th century up to now can best be described as a time of stagnation and declension for Baptists. The Maritime Convention Baptists were spared the trauma of a major schism and remain united as the only sizeable Baptist body in the region. But in spite of the increase of the total population in the three provinces—it has almost doubled since 1901—the number of Baptist churches and their membership is virtually the same today as it was in 1906.

The factors contributing to the decline are yet to be identified. In his latest book, *Champions of the Truth: Fundamentalism, Modernism, and the Maritime Baptists*, George Rawlyk observed that "Baptist mainstream theology in the Maritimes had always been basically syncretic, placing particular stress on personal religious experience and not on a specific religious ideology." From the late 18th century, the Baptist denomination has been committed "to a more experiential, Christ-centred rather than doctrine-centred faith."[10]

Such a primary focus on the experience of conversion and believer's baptism may have served the Maritime Baptists well during the 19th century when revivalistic spirituality was being rekindled in every generation. It likely helped also to prevent a schism over fundamentalism and modernism in the 1920s and 1930s.[11] But as genuine revivals faded away in this century, so did the dynamic motivation for evangelistic witness. Most congregations ceased to grow and outreach programs drummed up in denominational offices had only marginal effects on the churches.

One can picture this process of stagnation as the flattening of the Baptist balloon. The Baptist balloon in the Maritimes grew in size and flew high in the sky as long as the fresh breezes of the Holy Spirit kept inflating it in recurrent revivals during the last century. As these subsided and eventually disappeared and were not replaced sufficiently by other modes of Christian spirituality, many Maritime Baptist churches began to decline. An analysis of trends and influences, such as the Social Gospel during the 20th century, must be reserved for another occasion.[12]

Major Watersheds in Central Canada during the 20th Century

The trend to stagnation can be observed also in the churches affiliated with the BCOQ. There is no need to review the familiar story which has been the subject of close investigation by several historians in recent years.[13] We shall note only two watersheds which can be easily identified in retrospect.

In the decade from the mid-1920s to the mid-1930s, the BCOQ—as well as the Baptist Union of Western Canada (BUWC)—suffered a major schism over general theological orientation (fundamentalism vs. modernism) rather than over issues related to distinctive Baptist beliefs and practices, such as believer's baptism, regenerate church membership, and congregational autonomy.[14] However, contrasting interpretations of the Baptist understanding of religious liberty were a factor during the controversy. In the aftermath of the disruption, a significant shift in denominational identity and ecumenical cooperation occurred.

Earlier, the Baptist Convention had declined to enter into preliminary discussions of church union with the Presbyterian, Methodist, and Congregational bodies.[15] Therefore, Baptists were not included in negotiations leading to the formation of the United Church of Canada in 1925.

However, after the division associated with the name of T. T. Shields in 1927, the three regional conventions/unions—with the main leadership provided by persons in Ontario and Quebec—published a new *Hymnary* (1936) which was identical with the *Hymnary of the United Church of Canada* (1930) except for a few marginal revisions.

In 1937, Baptists also entered into a cooperative contract with the United Church for the publication of Sunday School and other materials for Christian education. Less formal links between the two denominations were developed in other areas of church work as well. In retrospect, the events which took place between 1927 and 1937 must be viewed as a major turning point which affected Baptist identity, image, theological orientation, and ecumenical cooperation. Baptist membership in the Canadian Council of Churches (organized in 1944) was consistent with the new course; all three regional conventions/unions voted to join the Council.

A generation later the Convention Baptists, loosely linked across the country in the Baptist Federation of Canada since 1944, approached another watershed. Their involvement with the large Baptist bodies in the United States during the Baptist Jubilee Advance from 1959 to 1964 might have strengthened the sense of Baptist identity and thus prepared the way for the important decisions which were to follow soon.[16]

The clear signal for the difficult process of theological and ecumenical reorientation was given in the vigorous debate on the new Sunday School curriculum. The positioning of opposing groups had ominous signs of another schism in the BCOQ. It was averted when the cooperation with the United Church in the production of Sunday School materials was ended in 1965. A few years later Federation Baptists published their own *Hymnal* (1973) which was radically different from the new *Hymn Book* the Anglican and United churches had produced jointly in 1971.

Both decisions had a symbolic value for an emerging new sense of identity. The process of distancing from the United Church led also to ecumenical realignments. The Atlantic convention and the French Baptist union (incorporated in 1969) terminated their links with the Canadian Council of Churches, through the Baptist Federation, in the early 1970s. Without the consensus of its four constituent bodies, the Federation had no choice but to withdraw from membership in the Council in 1980. The Ontario and Quebec convention decided to continue its affiliation with the Council whereas the BUWC, after a lengthy debate, joined the Evangelical Fellowship of Canada (EFC) in 1986.[17]

John Webster Grant summed up the recent trends: "The Baptists, once hospitable to religious liberalism, have moved perceptibly toward the conservative end of the theological spectrum." This substantiates his observation: "Within Protestantism there has been a resurgence of aggressive evangelicalism. The membership of denominations professing conservative forms of evangelical Protestantism has grown steadily as that of the major churches has stagnated."[18]

From the Past to the Future

With full awareness of the risks involved in the approach we have employed in the preceding review, we can, nevertheless, draw two conclusions.

(1) The contrast between the vitality of the churches in the Canadian Baptist Federation (CBF) stream during the 19th century and their stagnation in the present one is evident. To what extent the same conclusion can be applied to other Baptist groups not linked with the Federation is a question which cannot be answered without proper investigation. It should be noted in passing that a search for identity and a concern over the lack of growth have been voiced also among Fellowship Baptists. In a recent article, Larry Perkins of Northwest Baptist Bible College and Seminary asks whether Baptists are dying or growing.[19]

(2) Baptist churches affiliated with the Federation appear to have passed through crucial "watershed" events about once every generation. Is it reasonable, therefore, to anticipate another "decade of decision" which may begin in the mid-1990s but reach its climax in the early 21st century?

How shall we build a future which is always uncertain and has many options on a past which is fixed yet open to conflicting interpretations?

Building a Future on the Past:
The Role of Historians

Historians who are committed Christians are among the church leaders who must assume a major responsibility during any time (*kairos*) of reorientation to a different future. They should understand best the dialectic of continuity and discontinuity in the dynamic movement of history. Such a call to leadership extends to Christian historians serving in any context: to professional academics in church-related or secular institutions, as well as to lay persons who do research as a labour of love. The erection of a few guideposts may be in order on this occasion.

(1) The renaissance of Baptist historical studies in Canada in the 1980s has made available many valuable resources, among them two basic tools: the first bibliography and the first comprehensive review of "the Baptist story in Canada."[20] In both books, nearly all streams of the diverse Baptist tradition have been included, if not always in a satisfactory manner.

There are no limits to the opportunities for research in this field of studies: from oral history projects in which any volunteer can help, to doctoral dissertations and advanced research projects not only in history and theology but also in related disciplines such as literature and social studies. Comparative studies of Baptist and other denominational traditions are long overdue. Since opportunities for professional careers in Baptist history are very limited, persons trained in other fields had in the past, and hopefully will have in the future, a substantial share in Baptist research. Graduate students should be encouraged to specialize in Baptist studies.

(2) One of the specific tasks is the preparation, likely by a team of historians, of a book of sources representative of all Baptist groups in Canada. That opportunity was made even more urgent by the recent publication of the *Sourcebook for Baptist Heritage* prepared by H. Leon McBeth.[21] In vain does the reader search through the 639 pages of this otherwise remarkable book for any text from, or even a mention of, Canada. We need a sourcebook for Canadian Baptist heritage, a selection of texts which would reflect the regional, ethnic, cultural, and other differences, and yet document the fundamental unity of Baptist witness in Canada. Such a volume would not affect the continuing process of editing and publishing specific sources and other materials. The experimental series "Baptist Heritage in Atlantic Canada" has demonstrated that it can be done with very modest resources.

(3) Bibliographies, sourcebooks, and textbooks are incentives to further scholarly research and popular studies. But they are also indispensable tools for teaching courses on the Baptist heritage. Baptists of all shades and colours have made sacrificial investment in higher education for several generations. At the present time, they sponsor the Atlantic Baptist College (liberal arts) in Moncton, New Brunswick, and ten English-speaking, as well as two French-language, seminaries: five in Western Canada, four in Ontario, two in Quebec, and one in Atlantic Canada. There are also lay leadership training schools in Alberta and Ontario. Presumably, courses on Baptist heritage and distinctive beliefs are offered at each of these institutions.

Furthermore, several hundred Baptist students are enrolled in non-denominational seminaries in cities like Toronto, Winnipeg, and Vancouver, and in many Bible colleges, especially in Western Canada. All of these future Baptist leaders, whether lay persons or ordained ministers, should be familiar with the Baptist heritage. Without such awareness, the identity of many Baptist churches will be in jeopardy.

On the practical side, the potential sales of books to Baptist students in all these institutions, year after year, would provide a stable market for publications dealing with the Baptist heritage. Who will establish a network of the necessary personal contacts in order to promote the programs of Baptist studies?

(4) There are at least 2,000 Baptist congregations in Canada. How many of them celebrate the Baptist heritage in words, music, drama, and displays? Do they observe anniversaries or Heritage Sundays? Do they include material on Baptist heritage and distinctives in membership preparation classes? Baptist conferences (conventions, unions, fellowships) hold annual assemblies. Are issues of Baptist heritage and identity included on the program? Who will produce videos with popular discussions or dramatic presentations of Baptist heritage topics?

(5) Does the general population in any given area have opportunities to hear or watch informative radio and television programs on Baptists or to read reliable releases about Baptists in the secular press?

All the research into Baptist heritage and identity represents little more than academic or antiquarian interests unless the results are channelled into courses at schools, preaching and teaching in the churches, and news and features in the public media.

(6) Research and its utilization in publications require financial resources. It was a deliberate strategy of John Mockett Cramp when, in his lecture on "The Future of the Baptists" at Acadia College in 1852, he combined a lively interpretation of the past with a vision for the future and an appeal for an endowment fund. He understood the realities of life. If today the various Baptist archives and projects in Baptist heritage could depend more on designated capital funds than on the mercies of denominational charity, we could anticipate the future of Canadian Baptist studies with greater assurance. Without such stable support, many visions will remain dreams, recorded or forgotten.

(7) Another major hindrance to the pursuit of the objectives just outlined has been the lack of cooperation among the several Baptist bodies and their educational institutions in Canada. Do we have the faith to expect a change during this decade?

The annual pastors' conferences at Banff bring together the ministers from the Baptist Union of Western Canada and the North American Baptist Conference. The Fellowship Baptists and the General Conference Baptists now cooperate in the new evangelical seminary consortium, Associated Christian Theological Seminaries, on the campus of Trinity Western University, Langley, British Columbia. In December 1989, the chief executive officers of the five major Baptist bodies in Canada met for a consultation in Toronto and agreed to meet on an annual basis in the future. The Baptist Heritage Conference in Edmonton involved participants from nearly all larger Baptist bodies in Canada.

Are these unmistakable signs of a spring thaw in inter-Baptist relations in our land? Is it premature to propose the formation of one Canadian Baptist Historical Society with members recruited from all Baptist bodies and open to any other persons interested in the Baptist heritage?

Could one of the Baptist educational institutions sponsor and support a centre, or institute, of Canadian Baptist Studies?

David T. Priestley made a realistic assessment of the current situation when he wrote in 1988: "Admittedly, some would keep old antagonisms alive, maintaining old positions with the old intransigence and belligerence; but there is a greater theological and attitudinal unity among Baptists in Canada than their organizational diversity and its roots would suggest."[22]

Baptist historians can make a contribution to the courtship and cooperation among Baptists in such projects as: cooperative ventures in publications; exchanges of students and faculty members; joint celebrations of Baptist heritage in which congregations of different Baptist affiliations can see the whole rather than the fractured picture of the Baptist witness in an area.

It is high time to face the understandable but unacceptable contradiction in Baptist interchurch relations. For most of this century, Baptists in the various conventions and conferences have found it easier to relate to non-Baptist denominations, whether in the so-called mainline ecumenical or in the evangelical camps, than to build bridges of understanding and trust within the Baptist family. The same paradox applies to Baptist congregations in the same community ignoring one another.

Many factors have contributed to this fractured family tragedy. One of them which must be of concern to us is the role which some historians played in the process of alienation. Instead of an impartial examination and evaluation of past events, they distorted equally the heritage of their particular group by hagiographic or apologetic aggrandizement and the history of others by partial evidence, ascription of false motives, or total omission.

The time has come for a well-informed and integrated approach to Baptist historiography in Canada. Historians have a role to play in building a *better* future on the past. For generations, Baptists have affirmed—and still do today—that tradition is not an authoritative norm of faith and practice alongside the Bible. A better understanding of their history will help Baptists overcome the ever-present temptation of an uncritical acceptance of many "traditional" teachings and customs among them for which there is no basis in the Scriptures. Historians have an important role to play in building a future on the past.

Notes

NB: Given as the keynote address at the Baptist Heritage Conference in Edmonton on 19 May 1990. An unedited version of this chapter was published in the *McMaster Journal of Theology* 1, no. 2 (Fall 1990): 56-67; this corrected and slightly revised version is included here for wider access.

The documentation has been kept to a minimum since information on printed resources is readily available in Philip G. A. Griffin-Allwood, George A. Rawlyk, and Jarold K. Zeman, eds., *Baptists in Canada 1760-1990: A Bibliography of Selected Printed Resources in English*, Baptist Heritage in Atlantic Canada, 10 (Hantsport, NS: Lancelot Press, 1989); hereafter *Bibliography*.

[1] J. M. Cramp, *The "Future" of the Baptists and Their Duty to Prepare for It: A Lecture Delivered at Wolfville, N.S. March 25th, 1852* (Halifax, NS: n.p., n.d.); cf. *Bibliography*, No. 1116.

[2] Cramp, *"Future,"* 11-14.

[3] The influence of the past on the future of Baptists in Canada has been discussed by several authors in recent years: Roy D. Bell, "The Believers' Church in Canada: Future," in *The Believers' Church in Canada*, eds. Jarold K. Zeman and Walter Klaassen (Brantford, ON: The Baptist Federation of Canada; and Winnipeg, MB: Mennonite Central Committee, 1979), 55-62; Walter E. Ellis, "A Place to Stand: Contemporary History of the Baptist Union of Western Canada," *American Baptist Quarterly* 6 (1987): 31-51; and Harry A. Renfree, "Heritage and Hope: Reflections on the Canadian Baptist Pilgrimage," in *Costly Vision: The Baptist Pilgrimage in Canada*, ed. Jarold K. Zeman (Burlington, ON: G. R. Welch, 1988), 241-53.

[4] George Edward Levy, *The Baptists of the Maritime Provinces 1753-1946* (St. John, NB: Barnes-Hopkins, 1946), 78; see also George A. Rawlyk, *Wrapped up in God* (Burlington, ON: G. R. Welch, 1988), 76-95.

[5] On the various streams of the Free Christian tradition, see *Bibliography*, Nos. 163-76; and Philip G. A. Griffin-Allwood, "The Canadianization of Baptists: From Denominations to Denomination" (PhD diss., Southern Baptist Theological Seminary, Louisville, KY, 1986), 98-136.

[6] The title page has a title different from that on the cover: *Auto-biographical Sketch with Reminiscences of Revival Work by Rev. Isaiah Wallace, A.M.* (Halifax, NS: Press of John Burgoyne, [1903]), 17. On the 1855 revival, see S. W. DeBlois, *Historical Sketch of the 1st Horton Baptist Church, Wolfville...From A.D. 1778, to A.D. 1878* (Halifax, NS: Messenger Printing Office, 1879), 23-24. In his description of recurrent revivals, DeBlois singled out 1874 as the "year of grace throughout this valley" when "from all quarters came tidings of great ingatherings into the fold of Christ" (28). Perhaps the 1870s may be seen as the "watershed" decade. Cf. next note.

[7] "The revival in the spring of 1855 'came not of observation....' We could not trace this revival, we could not track it to its source, nor say how it came, save that it was of the Lord of hosts. It was not *got up, it grew....* I deem it my duty to place on record the conclusions on this subject to which I have been led by the observations of the last thirty years. Educated and trained in England, and in a Church which was not remarkable for liveliness, I was a stranger to the scenes which have fallen under my notice in this land, and in some degree prejudiced against them.... But now, having watched the progress and marked the effects of many events of this character, and believing that the treatment of religious phenomena is still susceptible of improvement, suggested by the teachings of Scripture, I am free to declare that, as a genuine revival of religion is an undoubted blessing, Christians should regard it as a standing obligation to seek renewed bestowments by earnest prayer and individual efforts for the conversion of souls. Revivals would be more frequent and more powerful if the members of our Churches were truer to their responsibility as witnesses for Christ." Cramp then mentioned revivals in Wolfville, "this truly hallowed spot," in the years 1857, 1865, 1871; in 1874, 103 persons were added to the Wolfville Baptist Church as the fruit of revival. Students at the Horton Academy and Acadia College were among the many converts. "Other churches, too, have partaken of the blessing. The tidings have been conveyed from place to place, and revivals have sprung up, whereby great numbers have been turned to the Lord." (J. M. Cramp, "Sketches of

the Religious History of Acadia College and Horton Collegiate Academy," in *Memorials of Acadia College and Horton Academy for the Half-Century 1828-1878* [Montreal: Dawson Brothers, 1881], 48-52). In her essay on "Theodore Harding Rand as Educator," Margaret Conrad described the effect of the 1855 revival on T. H. Rand: "As many as 300 were reported to have attended prayer meetings at Academy Hall.... Rand would be marked for life by the events of April 1855" (*An Abiding Conviction: Maritime Baptists and Their World*, ed. Robert S. Wilson, BHAC, 8 [Hantsport, NS: Lancelot Press, 1988], 159.

[8] For examples of outdoor baptisms, see Isaiah Wallace's account of a baptism at Freeport, NS, on Fundy Bay shore in February 1880 and in Campbellton, NB, in November 1885 (*Autobiography*, 58, 89).

[9] See the statistical tables in G. A. Rawlyk, *Ravished by the Spirit: Religious Revivals, Baptists, and Henry Alline* (Kingston and Montreal: McGill-Queen's University Press, 1984), Appendix B, 171.

[10] G. A. Rawlyk, *Champions of the Truth: Fundamentalism, Modernism, and the Maritime Baptists* (Montreal and Kingston: McGill-Queen's University Press for the Centre for Canadian Studies, Mount Allison University, 1990), 73 and 102.

[11] On the marginal influence of T. T. Shields in the Maritimes, see Rawlyk, *Champions of the Truth*, chaps. 2 and 3.

[12] A recent essay interprets the advocacy of the Social Gospel platform by the Maritime Baptist Convention in the 1920s, with its emphasis "upon individual conversion and community regeneration," as an authentic expression of "the Maritime Baptist Evangelical tradition" and suggests ideological links with the Allinite tradition: G. A. Rawlyk, "The Champions of the Oppressed? Canadian Baptists and Social, Political and Economic Realities," *McMaster Journal of Theology* 1, no. 1 (Spring 1990): 83-86; however, the cited evidence for his thesis is not convincing.

[13] See *Bibliography*, Nos. 101-26 (Ontario and Quebec), Nos. 731-57 (Ecumenism), and No. 776 (The Curriculum Controversy).

[14] See *Bibliography*, Nos. 471-82 (T. T. Shields), Nos. 786-853 (Higher Education, especially McMaster University and Brandon College), and Nos. 127-62 (Western Canada).

[15] The text of the Baptist reply was published in the 1907 *Year Book* of the Baptist Convention of Ontario and Quebec, 223-25.

[16] See J. K. Zeman, "Has the B. J. A. Any Meaning for Canadian Baptists?" *Canadian Baptist Home Missions Digest* 5 (1961-1962): 48-52; G. Gerald Harrop, "Whither, Canadian Baptists?" *The Canadian Baptist* 107, no. 18 (15 October 1961): 9, 15-16. On the Baptist Jubilee Advance in general, Davis C. Woolley, ed., *Baptist Advance* (Nashville: Broadman Press, 1964).

[17] See Jarold K. Zeman, "Baptists in Canada and Cooperative Christianity," *Foundations* 15 (1972): 211-40; Ellis, "A Place to Stand"; and *Bibliography*, Nos. 731-57 (Ecumenism).

[18] John Webster Grant, *The Church in the Canadian Era*, updated ed. (Burlington, ON: G. R. Welch, 1988), 237. Cf. Jarold K. Zeman, "The Changing Baptist Identity in Canada since World War II," in *Celebrating Canadian Baptist Heritage*, ed. Paul R. Dekar and Murray J. S. Ford (Hamilton, ON: McMaster Divinity College, 1984), 1-26.

[19] Larry Perkins, "Baptists: A Dying Breed or a Growing Force?" *The Gospel Witness* 68, no. 22 (8 March 1990): 5-7 (reprinted from the *Evangelical Baptist* [February 1990]); Perkins serves on the faculty of Northwestern Baptist Theological College and Seminary in Vancouver-Langley. See the similar sentiments of the president of Toronto Baptist Seminary: Norman H. Street, "Baptists: A Spent Force?" *The Gospel Witness* 69, no. 6 (7 June 1990): 1, 14.

[20] *Bibliography*; and Harry A. Renfree, *Heritage and Horizon: The Baptist Story in Canada* (Mississauga, ON: Canadian Baptist Federation, 1988). See also D. G. Bell,

"All Things New: The Transformation of Maritime Baptist Historiography," *Nova Scotia Historical Review* 4, no. 2 (1984): 69-81; and David T. Priestley, "Canadian Baptist Historiography," in *Faith, Life, and Witness: The Papers of the Study and Research Division of the Baptist World Alliance—1986-1990,* ed. William H. Brackney with Ruby J. Burke (Birmingham, AL: Samford University Press, 1990), 76-92.

[21] H. Leon McBeth, *A Sourcebook for Baptist Heritage* (Nashville: Broadman Press, 1990).

[22] David T. Priestley, "Canadian Baptists in National Perspective: A Narrative Attempt," *The Baptist Quarterly* 32 (July 1988): 321. Cf. Samuel J. Mikolaski, "Identity and Mission," in *Baptists in Canada: Search for Identity Amidst Diversity,* ed. Jarold K. Zeman (Burlington, ON: G. R. Welch, 1980), 1-19.

PART ONE
Ideas and Their Expressions

Chapter 2

The Recovery of Ontario's Baptist Tradition

William Gillespie

If one were to ask: "What was the most traumatic change to have taken place in the BCOQ [Baptist Convention of Ontario and Quebec] since its inception?" it is likely that almost every Federated Baptist in Canada would answer: "The schism which accompanied the Shields/Marshall controversy of the late 1920s." Yet as traumatic as this well-known event may have been for the BCOQ's tradition, it was not the most significant change. A later, but virtually unnoticed, development in the denomination's history has a claim to that title. To this later change the present chapter gives its attention.

In 1964, apparently commissioned by the BCOQ,[1] Gerald Harrop of McMaster Divinity College gave the following assessment of the BCOQ's tradition:

> In 1932, the convention joined with its sister Canadian conventions to the east and west in appointing a "Baptist Hymnary Committee of Canada...." The result of the committee's labour was the publication in 1936 of *The Hymnary for Use in Canadian Baptist Churches...*, basically a revision of *The Hymnary* of the United Church of Canada.... While some churches prefer the tabernacle type of "songbook," especially for evening services, the near-universal use of the Baptist *Hymnary* has assured a certain amount of dignity and uniformity in common worship. The period of the *Hymnary*'s use has coincided, perhaps not accidentally, with a trend toward more ordered liturgy and a type of church building featuring the chancel with pulpit and lectern. Gowned choirs are all but universal, gowned ministers common, and the wearing of the clerical collar no longer remarkable.
>
> In fact, Baptist worship, especially in the older urban churches and the new suburban churches, is hardly distinguishable from worship in the United Church of Canada.[2]

His words demonstrate unmistakably that the BCOQ's tradition had undergone a significant change from the 1930s to the 1960s which made its worship "hardly distinguishable" from that in the United Church of Canada (UCC).

Yet worship practice is not the whole story. The change in Ontario's Baptist tradition during this time was much more than a change in form. It involved structural changes as well, namely, the appointment of a general secretary and the accompanying centralization of denominational boards and leadership that entailed. But more than just these outward aspects, this change also involved the very essence of Ontario's Baptist tradition. It involved a modification in what it meant to be Baptist, an alteration in their identity, or at least a change from how they previously had defined themselves. Whether one's assessment is positive or negative, a change in tradition took place. It is surprising that little attention has been directed to a basic alteration. Such a development requires examination.

Those familiar with Anabaptist studies will realize that the title of this chapter, and the purpose it betrays, owe a debt to the pioneering spirit and example which Harold S. Bender displayed in the recovery of that constituency's forgotten vision and to the 1957 anthology prepared in his honour. Bender's initial step in opening the way for the recovery of the Anabaptist identity occurred in December 1943, on the occasion of his presidential address, "The Anabaptist Vision," before the American Society for Church History.[3] It is somewhat ironic that at virtually the same time that Bender was opening up the way for a recovery of the Anabaptist identity, Ontario's Baptist leaders were embarking on a course which, far from recovering Ontario's Baptist tradition, would redefine, reshape, and redirect its identity.

In 1945, the BCOQ authorized the executive "to appoint a committee to restudy our Baptist beliefs and polity."[4] At its first meeting, this appointed committee divided its task into five separate areas of study; the three which portended fundamental change were:

> 1. The re-statement of our faith and privileges in the language of today, and the wide promulgation of this statement.
> 3. A re-study of the co-operative relationships of our Baptist Churches through the Associations, Conventions and the Baptist Federation of Canada.
> 5. A consideration of Baptists in relation to the ecumenical movement—the possibilities of more fruitful co-operation through the Canadian Council of Churches and the World Council of Churches.[5]

At the November 1945 meeting of the subcommittee dealing with "the re-statement of our faith and privileges," one of the directions it set for itself was:

> Item 4, Of set purpose certain familiar phrases appear among the proposed questions seldom or not at all, among them being, "The Lordship of Christ," "the priesthood of believers," "soul liberty," "New Testament Churches," and "the guidance of the Holy Spirit." This is because they are not "Baptist principles," less cherished or not honoured elsewhere. Actually they are the common possession (in the present day if not in some previous generations) of very large numbers of Christians, and it neither commends us to them nor enables us to see ourselves clearly to repeat them without careful

definition. In fact, it can be argued that in some Baptist circles these phrases have become mere catchwords, and that the tyranny of the reactionary is more real than the lordship of Christ, the ingrained prejudices of the "old guard" at church meetings more real than the guidance of the Holy Spirit, the authority of secretaries and superintendents actually more unquestioned than that of bishops. Our inquiry commits us to examine real conditions and practical problems rather than to hold up ideals that we neither achieve ourselves nor hold more passionately in theory than do others.[6]

Apparently, the purpose for restating (and, in essence, changing) Ontario's Baptist tradition had more to do with ecumenical rapprochement than it did with affirming, or reaffirming, Baptist tradition. The next year's interim report confirms this estimate.

There is among us a widespread hope that we can participate helpfully in the ecumenical movement that is now bringing together Protestant Christians across barriers raised by ritual, order and doctrinal emphasis. Strictly, of course, it is impossible for us as a body (because ours is not a church but a brotherhood of independent churches) to be committed in this matter; but there appears to be no strong tendency among us to raise unnecessary difficulties. We all agree that organic union is still far distant, granted that it can or should come at all. But we are concerned to make sure that when the ecumenical movement raises, as it is likely eventually to do, such minimal suggestions as (1) interchange of church membership among the co-operating church bodies and (2) the "zoning" of thinly-populated areas in Canada where churches are either lacking or harmfully numerous, we shall have an answer ready that will appeal to us and to others as being unmistakably Christian both in spirit and in practical effects.[7]

In 1958, when the Convention eventually published this committee's findings in pamphlet form, the intertwining of ecumenical aspirations with the desire to redefine Ontario's Baptist tradition still remained in evidence. The conclusion of this pamphlet, in part, read:

If we believe in our interpretation of the Protestant view, surely the place to bear effective witness to it is within the largest possible fellowship of Christians. Furthermore, to remain aloof from the bodies that are striving for a unity that will preserve all that is essential in every distinctive witness is to weaken the impact of Christ upon the world by presenting a divided testimony.[8]

This ecumenical agenda (and the influence it had on Ontario's Baptist identity) is not the whole story of the change in the denomination's tradition. To gain a clearer understanding of this modification one must look at the so-called "Forward Movement." The Commission on Baptist Beliefs and Polity was one aspect of this movement.

The Forward Movement came into being in 1945. It originated in the UCC as that denomination's post-World War II program, "Crusade for

Christ and His Kingdom," to reach the nation. Through informal meetings between leaders from various denominations, before the year was out, it had become a joint movement involving the Anglicans, Presbyterians, and the Baptist Federation of Canada (BFC). In it, each denomination was responsible for "setting its own objectives and working out its own programmes" so that "a united impact" would be made "on each community and upon Canadian life." Each denomination also titled its branch of the Forward Movement, "Crusade for Christ and His Kingdom."[9]

Its appearance in 1945 among the conventions and unions constituting the BFC resulted directly from an impromptu meeting on 18 May which Dr. Gordon C. Warren, then president of the BFC, held at Toronto to discuss Canadian Baptists' response to the Forward Movement. It included "several members of the Federation Council, with all the Conventions represented." Its outcome was the recommendation of a Forward Movement Programme to the Federation Council and, through the Council, to the three conventions.[10]

In retrospect, from its inception in the BCOQ, this movement tied together ecumenical desires with a change in the denomination's faith and order. The motion to commit the BCOQ to this Forward Movement read:

> Out of the combined thinking of a group of ministers and laymen in recent weeks there has grown the conviction that the time has arrived for a thorough study and fresh statement of our Baptist beliefs in the language of today.
>   There is the conviction also that our whole programme of organized local church and denominational activities should be re-examined with a view to determining what beneficial changes can and should be made in our work. Therefore, this convention is hereby requested to appoint a commission of twelve members (who shall have power to add to their number) to undertake this endeavour.[11]

While the Assembly may not have understood that the agenda of the Forward Movement as formulated in the BCOQ tied ecumenical interests with a restatement of Baptist faith and order, its executive certainly did.

> At the last Convention the Executive was authorized to appoint a committee to restudy our Baptist beliefs and polity and to report at the next Convention; the committee to work in conjunction with the Forward Movement, which later was called 'The Crusade for Christ and His Kingdom.'[12]

Many of the leaders who initiated the Forward Movement also were advocating an ecumenical posture for the Convention.[13]

> Overtures have been received from the Church of England and the United Church of Canada asking that we meet with them to confer concerning a closer unity in Christian life and work. The Executive resolved to favour entering into conversations in order that our witness may be heard, and that we convey this decision to the Baptist

Federation of Canada, and also to the other Baptist Conventions and that we inform the United Church and Church of England of this decision.

A significant step has been taken during the past year, not only by our Convention, but by the Baptist Conventions of Canada, in linking up with the newly organized Canadian Council of Churches.

We believe the Convention should adopt the *forward programmes* incorporated in several reports to be presented. The Executive has been asked to appoint representatives to sit with leadersof the other large communions to consider a joint *forward movement* for *Christ and the Kingdom* during the coming year, each denomination to work out its own programme and objectives in its own way, but joining in services of witness so making a spiritual impact upon communities and the nation at the same time.[14]

What is so noteworthy about the BCOQ's Forward Movement (Crusade for Christ and His Kingdom) is not that it resulted from informal and impromptu meetings of representatives from various Canadian denominations nor that its impetus derived from the United Church. What is so noteworthy is the difference the Ontario-Quebec program exhibited from either the United Church's plan or the one which the Federation Council had recommended to the conventions. While all three programs included emphases on finance, evangelism, youth, Christian service, and stewardship, only the BCOQ's program incorporated a restatement of Baptist tradition. This means that a restatement of Ontario's Baptist faith and order was not an essential part of the Crusade for Christ and His Kingdom. Nevertheless, when the Forward Movement was presented step-by-step on the BCOQ's Assembly floor in June, it was inaugurated by a motion for a "fresh statement of our Baptist beliefs in the language of today."[15]

The most plausible explanation for the development of this unique Forward Movement in the BCOQ, combining ecumenical aspirations with a desire to change the denomination's tradition, is that some denominational leaders either saw a restatement of the denomination's tradition as essential to the program or saw an opportunity to piggyback a change they desired on a program they knew the rank and file of the Convention would not refuse. Although there was some resistance to the suspected wholesale change in Baptist tradition which a few Baptists feared this committee would make, an overwhelming change did occur.[16]

The starkest testimony to this change in the BCOQ's Baptist tradition and identity is found at the associational level. Here, during the early 1940s, a new type of association constitution began to appear. It replaced Ontario Baptists' hundred-year history of employing virtually the same constitution as the basis for their associational fellowships. The hallmark of this change was the alteration of the second article of these Ontario Baptist association constitutions. Until the 1940s, this article had been a compendium of doctrines which outlined the Baptist faith and order of the association and defined its membership.

Ontario's Baptist Tradition before 1940

The pre-1840 constitutions of Ontario's Baptists derived ultimately from the British Baptists but usually arrived in Ontario via Baptists in the United States. By the end of the 1840s, the majority (76.5%) of Ontario's Baptists had adopted a version of the 1833 constitution which the Niagara Baptist Association of New York state had developed. The Grand River Association illustrates the constitution's adoption and modification.

The keystone of tradition in this constitution was its second article, a compendium of doctrines. A doctrinal summary was designed as the theological standard for transcongregational fellowship in the association. Yet as the qualifying phrase which introduces the article, "as embrace in substance," makes equally clear, a compendium was not a static standard to which the churches were required to subscribe. To illustrate, the second article of the 1844 Grand River Association constitution is reproduced here:

> This Association shall be composed of such Churches only, as embrace in substance the following doctrines:
> The being and unity of God—the existence of three equal persons in the Godhead—the divine inspiration of the scriptures of the Old and New Testaments, as a complete and infallible rule of faith and practice—the total moral depravity and just condemnation of all mankind, by the fall of our first parents—the election of grace according to the foreknowledge of God—the proper divinity of our Lord Jesus Christ—the all-sufficiency of his atonement—regeneration and sanctification by the Holy Spirit—sanctification by grace alone—perseverance of the saints—immersion only baptism—believers, the only proper subjects of baptism—the Lord's supper, a privilege peculiar to immersed believers, regularly admitted to Church fellowship—and the religious observance of the first day of the week—the resurrection of the body, and general judgment—the final happiness of the saints, and the eternal misery of the wicked—the obligation of every intelligent creature to love God supremely—to believe what he says, and to practice what God commands.[21]

The only changes from the Niagara Baptist Association constitution of 1833 are stylistic ones. So, too, are the differences among the compendia adopted by the Western, Eastern/Niagara, and Haldimand Associations. This doctrinal foundation was passed on to seventeen other Ontario associations during the rest of the century.

Ontario's 19th-century Baptists understood these theological compendia to be essentially the same. This is evident in the way in which the Baptists interchanged various articles in their association constitutions from time to time. A case in point is the action of the churches which made up the Middlesex and Elgin Association and its subsequent derivatives. When this association was first formed in 1860 out of the Western Association, its constitution included a slightly redacted version of the Western Association's compendium of doctrines. In 1874, the Middlesex and Elgin Association, because of increased size, divided to form the Middlesex and Lambton Association and the Elgin Association; both bodies chose to use the 1844 Grand River Association's compendium in their constitutions. That they found these compendia to be interchangeable indicates a doctrinal consensus which could be expressed through any of the doctrinal articles derived from the 1833 constitution of the (American) Niagara Association.[18]

When the Toronto Association came into being in 1875 it employed another version of this consensus in its compendium of doctrines. The apparent immediate source for this article is the 1853 constitution of the Regular Baptist Theological School (RBTS) which had originated from the constitutions of the Grand River Association (1844), the Canada Baptist Missionary Society (CBMS, 1845), and the Haldimand Association (1849).[19] This means that the Toronto compendium, at least in part, was also a derivative of the compendium of the Niagara Association.

Toronto's theological article is important for two reasons. The first is because of its relationship to the compendia of the RBTS and the CBMS, two transassociational agencies organized thirty years earlier. The substance of their compendia came from Baptists in the Ottawa and Montreal Associations, although support was solicited across the province. Baptist historiography has uniformly insisted that there was hostility between these Baptists and the larger number of Baptists in the western part of the province. That the Regular Baptists in the west could choose to express their tradition in a compendium of doctrines derived largely from their eastern brethren rather than simply employing a statement of beliefs issuing from one of the western associations, while at the same time continuing to define their tradition, at the associational level, in terms of each association's individual compendium of doctrines, suggests otherwise. Rather than indicating division and hostility, it points to a province-wide Baptist consensus of faith.

As with the evidence for the doctrinal consensus arising from the compendia issuing from the Niagara Association's constitution, the proof for this province-wide doctrinal consensus is the interchangeable manner in which Ontario's Baptists used these various compendia in their 19th-century constitutions. A study of the minutes from the province's Baptist associations leaves no doubt regarding this interchangeability and the doctrinal consensus it revealed.[20] On account of this province-wide doctrinal consensus, it was not a divisive matter which compendia these Baptists employed to express their common Baptist identity.

The second reason for its importance is the spread of this compendium. In the same way that the Ontario compendia of faith had evolved and spread from the constitution of the Niagara Baptist Association of New York state, the Toronto version now proliferated among the associations in the denomination. Furthermore, in 1880, Senator McMaster had it enshrined as the trust deed of the Toronto Baptist College; and later, in McMaster University's charter. *The Canadian Baptist* at the time described the College's trust deed: "It will be seen from this document how carefully the interests of a sound, orthodox Baptist faith have been guarded in providing a new school of the prophets."[21] The University, during the dark days of theological controversy in 1910 and 1925, relied on this compendium as its expression of fidelity to the denomination's Baptist tradition.[22]

By 1900, thirteen of the sixteen associations in the BCOQ expressed this Ontario Baptist doctrinal consensus directly in their constitutions, which derived either from the Niagara Association (1833) or from the Toronto Association (1875). For them all, it represented a distinct and identifiable tradition.

A word should be said about the qualifying phrase, "such churches only *as embrace in substance* the following doctrines" (emphasis added). To 19th-century Baptists, this was the heart which made their tradition vital and dynamic rather than dead and static. For them, the compendium of doctrines was a standard of judgment, not a confession to be repeated "literally, sentence for sentence."[23] A church wishing to join an association was not expected to subscribe to the association's ready-made confession of faith, although it obviously had the right to express its beliefs in those words if it so desired. Instead, it presented a statement of its beliefs in its own words. This was then evaluated by the association to see whether, in the judgment of the association, its beliefs were "in substance" in accord with the association's standard.

This was the operative element in the process: namely, the decision whether a church's beliefs were "substantially" in accord with Ontario's Baptist tradition (as expressed objectively in the association constitution) rested, as all their constitutions styled it, solely "in the opinion of the Association." The matter was not left to the church wishing to become part of the association. It was the prerogative of the larger Baptist community, in this case the association, to render the subjective decision. A church whose beliefs were not "substantially" in accord with the heritage was refused fellowship.[24]

In this way, our Baptist forebears in Ontario were able to encourage religious freedom and vitality while at the same time maintaining Baptist orthodoxy and identity. Because of the demand for the local church to express its faith in its own words, the way for creativity and new theological insight was kept open. On the other hand, because the association had the prerogative to decide the issue, the local church was protected from the possible blindness of its own subjectivity; and the Baptist tradition was guarded against possible error. This is the genius of the Baptist tradition as exercised in 19th-century Ontario: an objective standard mediated by a subjective group judgment, the provision for liberty to guarantee the vitality of the faith combined with a mechanism to check licence.

The Reverend Elmore Harris, at the height of the 1910 controversy, focussed on Professor I. G. Matthews' alleged higher critical views of the Old Testament, captured in a vivid manner the spirit of Ontario's Baptist tradition in action as it applied to individuals.

> Professor Matthews, or any other person, can hold all the vagaries of the Higher Critics he pleases as to the Old Testament, and he is at liberty to proclaim them from the housetop, but he must not ask the Baptist denomination to give an endorsement to such views or to approve the inculcation of such views from his chair in the Theological Department.[25]

The Liberal Baptist Tradition

Throughout the first thirty years of the 20th century, the doctrinal consensus Ontario's Baptists had developed continued unquestioned. Even the secular courts during these years recognized this tradition, as expressed in the associational compendia of doctrines.[26] During the 1930s, however, some associations began to discontinue publishing their constitutions (and, therefore, the compendium of doctrines each contained) in their annual association minutes. Using that standard of measurement, this Baptist tradition had disappeared altogether by the end of 1940s. By that time, no association was employing any longer a constitution with an article on doctrine which expressed the hundred-year-old Baptist tradition in Ontario. Instead, every association had adopted a new type of constitution.

Three factors contributed to this change: centralization and the change in function this forced upon the association; advocacy of ecumenical relations; and the direction set by the commission on Baptist beliefs. The first factor resulted in the need for a new association constitution; the other two resulted in the need to abandon the various compendia.

Centralization began in 1942, shortly after Dr. H. H. Bingham became the BCOQ's first general secretary. An annual meeting for association moderators and clerks was inaugurated, and an Associational Relations Committee for the convention was begun. The focus of these annual meetings was:

First, to define the work for which the association is responsible and which it should *regularly* undertake. Second, to strengthen the relation between the convention and the association by discovering mutual sources and avenues of help. Third, to enlist the aid of local groups to put the program of the convention and association into effect in the churches, and thus to make effective in the local church, our Baptist program for these times.[27]

The Hamilton/Niagara Association illustrates how the associations changed function to adjust to centralization. At the 1942 sessions, Moderator S. R. McClung addressed those present on the subject, "The Place of the Association in Baptist Life":

He dealt with the fact that our function had changed of recent years by the convention taking over some of our powers, also by the difficulty in attending Association. He also emphasized the necessity of finding a real purpose. Some functions were suggested such as helping the local church put convention programme into operation, cultivating a spirit of brotherhood, a unified ordination service, and induction for ministers.[28]

A motion to strike a committee to revise the constitution followed quickly upon this address on the association's role. The next year, the newly appointed moderator, Mr. W. W. Richman, made a similar address. A year later, a new constitution was adopted which contained a new statement on function that made the association an arm of the convention.[29]

The second factor contributing to a change in Ontario's Baptist tradition was the ecumenical aspirations which seemed to some to require a change in the denomination's longstanding doctrinal tradition. As the various associations accepted the Crusade for Christ and His Kingdom program, not only did their long-standing constitutions disappear, but they adopted a new type of associational constitution devoid of any doctrinal statement. The end result was the quiet disappearance of Ontario's hundred-year-old Baptist tradition. In essence a new tradition came into being, although it was constantly referred to as the historic Baptist tradition.[30] Liberty of conscience, not a binding statement of faith, came to be accepted as "the fundamental axiom of the Baptist position."[31] The hallmark of this new tradition was an emphasis on individual religious liberty that lacked the former mechanism of a doctrinal article to guard against licence. So severe is this break in continuity that it can only be described as the complete abrogation of the century-old Baptist tradition the associational constitutions had conveyed in their doctrinal compendia.

But what name can be given to this new tradition? Perhaps the best name for it is one drawn from Watson Kirkconnell: "the liberal Baptist tradition." Appearing in another context, his summary of this liberal tradition would seem to parallel closely the tradition that resulted from the changes occurring in the BCOQ during the 1940s.

On the doctrinal side, I was reared in the liberal Baptist tradition, which believed in the competence of the individual believer to frame his theology in his own terms. This was not, of course, to believe just anything at all. If one did not accept theism, Trinitarianism, the atonement and lordship of Christ, a Zwinglian interpretation of baptism [sic!] and the Lord's supper, a "gathered" membership and the priesthood of all believers, one belonged to some other denomination and ought to leave the Baptist fold. On the other hand, one's definitions of basic terms were one's own right and any insistence on a uniform credal statement was an act of tyranny. Nominal Baptists who made such a demand were spiritual brothers of Torquemada and were aliens among us (emphasis added).[32]

The unchecked individualism of this new tradition, while it was asserted as the legitimate Baptist heritage, is strikingly different in spirit from Ontario's 19th-century Baptist tradition.

Outcome

The outcome of this research is rather straightforward. Ontario's Baptists had developed a rich and balanced tradition during the 19th century that lasted until the mid-1940s. This tradition provided for freedom but guarded against licence. By the 1960s, this heritage was replaced by a "liberal Baptist tradition" which no longer acknowledged an earlier consensus. Can such a dramatic shift in identity be described except as the most traumatic change in the history of the BCOQ?

If Baptists in Ontario want to shed the stagnation that has accompanied this liberal Baptist tradition and its United Church-like demeanour, perhaps it is time to consider whether vitality would be restored if Ontario's original Baptist tradition were recovered. If the denomination defined itself successfully for a hundred years with brief doctrinal compendia as described above, perhaps it is time it took this stand again, for the sake of a *Baptist* identity.

Notes

[1] At the very least, he was writing under the immediate editorship of Watson Kirkconnell, the Baptist Federation of Canada representative on the editorial committee of the "Baptist Jubilee Advance." The BJA was a five-year cooperative celebration by Canadian and American Baptists of the previous 150 years of Baptist witness in North America.

[2] G. Gerald Harrop, "The Baptist Convention of Ontario and Quebec," in *Baptist Advance*, ed. Davis C. Woolley (Nashville, TN: Broadman Press, 1964), 175.

[3] Guy F. Hershberger, ed., *The Recovery of the Anabaptist Vision* (Scottsdale, PA: Herald Press, 1957), 29-54.

[4] BCOQ, *Baptist Year Book (BYB)* (1946), 55.

[5] *Canadian Baptist* 91, no. 18 (15 September 1945): 1.

[6] G. P. Gilmour and I. C. Morgan, "Suggestions for Study Draft," "Minutes of the Committee on Baptist Faith and Order," November 1945, 2 (handwritten manuscript, Canadian Baptist Archives, McMaster Divinity College, Hamilton, ON [CBA]).

[7] "Interim Report of the Commission on Baptist Beliefs and Polity," June 1946, 10, CBA.

[8] F. W. Waters, *Protestantism—A Baptist Interpretation* (n.p.: Commission on Principles and Policy, BCOQ, May 1958), 67.

[9] "A Forward Movement Programme," in "Forward Movement" file (CBA); and "Forward Movement Programme," *BYB* (1945), 55.

[10] "Forward Movement Programme," *BYB* (1945), 55.

[11] *BYB* (1945), 35.

[12] *BYB* (1946), 56.

[13] The names common to the motions to establish the "Forward Movement" in the BCOQ were: Prof. R. J. McCracken, Rev. Ivan Morgan, Prof. Watson Kirkconnell, G. P. Gilmour, Prof. N. H. Parker, Prof. F. W. Waters, Dr. H. H. Bingham, and Rev. A. J. Moncrief—see *BYB* (1945), 35, 55; "Forward Movement" file, CBA; and the handwritten "Minutes of the Committee on Baptist Faith and Order," 15 October 1945, CBA.

[14] *BYB* (1945), 55.

[15] "Report of the Crusade General Campaign Committee," *BYB* (1946), 60ff; also, "Facing the Post War Years, The Moderator of the United Church of Canada Calls Ministers and People to a New Crusade for Christ and His Kingdom"; and "Forward Movement Programme," CBA.

[16] See, for instance, "McMaster Conference on Faith and Order," *CB* 91, no. 21 (1 November 1945): 3; "Conference Commission Studies," *CB* 92, no. 19 (1 October 1946): 5; and Rev. Harold Lewis' amendment to the "Interim Report of the Commission on Baptist Beliefs and Polity," *BYB* (1946), 37.

[17] "Minutes of the Grand River Baptist Association" (1844), 10.

[18] "Middlesex and Lambton Baptist Association" (1874), 7-9; "Minutes of the Elgin Baptist Association" (1877), 3-4.

[19] *Proceedings of the Meeting of Subscribers to the Endowment Fund of the Regular Baptist Theological School in Canada, Held January 19, 1853* (Toronto: John Carter Printer, 1853), 18.

[20] Cf. "Minutes of the East Ontario Regular Baptist Association" (1871), 13, and (1887), 18, with the "Minutes of the Toronto Association of Baptist Churches" (1875), 20; "Minutes of the Grand River Association" (1874), 15; "Minutes of the Norfolk Association of Baptist Churches" (1888), 5; "Minutes of the Brant Baptist Association" (1887), 4; "Minutes of the Woodstock Association of Baptist Churches" (1888); "Minutes of the Oxford and Brant Association" (1897), 4; "Minutes of the Midland Counties Association" (1892), 4; and "Minutes of the Guelph Association of Baptist Churches" (1899).

[21] See the trust deed of the Toronto Baptist College, "Toronto Theological College," *BYB* (1881), 99; "Minutes of the Toronto Baptist Association" (1875), 25; and William Muir, "Our New College," *CB* 27, no. 9 (3 March 1881): 4.

[22] *BYB* (1910), 168-69; these same pages also acknowledge the compendia of six other associations, which had derived from the 1833 constitution of the American Niagara Baptist Association, as similarly expressing the denomination's tradition. Also *BYB* (1925), 41-42, 176.

[23] Dr. Castle, "The Ministerial Institute," *The Christian Helper* 6, no. 24 (11 November 1880): 241.

[24] For example, "Minutes of the Toronto Baptist Association" (1875), 20; "Minutes of the Grand River Baptist Association" (1844), 11; "Minutes of the Niagara C. W. Regular Baptist Association" (1863).

[25] Rev. Elmore Harris, *Concerning the Attacks of Prof. Matthews on the Bible* (Toronto: Haynes Press, May, 1910), 17.

[26] Mr. Justice Kelly, "Ontario Supreme Court Decision in the Case of the Hughson Street Baptist Church, Hamilton," *Convention Notes for Convention Churches*, No. 4, (Toronto: BCOQ, 1929), 8.

[27] *BYB* (1946), 88; *BYB* (1942), 50-51; and *BYB* (1945), 55.

[28] Hamilton/Niagara Baptist Association, "Minutes" (1942), 2.

[29] Hamilton/Niagara Baptist Association, "Minutes" (1943), 2; (1944), 10-11.

[30] Charles M. Johnston, *McMaster University*, vol. 1 (Toronto: University of Toronto Press, 1976), 197-98; and J. K. Zeman, "The Changing Baptist Identity in Canada Since World War II," in *Celebrating the Canadian Baptist Heritage*, ed. Paul R. Dekar and Murray J. S. Ford (Hamilton, ON: McMaster Divinity College, [1984]), 10-11.

[31] Zeman, "Changing Baptist Identity," 10.

[32] Quoted in Zeman, "Changing Baptist Identity," 23 n. 43.

Chapter 3

Tradition and Traditionalism
in Baptist Life and Thought:
The Case of the Lord's Supper

Barry D. Morrison

With the appearance of *Baptism, Eucharist, and Ministry* (BEM),[1] the fruit of decades of labour by the Faith and Order Commission and others involved in the retrieval of the Church's heritage and mission in the world, Baptists have been challenged to reassess our tradition. The BEM document is a particularly important text for Baptists. Baptist theologians were involved in its formulation; yet the Baptist constituency has received it with a decided ambivalence. On the one hand, some Baptists are saying:

> Our attitude toward the BEM document can be nothing but ambiguous. While we appreciate the many hours of prayerful labour which have gone into its production, and while we recognize that, for the denominations involved in the World Council of Churches, this is an important step toward their mutual understanding, we find ourselves unsatisfied with it.
>
> The Document seems to favour historical tradition over the teachings of Scripture and a sacramental approach over the experience of the New Testament church. Thus, while Baptists may "recognize in this text the faith of the Church through the ages" as it has developed historically, we do not recognize in it the faith of the Church in the New Testament.[2]

With regard to the Lord's Supper specifically, the same respondent affirms that: "participation in the Lord's Supper gives us a fresh assurance and is a helpful *reminder*.... That is why we question the statement [of the BEM document]...that the celebration of the eucharist "continues as the central act of the church's worship."[3]

On the other hand, objecting to the Baptist tendency to speak of the sacraments as "mere symbols" (hence, preferring to call them "ordinances"), "a sizable number of Baptists think that this understanding greatly impoverishes the meaning of the ordinances." Some Baptists are coming to the conviction that much of Baptist thought and practice around the sacraments is inadequate to the biblical witness, for there is a "strong sacramental current which moves through the New Testament."[4]

The tension between these differing approaches indicates the continuing Baptist struggle for self-identity. Moreover, the divergences demonstrate something far more important than mere differences of taste or opinion. Rather, they have to do with radically different interpretations of the history and theology of the Baptist movement.

One element which, in Ernst Troeltsch's terms, may be called the "sect type," looks for a Baptist raison d'être in the Puritan movement of 17th-century England and the continental Radical Reformation of the previous century. For this group, the early Baptist view of the nature of the Church is considered foundational, even determinative, for future Baptist polity and practice. This view would concede that there is an observable evolution of ideas but still insist that the major Baptist principles are subject to rather strict interpretation along the lines laid in the first generation of the movement. A dominant thrust continues to be the articulation of "the Baptist distinctives"—how is this denomination different from other parts of the Church and what is its special reason for existence?

In contrast, another group, while appreciative of the historical exigencies which gave rise to the denomination, sees Baptist identity as rooted in the larger tradition of the Church. Tradition here is understood as "not simply the Church's past, but rather her present life viewed as in faithful continuity with that past."[5] According to this way of thinking, early Baptist principles must be followed through to their logical conclusions in the light of up-to-date historical and biblical research. When employed in the service of the Baptist desire to fashion the Church after the model of the New Testament, the use of such a methodology may lead to results quite different from those at which the founders of the denomination arrived 400 years ago.

The thesis of this chapter is that according to the original architects of the denomination there is no "Baptist position;" there is, at most, a "Baptist approach." At its inception, Baptist life and thought was rooted in what may properly be called a liturgical movement, inasmuch as it was the urgent desire of the founders to recover the worship of the New Testament and the early Church. Moreover, when the intentions of this original Baptist approach are retrieved, the case can be made that Baptists belong, not outside or in opposition to the ecumenical and liturgical movements, but in the forefront of these endeavours. The original Baptist "approach" is exemplified in John Smyth—Separatist, se-baptist, Anabaptist.

In *Principles and Inferences Concerning the Visible Church*, John Smyth lays out his ecclesiology and calls his readers to "read, consider, compare the truth here expressed with the frame, ministry, and government of the assemblies of the land; and accordingly give sentence, judge righteous judgement, and let practise answerable to the truth follow thereupon."[6] Defending each statement with a list of Scripture references,

Smyth begins by differentiating the catholic church—the invisible company of the elect—and the visible church—"a visible communion of saints...all which are to be accounted faithful and elect...till they by obstinacy in sin and apostasy declare the contrary." It is possible to be a member of one without being a member of the other. But it is the visible church—"a visible communion of...two, three, or more Saints joined together by covenant with God & themselves, freely to use all the holy things of God, according to the word, for their mutual edification, & God's glory"—which is "the only religious society that God has ordained for men on earth." All other religious societies including the Anglican local parish are thus unlawful. Moreover, since only in the visible church of "saints" may God be truly worshipped, all religious communion with others is forbidden: "whatsoever company or communion of men, do worship God, being not of the communion of a visible church, sin." According to Smyth, the one and only true shape of the visible church is described in the Scriptures. Any communions constituted on principles contrary to those set out in the Bible or whose constitutions are not adequately supported by the Scriptures are considered to be false; forged according to the "device of men [they] are real idols, and to join to them and to worship God in them is to join to idols, or to worship God in or by idols."[7]

By setting down the norms of the Bible in such rigid, absolute terms, Smyth divorces Scripture and tradition from one another; indeed, he calls into serious disrepute every intervening development after the time of the apostles. The "inventions of the man of sin" were to be ruled out in their entirety, leaving only the "pure" worship of the apostolic age. This absolute stand on the sufficiency of the Scriptures over against the sinfulness of the tradition would exert a strong influence on the development of Baptist life.

Of course, much of Smyth's writing on the nature of the Scriptures and its implications for the constitution and life of the church is polemical, addressed mainly to the Church of England and to other Separatist bodies which had fallen short of the whole truth as he believed himself to have discovered it. Late in his life, still as ingenuous as in his earlier days, Smyth sought to soften the blows:

> In the days of my blind zeal, and preposterous imitation of Christ, I was somewhat lavish in censuring and judging others: and namely, in the way of separation called Brownism, yet since having and finding my error therein, I protest against that my former course of censuring other persons, and especially for all those hard phrases, wherewith I have in any of my writings, inveighed against either England or the separation.... Generally all those biting and bitter words, phrases, and speeches, used against the professors of the land, I utterly retract and revoke, as not being of the spirit of Christ but of the disciples, who would have called for fire and brimestone from heaven, which Christ rebukes.[8]

Baptists in succeeding centuries continued to exalt the sufficiency of Scripture in opposition to tradition. Nearly 300 years later, an American Baptist could self-confidently and unapologetically introduce a collection of essays on Baptist doctrines by claiming that:

> In no spirit of controversy is this volume sent forth. Its aim is not to kindle strife, but to impart truth. Every religious denomination, perhaps, that wields a very extensive influence among men, has a formulated creed. The Mohammedans have their Koran; the Catholics, their long-established ritual; the Episcopalians, their Book of Common Prayer; the Methodists, their Discipline; the Presbyterians, their Confession of Faith; and the Baptists, the Gospel of their Lord. While Baptists have no rule of faith other than the Scriptures, and while they point every inquirer after divine truth to the Word of God as the ground of his belief, it has, nevertheless, been deemed expedient to give prominence to those great truths which separate them, more or less widely, from the rest of mankind.[9]

Those "great truths" were explained a quarter-century after that by a Southern Baptist historian in terms of the various "significances" Baptists have for the larger Church:

> The Biblical significance of the Baptists is the right of private interpretation [of], and obedience to, the Scriptures. The significance of the Baptists in relation to the individual is soul freedom. The ecclesiastical significance of the Baptists is a regenerated church membership and the equality and priesthood of believers. The political significance of the Baptists is the separation of Church and State. But as comprehending all the above particulars, as a great and aggressive force in Christian history, as distinguished from all others and standing entirely alone, the doctrine of the soul's competency in religion under God is the distinctive significance of the Baptists.[10]

All of these articles can be seen to be derived from the Baptist struggle with the established church; while stated positively as the teaching of the Scriptures, they inveigh against all whose ecclesiology, polity, and worship contain elements that lie beyond the orthodoxy which early Baptists saw prescribed by the New Testament.

Expressed more optimistically, the major principles of the Baptist desire to retrieve the shape of the New Testament church are: (1) openness to change, (2) openness to the Spirit, and (3) freedom of conscience.[11] The first is clearly set out by Smyth in his famous declaration, "We will never be satisfied in endeavouring to reduce the worship and ministry of the Church to the primitive Apostolic institution from which as yet it is so far distant." In this statement may be seen his earnest zeal to re-establish the true church, neither fractured by divisions nor compromised by an unhealthy entanglement with the state. The Church should be a holy society of the faithful, who are striving to live out the implications of the doctrine of the priesthood of all believers; yet he expects this ideal can never be actualized in human experience.

The second principle, openness to the Spirit, was initially the Separatist cry against the Church of England and its prescribed forms of worship. Access to God would be free and unmediated by ceremonies, the office of a hierarchical priesthood, or the dictates of the political authorities. The Holy Spirit would so reign in the hearts and minds of the members that government would be congregational and office would be undertaken according to already identified gifts for service. In practice this principle soon gave rise to a pneumatology which placed far more stress on the individual than on the Church. Worship came to be centred around the inspired utterances of individuals—spontaneous prayers, sermons, and songs contributing to the praise of God. While these elements were always expected to conform to the norms of Scripture and, therefore, were liable to censure, the principle of an autonomous, unmediated relationship with God gave rise to a great variety of expression in Baptist worship. This thinking was soon extended to refer to the right of the individual not only to read but also to interpret the Scriptures. Indeed, much of early Baptist dependence on the Bible as the only authoritative norm for faith and conduct relied on the Word of God *as it had been interpreted* by particularly influential persons.

Ever since these free, even charismatic, beginnings, one segment of Baptist thought has been characterized by a mistrust of sacramental worship and the so-called liturgical churches. A relatively recent Baptist writer illustrates this point: "To make baptism and the Lord's Supper forms or elements of worship is to admit the foot of the sacerdotal camel through the door of the church, and ere long the camel well may be presiding at the altar, whether he dons the insignia or not."[12]

This way of thinking is promoted by two significant and related pressures. The first is the perceived need to carry on the Separatist tradition which "regarded the Church from which it seceded as a 'false' Church."[13] So convinced is this school of thought of the rightness of their position that to countenance any of the doctrines or practices of such a "false" church is to compromise the truth. The second pressure, therefore, is provoked by those who court disaster by wanting to relinquish the historic Baptist position. Not only must the true faith be promoted, but it must also be defended against those who would undo the distinctiveness of the Free Church by admitting forms and doctrines of the adversaries.

A very different approach repudiates the view that Baptist polity and practice are complete, static, or finally defined. This segment of Baptist thought holds that to explore new ways of understanding the Church is not to break with Baptist tradition but rather to return to its original approach. A recent executive secretary of the Baptist Union of Great Britain and Ireland suggests that "above all, Baptists require a renewed baptism in the spirit of John Smyth, the spirit of the Gainsborough covenant. They possess a birthright of freedom which makes possible change and experimentation. It should make them courageous, adaptable, and resilient."[14]

Indeed, it was John Smyth's own urgency to guard the unity of the Church which prompted him to repudiate his self-baptism, the symbol of his own quest for a pure expression of the Body of Christ. For him, it had become unconscionable that the Church should be fragmented. Therefore, when he recognized the Waterlander Mennonites to be a "true church," he set about the process of articulating a theological consensus which would lead to visible unity. An appreciation of Smyth's submission of the individual for the sake of the corporate may help Baptists to realize that the seeds of a reconstitution of the Church and its worship lie buried within the soil of their own history.

The third principle of the New Testament church which Baptists sought to retrieve is identified in their common reference to "soul liberty":

> Along with our insistence upon Scripture as the *sole* criterion for the faith and order of our church life, Baptists have emphasized soul liberty—the conviction that individual believers and congregations of believers must allow the Spirit of God to speak to them afresh through the written Word of God. As John Robinson put it, "The Lord has yet more light and truth to break forth from His Word," and we must remain open to correction by the Holy Spirit.[15]

In practice, this "dogma" has often been seen as the right of private interpretation. As such, it has frequently served to divide, rather than consolidate, the Church's expression of faith. "Baptists recognize...that the freedom of individual interpretation invites all kinds of errors, but they are willing to take the risk of being wrong to preserve the freedom to find the truth for themselves."[16]

However, other Baptists deliberately refute this "anarchic" view by pointing out that the concept of freedom of conscience was originally derived from a

> belief in the sovereignty of God over the conscience, rather than upon human dignity and individual rights.... [T]oday this doctrine of liberty is often taken to mean that each individual is free to adopt whatever views he will, without any restraints at all.... Early Baptists, however, would have regarded such a conception of freedom as unwarranted licence, a view which can lead only to chaos.[17]

The net result has been that Baptists throw a very different light on the principle of *sola scriptura*. Originally, *sola scriptura* was heralded as the Protestant alternative to the dual authority of Scripture and tradition operative in the Roman Catholic Church. In reality, though, it would appear that one dual norm was simply substituted for another.

Baptist insistence on the dual norm of "Scripture and soul liberty," rather than on "scripture and tradition" (controlled hermeneutically by the authority of the church and its confessional statements), should set us free from bondage to any Baptist tradition which does not conform to Scriptures *as we understand them today.*[18]

Soul liberty should ensure freedom to entertain new understandings of the scriptures as new methods and discoveries make their message more intelligible. In other words, the concept of freedom of conscience, no less than openness to change or to the Spirit, is not intended to define a Baptist *position*; its purpose is to supply the mandate for a Baptist *approach.*

Such a view is consistent with the suggestion that "most of the modern reformers regard the Reformation as informative rather than normative and argue that the modern search for New Testament and patristic roots fulfils the aims of the Reformers through the use of scholarly methods not available in the past."[19] Difficulty arises to the extent that earlier interpretations are considered final. That produces the effect that "much Baptist scholarship, when it has dealt with such controversial subjects as baptism, eucharist, and ministry, has been captive to traditional denominational (confessional) interests in order to find support for certain positions and to refute others."[20]

The Canadian Baptist statement on the Lord's Supper, in response to the BEM document, illustrates this. To make the traditional Baptist point, it quotes an Anglican who declares that "sacrificial ideas are absent from the New Testament references to the Supper."[21] It chooses to ignore a Baptist commentator's opposite conclusion that "the idea of sacrifice is basic to the Lord's Supper, culminating in the Pauline-Lukan presentation of it in terms of the prophetic understanding of the covenantal sacrifice as self-surrender or self-sacrifice."[22] To complicate matters even further, however, the Canadian statement, after repudiating the "traditional" notion of sacrifice, concedes that there is a type of sacrifice in the Supper: "Embodied in his Church, [Christ] is redeeming it by drawing it into his kind of existence and life by first drawing it into his kind of sacrifice, not cultic but self-denying and self-giving."[23]

Further indication of these contradictory attitudes among Baptists may be seen in the Canadian Baptist criticism of the BEM document's sacramental tone; it considers that to be contrary to the experience of the New Testament church although, as indicated above, some Baptists are coming to the position that much of their denominational thought and practice of the sacraments is inadequate.

A major dynamic in the Canadian Baptist reaction against the sacramental theology of the liturgical movement can be seen as not so much one of "Scripture and tradition" as of "tradition and anti-tradition." The importance of this reactive impulse is noted by a Southern Baptist theologian:

In the Catholic and liturgical traditions, [the Lord's Supper] has tended to take precedence. Probably, in reaction, the churches of the "sect type" have tended to give it a minor role. We Baptists have often fallen into this category, relegating the Lord's Supper to an infrequent observance and forgetting that, in the New Testament Church, it was celebrated every Lord's Day.[24]

This anti-tradition attitude has affected Baptist thinking in a number of areas having to do with the Lord's Supper. The very word "sacrament" is little esteemed "among Southern Baptists, chiefly because it carries for them associations of the Roman Catholic mass." Likewise, the "real presence" of Christ, the Lord's Supper as "eucharist," and the sacrificial nature of communion have all been viewed historically with suspicion by Baptists.[25]

"Anti-tradition" has the insidious tendency to misconstrue the intentions of other theological systems. For example, as a Roman Catholic theologian has pointed out, many Protestants have wilfully misunderstood the Roman doctrine of *ex opere operato*. According to it, the sacraments derive their efficacy from neither the celebrant nor the faithful alone; rather they are gracious acts of God, "beyond the power of man." The tragedy of the situation is that

[the Protestant] way of looking at the matter is a complete caricature. It amounts to making a formula assume the exact opposite of its true meaning. Yet there is no misinterpretation, no tragic misconception of the meaning of Catholic doctrine, to which Protestants seem so closely and irrevocably attached as this. Herein lies the root of their own distrust of sacramentalism.[26]

This lament makes it plain that the task of theological recovery (for Baptists as well) must involve not only a comprehensive grasp of the Scriptures but also an enlightened understanding of other traditions. Such an approach fosters two major objectives. First, it encourages a more realistic appraisal of the biblical basis of the faith and order of other confessions, thereby clearing the way for consensus. Second, it unmasks the polemical nature of much theological formulation and invalidates an adversarial approach. At least one Canadian Baptist recognizes the need for his confessional fellows to apply these attitudes:

Only an honest admission and a critical assessment of the given "traditional" context of the current discussions on BEM, by Baptists and others, will lead to the necessary *freedom* for new insights and affirmations which can arise from fresh exposure to the Scriptures and to the living God who continues to speak *through them*.[27]

Not only is it essential for Baptists to know the meanings of their own and other traditions; it is necessary also to understand the meaning of the Great Tradition.

Baptist resistance to (indeed, disavowal of) tradition is not difficult to understand, as noted above, for the denomination grew up in a climate of dissent against the authority of the Church of England, of the British Parliament, and (by association with the continental Reformation) of the Roman Catholic Church. However, it would be wrong to assume that the early Baptists were opposed to the authority of the Church. As has been seen, their struggle had to do less with the authority, and more with the nature of, the "true Church." The authority of Westminster and Rome was denied, not because of any conviction that the Church should be without polity or jurisdiction, but because Westminster and Rome were considered to be false churches. One has to look only as far as the use of terms such as "ordinance," "mere symbol," "simple memorial," and "priesthood of the believers" to see that Baptists, having determined the shape of what they believed to be the true Church and its worship, were quite willing to enforce their particular interpretation of the Scriptures. Indeed, it would appear that the Baptist system of polity and practice—Baptist "tradition"—although unofficial, has itself frequently assumed magisterial proportions.

Recognizing that Baptists have not been able to stand aloof from the influences of tradition, the challenge is to see that the tradition, albeit at times in error and in need of correction, is not rightly understood as being opposed to the Scriptures. On the contrary, the tradition may be seen as the history of the Church's attempts to understand and live out the demands of the Gospel:

> Tradition is not *something other than Holy Scripture* and added to it, but rather the entire living transmission of the truth, whose central organ is the inspired Scripture. Scripture is not illuminated or completed by tradition as by something foreign to it and superadded. On the contrary, we must insist, Scripture keeps its true and complete sense only when it remains a vital part of that living tradition of the church in which the inspired writers actually composed it, making it as it were the essential deposit of this tradition. The Word of God is communicated to the Church and directs it through Holy Scripture, but through Scripture linked to all those things that make us see it as the deposit of a Word which is and will always be the Word of life, which cannot be preserved apart from the life it itself creates and sustains.[28]

For Protestants in general, the results of a divorce between the Scripture and the "living witness of the Spirit in the Church" has been that

> the letter of Scripture was abandoned to the entirely subjective variations of individual interpretations, and so Protestantism came to crumble into sects as hostile to each other as to the Catholic Church, disputing about texts torn from their context and isolated from Revelation as a whole, whose fundamental teachings were in danger of becoming more and more obscured through a narrow and falsifying attachment to details that were ill understood.[29]

The honest awareness that the Baptist tradition has been as offensive to other traditions as we find them to have been to ours will assist in the recognition that the continuing quest for biblical faithfulness completely transcends denominational lines. A prominent Southern Baptist historian observes that "in the past we at times sought to bury our competitors, at other times to blend our traditions into theirs in some syncretistic mix, and at still others simply to maintain some kind of detente." Now, he proposes, Baptists need to adopt a "catholic" outlook which strives "to embrace all of church history as the history of us all" to the end that the recovery of apostolic norms may be seen as the prerogative of the whole Church "within which each tradition may release the deepest witness within it."[30]

One sometimes gets the impression that many Baptists would rather use new forms of their own invention than employ anything reminiscent of Catholicism. Baptists, who have cherished the notion that God works unmediatedly in their midst, should be startled out of their complacency by a Roman Catholic observer who sees that Protestant thought appears to restrict the freedom of the Spirit; evidently, Protestants think that

> with the death of the last apostle the truth of the divine word within the Church ceased to be entrusted to a responsible body of men, invested for that purpose with the very authority of their master, ceased therefore to be the truth of a living Word kept in men's hearts, and became the wholly exterior truth of the unchanging letter of a book.[31]

Roman Catholics, however, understand that "the word of God cannot consist merely in something written, but is primarily a living Word. It is a living Word of which it is not enough to say that it is entrusted to the Church; its presence, ever active through the ages, being the presence of Christ himself, is what constitutes the Church."[32] This is to take very seriously the Christian doctrine of the Holy Spirit. A British Baptist educator echoes this view of the Spirit dynamically at work in tradition and immediate experience: "what controls our deciding is not only what was once done, but also what in the present situation will best forward the life and witness of the church. The authority is thus not only what God did in the past, but also what He calls us to do in the present."[33]

So much energy has been spent protecting the Free Church from so-called Catholic influences that to reflect on these matters might appear to compromise or, worse, concede defeat. To be involved in ecumenical and liturgical renewal is not to abandon the Baptist cause. It is, more correctly, to recover and pursue the original Baptist vision. The kernel of John Smyth's teaching bears quotation:

> The matter of our spiritual worship [is] Christ Jesus & His merits: the word of God contained in the Scriptures which offers Christ Jesus to us: the seals of the covenant with all the actions thereto appertaining...the form of our Spiritual worship consists in the fire

of the Spirit working with the word.... As the fire came down from heaven, wherewith the sacrifices were offered,...so the Holy Ghost like fire came down upon the primitive Church, to make their spiritual sacrifices acceptable: so must it do also upon ours.[34]

Spiritual worship is the prayer of the heart. Whatever the outward forms, it is to offer oneself to God with absolute attention and to trust that the encounter is consummated by the living presence of Christ. A later Baptist thinker expresses it like this:

We may need a different doctrine in regard to the Lord's Supper in order to keep in mind the fact that the realities of such an act are much more complex, much larger, and more difficult to achieve than the simple dimensions of sentimental memory. But once that has been accomplished, our harder task will be to resuscitate the deeper levels of our souls to match the profundity of revelation by which we may be redeemed. To do this will mean to take upon ourselves new disciplines of mind and heart, a new way of life, a different sense of values, a radical shift in our way of looking at truth and reality.[35]

For Smyth, these "disciplines of heart and mind" were never undertaken in isolation, but always in the context of his desire to recover the "true outward, visible church which Christ and his Apostles, at the first instituted." It was this sense of vision which enabled him to risk change:

Now I have in all my writings hitherto received instruction of others and professed my readiness to be taught by others and, therefore, have I so often times been accused of inconstancy. Well, let them think of me as they please; I profess I have changed, and shall be ready still to change, for the better.[36]

Surely, if there is one attitude bequeathed by Smyth to be cultivated by Baptists in the current climate of liturgical renewal and ecumenical relations, it is this one. It will be of immeasurable worth in our attempts to understand our identity within the larger Church. More broadly, in addressing the pastoral challenges of one denomination, it also will serve the work of the Great Church in its endeavour to regain a comprehensive sense of its future as the living harbinger of the Kingdom of God.

Notes

[1] Faith and Order Commission, *Baptism, Eucharist, and Ministry*, Faith and Order Paper No. 111, Lima, Peru (Geneva: World Council of Churches, 1982).

[2] Ronald F. Watts, *The Ordinances and Ministry of the Church: A Baptist View* ([Mississauga, ON]: InterChurch Relations Committee, Canadian Baptist Federation, 1986), 43.

[3] Watts, *Ordinances and Ministry*, 35.

[4] James Tull, "The Ordinances/Sacraments in Baptist Thought," *American Baptist Quarterly* 1 (December 1982): 191.

[5] Geoffrey Wainwright, Newsletter of Societas Liturgica 2, no. 1 (Summer 1984), 11.

[6] John Smyth, "Principles and Inferences Concerning the Visible Church," in *The Works of John Smyth*, ed. W. T. Whitley, vol. 1 (Cambridge: Cambridge University Press, 1915), 268.

[7] Smyth, "Principles and Inferences," 251-53.

[8] John Smyth, "Retractions and Confirmations," in *Works*, 1:753-54.

[9] Charles A. Jenkins, ed., *Baptist Doctrines* (St. Louis, MO: Chancy R. Barns, 1880), iii.

[10] E. Y. Mullins, *The Axioms of Religion* ([1908], 56-57), quoted in *The Life and Faith of the Baptists* by H. Wheeler Robinson (London: Methuen, 1927), 18.

[11] Thomas R. McKibbens, Jr., "Our Baptist Heritage in Worship," *Review and Expositor* 80 (Winter 1983), 56.

[12] H. E. Dana, *A Manual of Ecclesiology* (Kansas City, KS: Central Seminary Press, 1944), 324.

[13] Horton Davies, *The Worship of the English Puritans* (Westminster, MD: Dacre, 1948), 77.

[14] Ernest A. Payne, *The Fellowship of Believers* (London: Carey Kingsgate, 1952), 129.

[15] Watts, *Ordinances and Ministry*, 3.

[16] C. Brownlow Hastings, *Introducing Southern Baptists: Their Faith and Life* (New York: Paulist Press, 1981), 22.

[17] Norman Maring and Winthrop Hudson, *A Baptist Manual of Polity and Practice* (Valley Forge, PA: Judson Press, 1963), 5.

[18] Jarold K. Zeman, comp., "*Baptism, Eucharist, and Ministry*: Selected Aids to Baptist Interpretation" (Wolfville, NS: Acadia Divinity College, n.d.), 1.

[19] James F. White, "Recent Developments in Worship," *American Baptist Quarterly* 1 (December 1982): 21.

[20] Zeman, "Selected Aids," 1.

[21] C. E. B. Cranfield, "Thank, Give Thanks, Thanksgiving (Eucharist)," in *A Theological Word Book of the Bible*, ed. Alan Richardson (London: SCM, 1951), 256, quoted in Watts, *Ordinances and Ministry*, 15.

[22] Eric C. Rust, "The Theology of the Lord's Supper," *Review and Expositor* 66 (Winter 1969): 13.

[23] Frank Stagg, "The Lord's Supper in the New Testament," *Review and Expositor* 66 (Winter 1969): 13-14, quoted in Watts, *Ordinances and Ministry*, 15-16.

[24] Rust, "Theology of Lord's Supper," 35.

[25] Rust, "Theology of Lord's Supper," 35.

[26] Louis Bouyer, *The Word, Church and Sacraments in Protestantism and Catholicism* (Paris: Desclé, 1961), 66-67.

[27] Zeman, "Selected Aids," 1.

[28] Bouyer, *Word, Church, and Sacraments*, 53-54.

[29] Bouyer, *Word, Church, and Sacraments*, 27.

[30] E. Glenn Hinson, "The Lima Text as Pointer to the Future: A Baptist Perspective," *Studia Liturgica* 16 (1986): 99.

[31] Bouyer, *Word, Church, and Sacraments*, 51.

[32] Bouyer, *Word, Church, and Sacraments*, 76.

[33] W. M. W. West, "Church, Ministry, and Episcopacy: Reflections on a Baptist View" (Baptist Union of Great Britain and Ireland, March 1981), 3, quoted in Watts, *Ordinances and Ministry*, 28.

[34] John Smyth, "The Differences of the Churches of the Seperation," in *Works*, 1:302.

[35] Samuel H. Miller, "Reducing the Reality of the Lord's Supper," *Review and Expositor* 66 (Winter 1969): .

[36] John Smyth, "The Last Booke of Iohn Smith," in *Works*, 2:753 and 752.

PART TWO
Movements and Their Structures

Chapter 4

The Effect of Baptist "Home Mission" among Alberta's German Immigrants

David T. Priestley

The settling of Canada's northwest—travel, weather, money, immigration, politics—is an epic backdrop for the narrative of the planting and growth of churches in Alberta. Baptists also have their beginnings here among the people who spilled across the region east from the Rockies to the 110th meridian.[1]

Five different Baptist bodies have member congregations in the province, distinguished fortuitously or intentionally by ethnic and theological differences. The largest union stands in the Anglophone mainstream which traces its roots to the Nova Scotia Great Awakening of the late 18th century. The second-largest originated from the immigrations of Germans a century and more later. Around the histories of the ten North American Baptist[2] churches in Alberta which are presently over seventy-five years old, this chapter seeks to review the drama and tedium of church planting and the vicissitudes of church growth which has been duplicated to varying degrees in the experiences of other Baptists as well. Like all church history, it is a story of sin and grace with large doses of dumb luck.

The Germans who settled Alberta came primarily from the Russian and Austrian territories of eastern Europe.[3] They had migrated there since the 1770s at the invitations of Catherine of Russia and Joseph of Austria. After 1870, Austro-Hungarian political setbacks and russification of czarist territories were jeopardizing German privileges. At just this time Canada and the United States were intensifying efforts to draw immigrants into North American prairies.[4]

German Baptist pioneers in Alberta and the southwestern corner of Saskatchewan organized nearly twenty-five churches in the years before World War I.[5] They ranged from south and east of Medicine Hat north to Edmonton wherever concentrations of Germans accumulated. The earliest, Rabbit Hill, southwest of Edmonton, organized in 1892; the latest, now Grace Baptist of Calgary, got its start twenty years later.

While demographically German Baptist work in Alberta is part of the larger story of the province, ecclesiologically these churches share in the institutional evolution of *deutschen Gemeinden getaufter Christen (gewöhnlich Baptisten genannt).*[6] Initially, churches were organized by immigrant German Baptists and their converts among fellow immigrants in the United States. In 1851, the movement began forming convention structures which multiplied regionally as Germans followed the frontier westward. German Baptists were greatly indebted to the help of the American Baptist Home Mission Society and the American Baptist Publication Society, although they remained self-consciously distinct from the bodies whose help was so valuable. Likewise, English-speaking Canadian Baptists supported German Baptist work in the west as a consequence of the vision of people like Alexander Grant, pastor of Winnipeg's First Baptist Church from 1889-97, and of C. C. McLaurin, who from 1901-26 was missionary-at-large and superintendent of predecessor bodies to the Baptist Union of Western Canada (BUWC).

The Years of Planting (1890-1920)

The earliest German Baptist churches appeared in an arc of forty to sixty kilometres that stretched from west of to southeast of Edmonton. They originated among immigrants from Volhynia, a region in eastern Poland-western Ukraine. Some of these had embraced Baptist convictions as a consequence of a Lutheran religious awakening and Baptist evangelism among the *diaspora* Germans (*Volksdeutsche*) of eastern Europe in the 1850s.[7] The first Baptists began to move into the area south of Edmonton in 1889, scattering among Moravians and Lutherans. Some came directly from Europe; some had tried making a livelihood in the Winnipeg area for a time; most had tried to farm the arid townships south of Irvine and Dunmore;[8] at least one had gone to Texas first where he heard of more favourable prospects in Alberta.[9]

Seventeen charter members organized the Heimthal (now Rabbit Hill) Baptist Church in 1892. German and Canadian Baptists concurred in a recognition council that September. Only after the Rabbit Hill church was organized and recognized did its first pastor arrive.

F. A. Mueller had been a German Baptist missionary in Volhynia until the summer of 1892. Then he was banished from czarist territories because he had baptized two Russians in defiance of the law. He came to North America partly to find a new home for his former parishioners. First he tried Texas. Presumably, while he was there, the Rabbit Hill leadership learned that he was available. When Mueller accepted the call of the newly organized church, he set about not only ministering to those already there but arranging for families in Volhynia to come also. More than thirty families arrived in 1893. Most of them settled about twenty-five kilometres southeast of Rabbit Hill, in the Fredericksheim neighbourhood south of Leduc, though all were members of the one church. When Rabbit Hill applied to join the Northwestern Conference of German Baptist churches,[10] their letter of July 1893 reported:

> The church holds its worship services in Heimthal and Leduc which are well attended. In the city of Edmonton, we hold a service twice a month; and once [a month], in Wetaskiwin. The prayer meetings enjoy lively participation. The church is united in love. The Sunday School is being blessed. This is a good field for the distribution of Bibles, Testaments, and tracts.[11]

The church, obviously, was dependent on lay leadership in worship and Sunday School; the pastor's frequent travels to other preaching points left them dependent on the expository skills of the men of the church. Occasionally a visiting German Baptist, English Baptist, or German Moravian pastor would preach for them.

More than 140 Baptist immigrants joined the Rabbit Hill church by letter in the first two years of its existence; Mueller baptized another forty. The distance from Rabbit Hill and the density of German Baptists in the Fredericksheim area justified the Leduc station in establishing itself as an independent congregation in 1894; 141 members were dismissed from Rabbit Hill to found the new church at Fredericksheim. The large charter membership at Leduc is unique. Of fourteen opening rolls from this period, the average is twenty-one; the largest is thirty-two. Two of Leduc's stations soon organized as separate churches in their turn—Wetaskiwin in 1896 and Wiesental in 1908.

Church life for German Baptist congregations followed a pattern. First, they undertook the task of gathering the Baptists who were coming into the area, then, of evangelizing the unconverted. Personal evangelism tended to be confrontational; annual revival meetings (in earlier years referred to as "prayer meetings") emphasized hellfire and brimstone.

Families lived in log houses with sod or "thatched" roofs; but the church was lumber, built by volunteers who in some cases had sawn the planks themselves during the winter months. Hardware and glass were purchased with gifts from German Baptists elsewhere and funds from Canadian and American Baptists. Sunday Schools were quickly organized at each of the stations as well as in the mother church but not always faithfully maintained. Youth work, choir, Women's Missionary Fellowship, and a band or orchestra often followed.

Russian-Germans formed another congregation among settlers to the west of Edmonton in another manner. There a homesteader-preacher, Edward Wolfe, was the catalyst. In the Glory Hills neighbourhood north of Stony Plain, the immigrants were primarily German Reformed. They did not organize a church immediately but met for a lay-led Sunday School.

Wolfe often spoke at these services and planted seeds of Baptist concerns—personal conversion, separation from the world, believer's baptism, and the like. Finally in 1903, those persuaded that Baptist understanding of Christian faith and practice was preferable to the Reformed tradition in which they had been reared organized themselves into a Baptist church.[12] Some years later Wolfe simultaneously served Glory Hills and the Rabbit Hill church, forty kilometres and a river crossing to the southeast.

Rabbit Hill had shown a concern for Edmonton from the beginning; but Mueller's successor, Abraham Hager, managed to found a church only after he moved into the city. Girls from the Leduc and Rabbit Hill churches worked as domestic servants and clerks in the two towns which straddled the North Saskatchewan River; they and immigrating tradesmen formed the nucleus and prospects of the First German Baptist Church of Edmonton (1900). Hager helped people to find housing and employment and to deal with government offices as well as evangelizing and nurturing the saints.[13]

On the dusty southern prairies abandoned in 1890 for the better promise of the Edmonton area, other homesteaders continued to battle the aridity of the Palliser Triangle. Among those who remained for some years, German Baptists were reported in 1894.[14] Five years later a congregation was organized at Josephsburg, a rural post office. As the years passed they also bought a meeting place in Irvine and began a station in Medicine Hat. Despite the climate, things went moderately well for Josephsburg until its Medicine Hat station became independent in 1917. Then the mother church declined in three years from over ninety to less than forty.

The first decade of the century produced three congregations which were not composed of direct Old World immigrants. Since the 1880s many Russian-Germans from settlements along the Black Sea around Odessa (Moldavia and southern Ukraine) had been prospering in Oregon and the Dakotas. Although all the homestead land below the 49th parallel was by no means taken in 1900, some were attracted to the Camrose, Trochu, and Carbon areas because the possibilities for expansion near them in the United States were becoming limited. These families were quite acculturated in comparison to the latest arrivals at Halifax and relatively well-endowed with household goods, equipment, cattle, and cash. A number came from Oregon to settle along Bittern Lake, near Camrose, and formed a church there (1901). A Dakota contingent of seven families required fifty-two boxcars and two coaches to get as far as Strathmore; from there, they trekked overland to settle along Knee Hill Creek east of Crossfield in 1909. The land agent had arranged the homesteaders in distinct ethnic and religious blocks in this area.[15] The former Dakotans soon organized Freudenthal Baptist Church, near Carbon (1910). About fifty kilometres farther up Knee Hill Creek an earlier group of Dakota Germans had organized a slowly growing church in 1902. When the town of Trochu was founded in 1911 along the new rail line, a majority of these Knee Hill Creek families moved east about thirty kilometres and organized another German Baptist church in the new town. A parsonage was built, but their first services were held in the Presbyterian church.

Homesteaders were also being attracted into the grasslands east of the Red Deer River. German Baptists were drawn east from the Wetaskiwin area; others came directly from Europe. Enthusiastic reports of the prospects there were justified when a church was organized in Forestburg in 1913. Three years earlier another church had formed out of the same influx of settlers near Richdale; Craigmyle was a Richdale station which, five years after the mother church came into existence, hived off as an independent church.

In the same decade, German immigrants were spreading over the prairies on either side of the Alberta-Saskatchewan border, south of the South Saskatchewan River. German Baptist efforts near Herbert (1903-05) and Hodgeville, Saskatchewan (1914-23), failed in the face of the overwhelming predominance of Mennonites. But those who homesteaded near Lutherans around Hilda (Alberta) and Leader, Burstall, Glidden, and Maple Creek (Saskatchewan) were able, despite impoverished beginnings, to establish churches which in time grew to require stations. These churches usually shared pastors; more often, they had to conduct their spiritual lives under lay leadership, for pastoral placements among them were short and irregular. The regional fellowship they organized in 1916 (the Saskatchewan-Alberta Central Association) welded them together and sustained their determination in the hard times ahead.

Efforts to begin a church among German immigrants in Calgary were not so successful as in Edmonton. This may be due to the lack of a resident pastor until the 1920s. A church was built and services conducted for a time. But by 1919, the building was rented to others; and the Germans were attending Calgary's First Baptist Church which had helped them start.

Mission assistance from the German Baptists and Canadian Baptists was essential to support most pastors. Perhaps because they were dependent on this outside help, these preachers were astonishingly peripatetic; on foot, by buggy, and by train, they ranged far beyond the natural borders of their own church's community to edify and to redeem.

Three types of full-time itinerant ministers (*Reiseprediger*) were used by the German Baptists to plant and nurture churches. A colporteur was a Bible, tract, and literature salesman. He went from farm to farm, house to house, selling his books. He sought to lead people to Christ, then gather them into Bible study and prayer groups, and as soon as possible organize them as a local church. He was also on the lookout for German Baptists to include in an existing circle or to provide the focus around which a permanent group could be gathered.

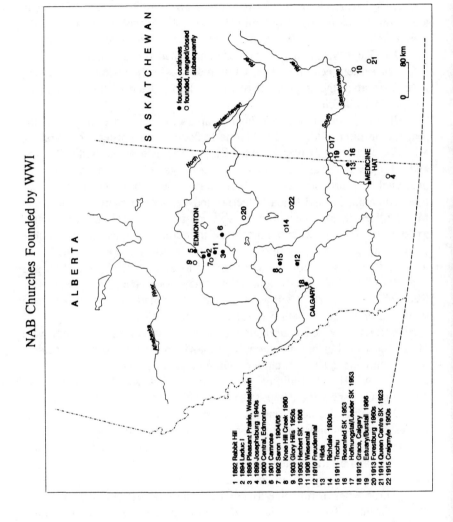

NAB Churches Founded by WWI

1 1892 Rabbit Hill
2 1894 Leduc I
3 1896 Pleasant Prairie, Wetaskiwin
4 1899 Josephsburg 1940s
5 1900 Central, Edmonton
6 1901 Camrose
7 1902 Saron 1904/06
8 Knee Hill Creek 1960
9 1903 Glory Hills 1950s
10 1905 Herbert SK 1906
11 1906 Wiesental
12 1910 Freudenthal
13 Hilda
14 Richdale 1930s
15 1911 Trochu
16 Rosenfeld SK 1953
17 Hoffnungstal/Leader SK 1953
18 1912 Grace, Calgary
19 Estuary/Burstall 1966
20 1913 Forestburg 1960s
21 1914 Queen Centre SK 1923
22 1915 Craigmyle 1950s

● founded, continues
○ founded, merged/closed subsequently

The second was a conference or district missionary; he was responsible to serve the pastorless churches as advisor and preacher, much as does an area minister presently. He built on the colporteur's work and on leads suggested by others.

The third itinerant provided by the denomination was an evangelist, available to churches anywhere in Canada or the United States for special meetings. From 1889-1920, Heinrich Schwendener served in this capacity; several times he held memorable campaigns in Alberta churches. Churches were not dependent upon Schwendener for evangelistic outreach, however. Annual crusades were customary, usually lead by a visiting pastor from elsewhere in the province, sometimes by the local pastor himself. Apart from reviving the church, these services had the primary effect of bringing their children and neighbours to declare their faith in Christ and soon to join the church.

The Years of Rooting (1920-50)

The twenties did not roar much in the largely rural German Baptist churches. Generally, the churches had experienced no problems as a result of the *Alien Enemies Act* during World War I. Their perceived "spiritual arrogance" caused more resentment among their neighbours than their ethnic roots did. The influenza epidemic of 1918 emptied many a child's chair, but the adult membership of the churches seemed little effected by deaths. The more established churches began to experience the prosperity of the members as farms were paid off and facilities improved. Educated in public schools, the children were being Canadianized; and the churches, even without the pressure of wartime hysteria, were beginning to use English in literature, Sunday School, worship, and sermon.

The patterns of the English-speaking Baptists increasingly were adopted. Sunday Schools often were intended to teach the German language as much as Scripture lessons; but the principles and standards of the Sunday School movement were pushed by *Der Sendbote* and other denominational publications. Young people's societies provided leadership training for the coming generation.

Apart from the immigrant pastors and early conference workers recruited from the Alberta churches in the first twenty years of German Baptist work here, virtually all the pastors serving in Alberta after 1910 were alumni of the German Department of Rochester (NY) Theological Seminary. This education at a single seminary created a cohesion and institutional homogeneity not only for Alberta but across the denomination which has been of incalculable influence in its corporate life.

In language, organization, and style of church life, German Baptists quickly naturalized. Because of the dependence on the Rochester seminary and denominational "headquarters" in Cleveland and Chicago, they were quite Americanized in church life; because of school, community, and business, however, they were clearly Canadianized, content to follow the lead of the "Ontario-based British elite."[16]

This second period saw the formation of only seven new churches, four of them outgrowths of existing congregations. But 1920-50 was a period of great national change in which all the churches shared; the key events were the drought and depression of the thirties and the challenge of World War II. The German Baptist churches in these years were not just getting older and bigger; they were beginning to urbanize.

Germans, since the 1880s, had been settled in towns like Leduc, Wetaskiwin, and Onoway; and German Baptists, despite their preponderantly rural memberships, viewed these townspeople, too, as candidates for evangelism and pastoral care. Now, however, some of the farmers formerly active in the country churches of Fredericksheim, Pleasant Prairie, and Glory Hills were retiring to the villages where they were accustomed to do business. First, occasional services were held in the homes of the pensioners in town; but as the fellowship grew, churches were organized which continue to the present. The second Leduc church (Temple Baptist) was formed in 1927. The Westside Baptist Church in Wetaskiwin organized in 1929. The Glory Hill church began a branch Sunday School and station in Onoway in 1932 which later became an independent congregation.

Troubles shook the Freudenthal church in the early thirties to the extent that some families withdrew to form Bethel Baptist less than ten kilometres away. Alberta pastors and denominational workers tried to mediate; but the two went their separate ways in 1933. Only twelve years later the churches reunited; symbolic of the reconciliation and the changing farm population, they dismantled both country structures and built a new church in the town of Carbon.

Another church began when the large Reed Ranch east of Olds sold its ranges for farmsteads. News of this opportunity was spread among the German Baptist churches in the hope that new families would revitalize the Knee Hill Creek congregation. Numbers came in 1928 and 1929; but instead of augmenting the adjacent senior church, a new one was organized.

The thirties forced massive relocations throughout the province, as farms dried out and small towns shrivelled across once lush prairies. While some areas gained as a result—Valleyview and Onoway—others lost. The Richdale church died and Craigmyle went into an irreversible decline in a region which since the thirties has had peculiar governmental and agricultural structures.[17] Forestburg, north of the worst-hit parts of Special Areas, limped along in the aftermath of "the winter years;"[18] and Josephsburg, in the arid south, just drops from denominational reports without comment. Efforts to found a work near Success, Saskatchewan, failed. The Golden Prairie church seems to have been begun in 1945 to gather the remnants of the fading churches west of the Sand Hills.

The Anglicization of the German Baptists was interrupted somewhat in the early part of this second period by the arrival of another wave of immigrants. In the aftermath of the Bolshevik Revolution and during the power struggle after Lenin's death, thousands of Germans contrived to leave the Soviet Union and come to North America. German Baptists organized a Immigration and Colonization Society to assist these prospective Canadians.[19] The new arrivals brought with them an older pattern of church life, more lay-led and less literate, which caused some tensions; but generally, the new Canadians fit in well with the Canadianized German Baptists. Nonetheless, they did somewhat revive the need for the German language in worship services and Bible classes.

In 1922, the denomination organized a Young People's and Sunday School Worker's Union (YPSSU). "It would be difficult to estimate the importance of this organization in conserving the young people for the denomination and in assisting in the transition from the German to the English language."[20] The Bible school movement was one specific outcome of this denominational decision.

In 1929, the Northern Conference adopted a plan to hold four-week Bible schools in each of its four associations to supplement the occasional provincial youth rallies. The ad hoc Bible schools held previously had been well received.[21] Now each year a church was expected to host a Bible school for all the German Baptist churches in its area. In the daytime, courses in Bible, teaching skills, instrumental and vocal music, conducting, and the devotional life were taught by pastors from the participating churches and by guest lecturers. Evenings were given over to evangelistic meetings at which the instructors preached and the young people sang, played, and testified.

After 1933, F. W. Benke, pastor at Wetaskiwin, became the principal organizer for Alberta. For a few years, the German Baptists used the building in Wetaskiwin that the Swedish Baptists had purchased for similar purposes. E. P. Wahl, previously an Alberta pastor, had become director for these Northern Conference Bible schools in 1937. His energy and vision soon led to the purchase of land in Edmonton and the construction of a residential school in 1939—the Christian Training Institute. The "floating" Bible schools had contributed greatly to knowledge, skills, friendships, and marriages, despite their limitations. With the construction of a permanent residential school, the courses could be extended in length and greater care could be given to developing faculty and library. Since the first course in January 1940, CTI has united the German Baptist churches and contributed to their growth, especially in Alberta.

The Sunday School Union, the Young People's Union, and the Choir Union began to hold simultaneous annual conferences. A camp program for children and youth was begun in the mid-1940s. Benke, while a key figure in Alberta's Bible school movement, passed on to his students and finally to the whole denomination his passion for the salvation of Alberta's Cree Indians. In 1946, the NAB Board of Mission undertook ministry on the Bull and Montana Reserves near Wetaskiwin. These institutional developments within and between the churches conformed to practices in various denominations. But though the form was Canadian or American, the constituency still was explicitly German.

These years of rooting were times of deepening, maturing, and institutionalizing. The Germanness of the churches was waning. Typically, it was only after 1940 that the Edmonton church changed its name from *Erste deutsche Baptisten Gemeinde* to Central Baptist Church; in 1943, it took the major step of conducting the evening service in English. The denomination dropped its ethnic label in 1946 for a name which intended to declare that its member churches were located both in Canada and in the United States. By the end of the period fewer and fewer services were conducted in German; only a German Bible class for older members remained in many churches. In some cases, the pastors spoke only English. Yet the network of fellow-ship and ministry which had been forged in the early years still had an ethnic quality. In the next period, the ethnicity both intensified and collapsed.

The Years of Branching (1950-70)

The post-war years brought optimism, prosperity, and change. A long-time station of the Carbon church organized as a daughter church (which after one year celebrated the twenty-fifth anniversary of its Young People's Society!).[22] The rural churches outside Camrose and Wetaskiwin merged with their daughter churches in town. While prosperity enabled many of the churches to build and remodel parsonages and churches and to support local and denominational programs more generously, other fragile churches from the first era gave up the ghost. Glory Hills disappeared; Forestburg dwindled away; Knee Hill Creek disbanded to join the East Olds church to the west. In southwest Saskatchewan, stations closed and the churches at Glidden, Leader, and Burstall vanished. Rosenfeld's last members joined Golden Prairie.

Suburbanization became a trend in the larger cities. Central Baptist, Edmonton, organized two daughter churches in 1951. Lauderdale had been a northside mission station for many years; McKernan was built in the south near CTI to draw NAB families spreading into the southern developments of the city. Central gave some additional members twelve years later who combined with the Lauderdale congregation as Northgate Baptist. In 1960, Central released seventy members to found Capilano Baptist.

Some of this outgrowth would have developed in any case; but it would not have been so frequent or so large had it not been for the massive immigration of Germans displaced during WWII and its aftermath. Generous relief shipments of food and clothing first forged ties of compassion. Then Canada opened her doors to the refugees. Over 7,000 were assisted entirely or in part by the revived NAB Immigration and Colonization Society.[23]

Edmonton, Calgary, and Lethbridge were the three major centres of influx in Alberta, with some gains also in Medicine Hat. As Abraham Hager had done in Edmonton fifty years before, Henry Pfeiffer, Central's pastor from 1950-56, now energetically duplicated. He met immigrants at the train depot; he found housing; he directed them to employment; he accompanied them to government offices. His energy, and above all, his evangelistic challenge astounded, overwhelmed, and persuaded the newcomers of the claims of Christ; so by conversion and baptism as well as transfers of church letters, church membership mushroomed. Numerically, the new Canadians came to outnumber the old ones; so in Calgary, Edmonton, and Medicine Hat the churches which welcomed them soon took on the complexion of the newcomers.

The established NAB churches suffered numerous strains over the recent arrivals. The new freedoms, the unfamiliar ways, the Canadianness of the welcoming churches, the different customs and standards even among the immigrants, the strong personalities of lay leaders and pastors now coming from Europe, and nameless more subtle differences generated tensions which could not be contained. These contributed in part to the formation of the new English-speaking NAB churches mentioned above.

But old "First German Baptist" could not retain all of the immigrants. Calgary spawned two German- and one English-speaking daughter churches between 1953 and 1960, largely as a result of the inflexibility and insensitivity of its Canadian-born pastor. In Medicine Hat, the more Canadianized families also left to found a new church. Even before Pfeiffer left Edmonton, a German group had withdrawn to form Emmanuel; on the heels of his resignation, Zion was organized by some of the recent arrivals. Central, with Emmanuel and Zion, contributed to the membership of two other "German" churches which arose in the sixties.

The post-war years also brought the inauguration of a conference-wide "church extension program" which caught the imagination of Alberta's "elder sisters" also. Leaders recognized that the immigrants would inevitably (and probably more rapidly) follow the same process of acculturation which the existing NAB churches had undergone. They also saw that the move to the suburbs not only threatened to drain the membership of established NAB churches but offered opportunities for evangelism and planting new churches. So with assistance for pastors' salaries, land purchase, and building construction, Alberta NAB churches set about starting new churches in growing areas of cities where there were existing churches who could "mother" the infant effort. Soon the vision expanded to encompass growing communities which lacked strong evangelical ministries even though no NAB family lived there.

In the post-war years, CTI continued to train lay leaders; increasingly, it came to be a stepping-stone to university and, hence, for the urbanization of the farm-reared. Likewise, it played a key role in the assimilation of the immigrants. Many of these young people were "determined to make a clean break with the past and start a new life with Christ in the country of their choice."[24] They wanted Bible training; they needed high school diplomas and English language skills.

Some of the students also felt called to pastoral ministry, but the Bible school courses failed to provide training in pastoral skills and many of these young men lacked the academic foundations for a full seminary program. So in 1958, the school was authorized to inaugurate a three-year undergraduate theological course for men (!) to "serve our Canadian churches in a bilingual capacity."[25] Within a decade, the school was renamed NAB College, a revised mandate dropped the "German-speaking" restriction on pastoral training candidates, and a new Bachelor of Religious Education program admitted women. The College relocated to its present site, a gift of the Alumni Association.

The Years of Spreading (1970-90)

Structural changes in the denomination eliminated the regional Northern Conference in 1972; the Alberta Baptist Association became the focus of fellowship and cooperative ministry. F. W. Benke's beloved Indian mission, faulted by some for "trying to make good Germans out of Cree Indians", was entrusted to the Northern Canada Evangelical Mission in 1971. In Edmonton, Leduc, and Medicine Hat, retirement homes were built under the auspices of individual churches or with wider association (and government!) support. CTI's undergraduate pastoral training matured, in 1980, into a full post-baccalaureate seminary (Edmonton Baptist Seminary). Central Baptist Church relocated in 1973. Recently, they repurchased their old building for use as a "street people church;" this intriguing response to urban needs is supported jointly by NABs and BUWC.

To what degree ethnicity remains a factor is difficult to assess. Virtually all the churches which grew out of the post-war immigrations, and in some cases were begun in trauma to preserve the German traditions, have faced and survived the transition to English. Ironically, the two urban churches, Central (Edmonton) and Grace (Calgary), are the most German of the surviving ten elders. The vision once focussed on Germans has become a vision for growing places and empty lives regardless of ethnicity. Church extension is a continuing thrust. None of the "first ten" is in imminent danger of extinction; even some of the more rural ones have optimistic prospects in the long range.

Conclusion

Alberta's more than 7,700 NABs, in their fifty churches, with the children and friends who study and worship with them, are the heirs of heroic efforts among immigrant pioneers on prairie and in parkland. Of the eighteen churches organized more than seventy-five years ago in Alberta, ten survive. Etched on their histories, but ignored, is the wider story of Alberta's development; ethnicity had little to do with how they handled drought and depression in the thirties or prosperity and suburbanization in the sixties. Preserved in their heritage, but unexamined, is the larger story of German immigration over 100 years. Reflected in their present character, but unnoticed, is the spiritual milieu of American evangelicalism. It is not their ethnicity, but their Baptistness which stands in jeopardy. NABs stand at special risk, for the ethos which first addressed and has constantly nourished us was the much-transformed Anglo-American evangelicalism of the mid-19th-century and the successive permutations it has undergone since then, particularly in the United States. Alberta's NABs, and their sister congregations across the prairies and in British Columbia's valleys, are a product of distinctive ethnic, cultural, and religious forces which are traceable in the narratives of these ten eldest.

Notes

[1] John E. Foster, ed., *The Developing West* (Edmonton: University of Alberta Press, 1976); R. Douglas Frances and Howard Palmer, eds., *The Prairie West* (Edmonton: Pica Pica, 1985); Gerald Friesen, *The Canadian Prairies* (Toronto: University of Toronto Press, 1984); James G. MacGregor, *A History of Alberta*, rev. ed. (Edmonton: Hurtig, 1981); Howard and Tamara Palmer, eds., *Peoples of Alberta* (Saskatoon: Western Producer Prairie Books, 1985); Howard Palmer and Donald Smith, eds., *The New Provinces, Alberta and Saskatchewan: 1905-1980* (Vancouver: Tantalus Research, 1980); Benjamin G. Smillie, ed., *Visions of the New Jerusalem* (Edmonton: NeWest, 1983); and Lewis H. Thomas, ed., *Essays on Western History* (Edmonton: University of Alberta Press, 1976).

[2] The "German Baptist General Conference" changed its name in 1946 to "North American Baptist General Conference," then later dropped the "General." Hereafter, "NAB" even when anachronistic.

[3] Heinz Lehmann, *The German Canadians, 1750-1939*, trans. Gerhard P. Bassler (1937; ET, St. John's: Jespersen Press, 1986).

[4] E.g., J. N. McCrorie, "Historical Background to Prairie Settlement," in *New Jerusalem*, ed. Smillie, 19-20.

[5] Denominational statistics and decisions are recorded in "Verhandlungen" [Proceedings] and "Minutes" of general (triennial) conferences, regional conferences, and (since 1972) provincial/state associations, published annually since 1851. The most complete history is Frank H. Woyke, *Heritage and Ministry of the North American Baptist Conference* (Oakbrook Terrace, IL: North American Baptist Conference, [1976]); cf. Edward B. Link, "North American (German) Baptists," in *Baptists in Canada*, ed. Jarold K. Zeman (Burlington, ON: G. R. Welch, 1980), 87-103. During a sabbatical, January-June 1989, in extended visits to most of these ten, I collected church histories, interviews, archival materials, and impressions; specific local sources found will be noted only rarely.

[6] "German Churches of Baptized Christians (Usually Called Baptists)"— cf. Woyke, *Heritage and Ministry*, 3-106.

[7] Robert L. Kluttig, *Geschichte der deutschen Baptisten in Polen von 1858-1945* (Winnipeg: By the author, 1973).

[8] MacGregor, *History of Alberta*, 165-66.

[9] [Helen Hieberts et al., eds.,] *South Edmonton Saga* (Edmonton: South Edmonton, Papaschase Historical Society, 1984), 610-11, 950, 1046-47.

[10] The Northwestern Conference at that time comprised the churches of Iowa, Wisconsin, Minnesota, North and South Dakota, and "the British Northwest." In 1902, the churches in the three prairie provinces withdrew to form the Northern Conference.

[11] "Verhandlungen," Nordwestliche Konferenz (1893), 100.

[12] Nora Albrecht and Doris Horne, eds., *Along the Fifth* (Stony Plain: Stony Plain Historical Society, 1982), 105; and "Verhandlungen," Nördliche Konferenz (1905), 4, 9-10.

[13] Minnie A. Falkenberg [daughter of Abr. Hager], "Beginning of Our Church Work Here in Edmonton," manuscript of public address, 1956.

[14] "Verhandlungen," Nordwestliche Konferenz (1894), 56.

[15] *50th Anniversary of the Carbon Baptist Church, 1910-1960*.

[16] Lewis G. Thomas, "Alberta 1905-90: The Uneasy Society," in *New Provinces*, ed. Palmer and Smith, 28-33.

[17] Jack Gorman, *A Land Reclaimed* (Hanna, AB: Gorman and Gorman, 1988).

[18] See James H. Gray, *The Winter Years* (Toronto: Macmillan, 1966), on the Depression in Canada.

[19] William J. H. Sturhahn, *They Came from east and west...*[sic] (Winnipeg: North American Baptist Immigration and Colonization Society, 1976), [1]-93, 289-93.

[20] Woyke, *Heritage and Ministry*, 299.

[21] "Verhandlungen", Nördliche Konferenz (1929), 32; (1930), 62.

[22] "Church Letters," "Minutes," Northern Conference (1956), 85.

[23] Sturhahn, *...from east and west*, 65-117.

[24] Richard Hohensee, *Seventy-fifth Anniversary* (Edmonton: Central Baptist Church, 1975), 11.

[25] "Minutes of the 32nd General Conference Sessions" (1958), 39.

Chapter 5

The Sociocultural Transformation
of the North American Baptist Conference

Ernest K. Pasiciel

The transformation of the German Baptists of the mid-19th century into the North American Baptists of today was a metamorphosis involving both cosmetic and genetic changes. The structural history of the denomination recounts the normal maturation and institutionalization of an organization. The social history, however, reveals a transmutation of the very form and function of the organism.

With the founding of German Baptist churches, a new and unique denomination was established; the original structure, composition, and ministry of the German Baptist Conference were distinctive on the North American religious landscape. Subsequently, as the individual churches and the entire conference increasingly adjusted to their societal environment, the sociocultural background, characteristics, and orientation of the denomination changed dramatically.

The analysis of the changes in the North American Baptist Conference is the aim and scope of this study. What was distinctive about the original German Baptist churches? How has the sociocultural composition of the denomination changed? Does the present NAB Conference have a distinctive sociocultural character? Before dealing with these issues, a brief survey of the history of the denomination will help place the study in its proper context.

The German Baptists in Canada

German Baptist beginnings in Canada were the result of an American-led revival among German immigrants living in Canada West (Ontario). In 1851, August Rauschenbusch, then in the employ of the American Tract Society, conducted evangelistic services in Waterloo County. Upon baptism, the converts were organized as the Bridgeport German Baptist Church with Heinrich Schneider as pastor. Great distances separated the members so the next year the church voted to divide into three; the Bridgeport group relocated to Berlin (Kitchener). These and other fledgling churches organized the

German Baptist Conference and, when the ethnic fellowship later divided regionally, remained part of the Eastern Conference of German Baptist Churches.

The German Baptist denomination also participated in the progressive westward shift of the North American frontier. In Dakota Territory and in the British Northwest, German-speaking Baptist immigrants from eastern Europe also formed new churches. The first German Baptist church in Canada west of Ontario was started in New Toulcha (Edenwold), near Regina, Saskatchewan, in 1886. By the turn of the century, seventeen churches had been founded in western Canada.[1] With this growth, a separate "Northern Conference," encompassing the churches of Alberta, Assiniboia (southern Saskatchewan), and Manitoba, was organized in 1902.

During these years of growth and expansion, most denominational ministries involving the Canadian churches, particularly the domestic and overseas missionary enterprise, were coordinated by the leadership in the United States. Literature, too, was produced centrally. Provision for pastoral training was made at the Rochester Theological Seminary in New York State. In 1940, a Bible school—the Christian Training Institute (CTI; since 1968, North American Baptist College)—opened in Edmonton, Alberta, specifically to contribute to "the mental and spiritual culture" of the young people in the Northern Conference.[2] The ministry of CTI was expanded in 1958 with the addition of a pastoral education program; this was upgraded to a separate theological seminary in 1980.

Over the years, the German language, name, and associations became increasingly problematic. The difficulties were heightened, of course, by the hostilities of the two world wars. The ethnic tensions and adjustments prompted the renaming of the denomination as the "North American Baptist General Conference" in 1944 (shortened in 1975 by dropping "General"). This did not conclude the ethnic issue, for World War II triggered another wave of German refugees. Canada, especially, received a flood of these immigrants, many being resettled by the NAB Immigration and Colonization Society. At least twenty-three new Canadian NAB churches came into existence as a result of this immigration.[3]

The generally good relations between the US and Canada have been strained occasionally by expressions of political nationalism and economic protectionism. To date, the NAB Conference, however, with its 122 churches and church extension projects in Canada and 275 in the US, has chosen to remain an organically united body.[4]

This historical sketch provides the background for analyzing the social history of the denomination. The analysis will use H. Richard Niebuhr's classic thesis of "the social sources of denominationalism" as a framework.[5]

The Social Sources of Denominational Divisions

Niebuhr's pioneering discussion of the social character of the Christian churches was intended to be "a practical contribution to the ethical problem of denominationalism."[6] The traditional, orthodox explanation of divisions in Christianity had been sought in the official creeds and doctrinal interpretations of the churches. This Niebuhr rejects as both artificial and fruitless.

Instead, he suggests that theological opinions have their roots in cultural conditions, for "the religious life is so interwoven with social circumstances that the formulation of theology is necessarily conditioned by these" (16). Denominational divisions within Christianity are, therefore, basically and ultimately the result of sociocultural differences.

Niebuhr deals with four especially divisive social factors: nationality, economics, geography, and race. Each is a major principle of differentiation among denominations; the division of the churches "closely follows the division of men into the castes of national, racial, and economic groups." Since such denominationalism represents "the accommodation of Christianity to the caste-system of human society" (6), it also represents "the moral failure of Christianity" (25).

Niebuhr shows convincingly that churches and denominations are not only spiritual entities; they also reflect social variables and exhibit cultural patterns. These factors will now be used to develop the sociocultural profile of the early German Baptist Conference.

Early Sociocultural Profile

The year 1883 was a high point for the German Baptists in North America. Forty years had elapsed since the first church had been organized in Philadelphia. They had grown to 138 churches with a membership of 10,899.[7] The founding of the General Missionary Society that year completed the Conference's basic organizational structure. Numerically and structurally, the denomination was firmly established.

Even during those early years, the movement reflected definite sociocultural features; the churches, pastors, and members exhibited marked ethnic, linguistic, economic, and geographic characteristics.

National Background

Although the German Baptist Conference was indigenous to North America, during that early period it was thoroughly German in composition, operation, and mission. Virtually all the early leaders and the majority of the early members had originated in Europe. Whether they were sociopolitical refugees from Germany, homesteaders from Russia, or religious pioneers with a separatist, Pietist, or state-church background from other parts of Europe, ethnically and culturally they were Germans. The German Baptist churches developed to meet the religious and social needs among the German settlers; they were bases of fellowship and avenues of evangelism.

The American Baptists contributed much to the rise and development of the German Baptist Conference; Canadian Baptists invested proportionately, also. Although the German Baptists appreciated the assistance, they were sensitive to the cultural differences and critical of the religious distinctions. No less a leader than Konrad Fleischmann, the founder of the first of their churches in 1843, claimed that the spiritual life in the American Baptist churches was not of the same high calibre as in the newly organized German ones. He lamented the shallower life with Christ of the American Baptists, their great weakness for the latest fashions, their worldly mindedness, and their acceptance of secret fraternal organizations, mixed marriages, and the keeping of slaves. He concluded that a separate German Baptist work could and would avoid such spiritual shortcomings and administrative errors.[8]

The German Baptists thus considered the evangelistic outreach to and brotherly consolidation of the German immigrants to be their special mission. This missionary concern was vividly expressed at the Eastern Conference in 1881:

> In recognition of the fact that during the past two years, immigration from our old Fatherland has again attained such colossal dimensions, and since it is to be expected that in the near future, if the favourable economic conditions continue, further thousands—yea, hundreds of thousands—will arrive to establish a new homeland for themselves here, we believe that progress in our mission endeavour must be the watchword of this time so that the churches in the East and the West will recognize anew the importance of their responsibility to utilize all our available means to bring salvation in Christ to our countrymen.[9]

As scattered and struggling congregations, the German Baptist churches looked to each other for fellowship and support. In a strange and often hostile environment, religion was a stabilizing influence; and the church served as a unifying agency. For fellowship around similar interests and the promotion of common objectives, the German Baptists gathered into separate churches and organized their own denominational structures.

The unique ministry of the German Baptists centred in and was reinforced by the German language. German Baptists longed to worship with those who spoke their language; for them, religion lost something when it was conveyed in a strange tongue. This language concern was prominent from the beginning. At the first conference in 1851, the participants unanimously resolved: "We consider it most important and desirable that our children be instructed in the German language and, therefore, recommend to our churches to start German Sunday schools and, when practical, German week-day schools."[10] During these early years, consequently, the denomination functioned exclusively in German. The local worship services, the Conference business meetings, the various publication efforts—all used the German language.

The German Baptists constituted only a small segment of the evangelical Christian element in America during the 19th century. A. J. Ramaker, an early denominational historian, suggests that the adjective stood for the particular mission which they felt themselves called upon to perform.[11] Ministering in German to Germans already or potentially Baptist was their distinctive service.

Socioeconomic Class

German Baptist beginnings were humble economically as well as numerically. Although most socioeconomic levels were represented among the German immigrants, the early German Baptists belonged predominantly to the poorer classes. The German settlers of the early 19th century were mainly peasant farmers; following the failed Revolution of 1848, they were more typically artisans and labourers; the later influx of Germans consisted mostly of farmers from eastern Europe. Of almost every one of their churches it could be said that "the company of believers was small, and there was the traditional poverty among the members."[12]

Despite financial assistance from the American Baptists, the scattered German Baptist congregations led a precarious existence. A recent denominational executive/historian lists their poverty as one of the general characteristics of the churches:

> The German immigrants of those years, except for some "forty-eighters," were virtually penniless when they arrived in America. While some soon achieved affluence through farming or in business, most of them remained relatively poor for many years. Obviously this made it very difficult for the churches to support qualified pastors and to provide adequate facilities for worship.[13]

Such circumstances were bound to affect the educational interests and provisions adversely. Generally, both the membership and the leadership lacked formal training. In their poverty, the constituents had difficulty supporting their local work, much less a denominational educational program. The conclusion must be that during the early years the German Baptist denomination was largely composed of unskilled workers and farmers who were basically poor and uneducated and who had only minimal concern for pastoral education.

Geographic Distribution

The early German Baptists spread across the country in relation to their socioeconomic background. The labourers and tradesmen tended to remain in the cities while the farmers moved on in search of suitable land. Each group settled where sentiment and occupation were most compatible.

From the beginning, German Baptist strength and growth were in the regions of greatest German settlement. Because the German immigrants were heavily concentrated throughout the Great Lakes region, originally the area of German Baptist strength was the northeastern section of the US and southern Ontario.

But already during those early years, the denomination experienced the shift in the frontier as successive waves of immigrants moved increasingly further west in search of virgin land and golden opportunities.

> During the sixties, immediately after the bloody Revolution of 1848, the German immigrants tended toward Michigan, Texas, and Minnesota, and here also churches were founded. In the seventies the prairie states of Kansas, Nebraska, and Dakota followed in order. In the eighties the destination was the Pacific coast, and in the nineties it was the newly-opened British provinces in the northwest.[14]

These immigrants tended to settle in the type of territory to which they were accustomed; and where they settled, German Baptist churches emerged and expanded.[15]

The westward shift is evidenced in early discussions concerning the possible relocation of the seminary. In 1874, the general conference reserved for itself the right at any time, should it become advisable to move the seminary further west, to sell the property in Rochester and to use the proceeds for a new institution elsewhere.[16] The next general conference in 1877 provided that relocating the seminary further west could be considered when the membership of the Conference in Ohio and the states to the west exceeded twice the numbers in Ontario and the eastern states.[17] Although the German Baptists had begun as a predominantly eastern group of churches, their centre of gravity quickly shifted to the heart of the continent, though the symbolic move of the seminary did not occur until after World War II.

Miscellaneous Factors

The national background, socioeconomic status, and geographic distribution of the early German Baptists were their more distinctive features. The total sociocultural composition of the denomination, however, involved additional variables. Several of these are included to complete the picture.

Race was not an issue in the policy of the denomination or the membership of the churches. As a group of German-oriented churches located largely in the northern section of the US, the Conference did not experience many of the tensions associated with the animosity between the races. Although the racial composition of the churches was not involved, many German Baptists were actively against slavery.[18]

The attitude of the young denomination toward women was ambiguous. Since German society of the mid-19th century was radically male-oriented, men were the dominant element in the German Baptist churches and the Conference leadership. Although the women were allowed to pray, to share their experiences in the assemblies, and to participate in the business of the church, they were prohibited from admonishing and teaching publicly.[19] Nevertheless, both numerically and functionally, women were a significant element in the denomination from the beginning.

The age distribution in the churches during those early years was equally ambiguous. Since many of the first leaders had come out of German Pietist and separatist backgrounds where a definite religious experience was generally made later in life, the early German Baptist work was essentially an adult movement. This orientation did not mean indifference toward children, however; from the beginning special provision was made for their spiritual nurture.[20]

Such was the sociocultural composition of the German Baptist Conference toward the end of the 19th century. North American society and its culture, however, were too powerful to permit the indefinite perpetuation of such restricted identities. In interacting with other institutions of society, the German Baptists gradually became victims of the inexorable forces of accommodation and assimilation.[21]

Modern Sociocultural Profile

The beginning of the 20th century was a time of sociocultural transition for the German Baptists of North America. With the passing of the first-generation pioneers, the emphasis on the Germanness of the work seemed to diminish. The use of the German language, especially, was not as necessary or as desirable for later generations. A process of assimilation had been started that could not be stopped, much less reversed.

Despite the changing circumstances and the corresponding adjustments by the German Baptists, it is possible to construct a sociocultural profile of the denomination for the modern period. A composite of the general characteristics approximately 100 years after the early profile is developed next, based partly on an earlier sociological survey by the author.[22]

Ethnic Orientation

The German Baptist churches prospered initially from the strong ethnic orientation of the newcomers and, in turn, fostered a national exclusiveness in their constituents. The inevitable interaction of the immigrants with the larger society, however, precipitated a process of assimilation which occurred imperceptibly for some and was promoted deliberately by others.

Acculturation is extremely complex, involving various stages and dimensions. Religion is often a complicating and even excruciating factor in assimilation.

> The church and religion were for the parents the one element of real continuity between the old life and the new. It was for most of them a matter of deepest concern that their children remain true to the faith.... Their children, however, could not and did not look upon it in the same way. To the first generation, the immigrant generation, church and religion were part of their "natural" immigrant heritage; they were embedded in their very life and culture. To the second generation, including the younger people among the immigrants themselves, church and religion were also that—part of the immigrant heritage—but their attitude toward the immigrant heritage was no longer so unequivocal.[23]

For succeeding generations, religion may be part of the baggage of foreignness they are eager to abandon.

As the vehicle of culture, language is often the key to assimilation. For the early NABs, the German language was frequently the most efficient mode of communication and often the only effective manner of expression. But subsequent generations were quickly faced with a dilemma—as the young people became Anglicized, they could no longer worship properly in German; yet, having been raised in a German religious environment, many could not worship properly in English.

The internal pressures to acculturate were transformed into an enormous force for full assimilation by the tensions of World War I. Some did not want to be identified in any way with the German group. The losses to the Conference were especially great in Ontario. As a member of the British Empire, Canada was in the war from the beginning; Canadian NABs could not understand the pro-German sentiments of their American brethren before the US entered the war.[24] A recent denominational editor notes further differences between responses in the established east and the frontier west of Canada:

> The eastern provinces were staunch [sic] British and followed the rule "right or wrong, my country," whereby they applied this motto mainly to people of British descent. The prairie provinces in comparison, were not so much interested in a British alignment. They offered to the immigrating masses greater freedom to live according to their accustomed life-style. The Anglo-Canadian pressure in the eastern

provinces therefore led many immigrants to want to be absorbed in the present culture as quickly as possible. However, the Germans in Manitoba, Saskatchewan and Alberta, in whose vast territory good citizenship was measured by the degree of comradeship and willingness to [give] neighbourly assistance, and not by ethnic origin, saw no reason for a fast assimilation. They maintained their old ways and knew that not too many others would object to it, since they themselves were immigrants from one land to another.[25]

In time, western Canada also was caught up in the pressures to assimilate. Gradually, but definitely, the German Baptist Conference became acculturated. Increasingly, the English language was used in the local churches. In 1923, an English periodical, *The Baptist Herald*, was started; it ultimately replaced *Der Sendbote des Evangeliums* as the major publication of the denomination. Progressively, both the fellowship and business of the denomination came to be conducted in English. At the twenty-sixth general conference in 1940, the program was entirely in English for the first time.[26] The climax of this development came with the change of name to "North American Baptist General Conference" in 1944. This represented a transformed self-concept and outlook; it meant a change in identity and a reorientation of perspective.

The ethnic transformation of the denomination has continued steadily since then. Slowly but persistently, the narrow ethnic mission of the early German Baptists has become a socially inclusive vision for today's NABs.

Socioeconomic Status

The socioeconomic stratification of the NABs also evidences significant changes. During the early years, the denomination had reflected the general poverty and proletarian backgrounds of the German immigrants; but the diligence and industry of these newcomers steadily raised the general socioeconomic level of the denomination.

This increasing prosperity of the NABs is evident in much of their later activity. Initially, the German Baptists had been heavily dependent upon the financial support of the American and the Canadian Baptists. As they prospered, they in turn assisted the mission agencies who had helped them; finally, they dropped their ties with the other bodies altogether.[27] More recently, they have conducted periodic fund drives entirely among themselves for projects beyond the general operating expenses of the denomination. These special offerings were largely for the establishment and expansion of educational and mission efforts.

Other indicators also suggest the improved socioeconomic condition of the modern denomination. In 1971, the contributions for conference ministries were $171.07 per member, placing NABs third highest in giving among the Baptist groups compared. For 1988, the total contributions of NAB churches was $48.9 million, or $811 per member.[28]

Occupation is often considered the best single indicator of status. In a 1974 survey of the denomination, the responding churches had 41 percent of their constituents in the professional and semi-professional categories; and 37 percent were classified as skilled and clerical workers. Only 22 percent were categorized as semi-skilled or unskilled workers.

Both individually and corporately, NABs have ascended the socioeconomic ladder. While not every church nor every family has participated equally in the increased prosperity, the NAB Conference generally has grown financially and materially. Gone are the early years of poverty; NABs have become a middle-class denomination.

Geographical Distribution

The NAB Conference had started within the German concentrations of the northeastern US and southern Ontario. The persistent movement of people westward affected the growth and structure of the denomination.

This progressive movement westward was not a simple expansion, however. It represented a shift in concentration. As new churches were started further west, older ones in the east died out or assimilated with Anglophone conventions. At the turn of the century, the heaviest concentration of NAB members and churches was in the midwest; then it shifted to the Dakotas, the Pacific states, and western Canada. At present, the greatest growth, as demonstrated by new church-planting projects, is in Alberta, British Columbia, and California. The strength and momentum of the denomination have definitely shifted westward.[29]

Just as the Conference has expanded to nearly every section of the continent—from the Atlantic to the Pacific, and from Canada to the Gulf of Mexico (with the exception of the "Deep South")—NAB churches also can be found in virtually every setting: in rural communities, in small towns, in metropolitan centres, and in the suburbs. Although the persistent shift westward and steady urbanization are noticeable, no section of the continent and no demographic area are predominantly represented. Geographically, modern NABs are widely dispersed and diversified.

Miscellaneous Factors

With the decline of the German orientation, the exclusively Caucasian character of the denomination has also been eroded. Numerous churches have at least some non-Caucasian members; several in the US are even predominantly non-white. Various churches have introduced ministries specifically to non-Anglo elements in their communities. Although non-Caucasians still amount to only a small percentage of the total membership, these developments represent the beginning of a change in the racial composition of the denomination.

Through the years, NAB women have become a progressively more significant element within the churches. Numerous women serve on church staffs as directors of Christian education or other church ministries. Many others have served as foreign missionaries—nurses, teachers, and evangelists. As a reflection of these developments, the denominational Women's Department received its first full-time director in 1973. While, at present, women outnumber men in NAB churches only slightly, the women's work is much more active than programs designed for men.

The parallel increasing significance of young people within the denomination is evident. The younger generation had been in the forefront of the agitation leading to the transformation from an exclusively German orientation. To serve their interests better, throughout the years various structures and programs have focussed on youth activities and ministries. Although the emphasis on youth is subject to regional variations, the age distribution within the denomination is quite consistent with the national pattern.

NABs have experienced many sociocultural changes, yet they continue to exist and function as a denomination. The impact of such sociocultural adjustments on the NAB Conference and ultimately on the essence of denominationalism is considered next.

Sociocultural Factors and the German Baptists

The German Baptists of the early period were a quite distinct and readily identifiable group within North American society. The sociocultural profile of the denomination centred around the German heritage and outlook. The early NABs were essentially Germans, ministering to the continuing tides of German immigrants, in their common German language. There were other German-speaking groups; there were other Baptist bodies; but there was only one German Baptist denomination. Their distinctiveness was expressed by Walter Rauschenbusch as late as 1916 at the 18th General Conference: "In the providence of God an important work has been entrusted to us, because we are able through the medium of the German language to do missionary work among the newly immigrated peoples. English-speaking Baptists could not have done this work."[30] The combination of German background and Baptist conviction was unique in North America. But the German orientation was basic to the existence of the early NAB churches; it promoted their unity, provided their identity, and prompted their ministry. The emergence and establishment of the German Baptist Conference during the mid-19th century thus supports Niebuhr's thesis of the social sources of denominationalism.

In the 20th century, however, the sociocultural characteristics of the NAB Conference became greatly diffused. The inevitable contact with North American society prompted adjustments and transformations which gradually eroded the narrow sociocultural profile of the early German Baptists. Geographically, the denomination has spread to most sections of the North American continent. The socioeconomic status of its members has greatly improved. Non-Caucasians, women, and young people have become increasingly represented in the constituency and involved in the ministry of the denomination. And, most significantly, the almost exclusive German orientation has persistently been dissolved. These changes have drastically altered the identity of the NAB Conference. Socially and culturally, NABs are virtually indistinguishable from the larger Baptist segment of Protestant Christianity in North America.

The implications for the social sources of denominationalism are significant. Having lost the foundational ethnic orientation, no other characteristic has become the dominant unifying factor for the NAB Conference. In fact, no sociocultural feature is sufficiently distinctive to define and identify the denomination within contemporary society. Modern NABs are without a "social source" to support their existence.

Yet the NAB Conference continues to exist and function as a separate denomination. Evidently, therefore, modern denominational divisions cannot be attributed to sociocultural differences alone. While such factors may still be significant in explaining the varying compositions and backgrounds of denominations, the transformation of the early German Baptists into the modern NABs shows that ethnicity, socioeconomic status, and regionalism are not necessary for the perpetuation of denominational divisions.

Notes

[1] Frank H. Woyke, *Heritage and Ministry of the North American Baptist Conference* (Oakbrook Terrace, IL: North American Baptist Conference, 1979), 210; these seventeen churches had 1,133 members. Cf. Edward B. Link, "North American (German) Baptists," in *Baptists in Canada*, ed. Jarold K. Zeman (Burlington, ON: G. R. Welch, 1980), 90-92.

[2] North American Baptists, "Verhandlungen," Bundes-Konferenz (1940), 40. The spelling "Konferenz" or "Conferenz" is inconsistent through the years; here uniformly, "Konferenz." "North American Baptists" and "NAB" are anachronistic before 1944.

[3] William J. Sturhahn, *They Came from east and west...[sic]: A History of Immigration to Canada* (Winnipeg, MB: North American Baptist Immigration and Colonization Society, 1976). This figure does not include "the small congregations which grew to substantial size, or the English congregations which separated because of language" (219).

[4] 1994 Statistics, *N.A.B. Directory* (Oakbrook Terrace, IL: North American Baptist Conference, 1996), 5.

[5] H. Richard Niebuhr, *The Social Sources of Denominationalism* (New York: Henry Holt, 1929).

[6] Niebuhr, *Social Sources*, vii; succeeding quotations identified by page number in text.

[7] Albert John Ramaker, *The German Baptists in North America* (Cleveland, OH: German Baptist Publication Society, 1924), 48, 94.

[8] Konrad A. Fleischmann, "Unsere Stellung und Aufgabe als deutsche Gemeinden gläubig-getauften Christen," *Der Sendbote des Evangeliums* 6 (July 1850): 2.

[9] "Verhandlungen," Eastern Conference (1881), 14.

[10] "Verhandlungen," first conference (1851), 8.

[11] Ramaker, *German Baptists*, 120.

[12] Albert J. Ramaker, "Earliest Beginnings of Our History," in *These Glorious Years: The Centenary History of German Baptists of North America, 1843-1943*, by Herman von Berge et al. (Cleveland, OH: Roger Williams Press, 1943), 30.

[13] Woyke, *Heritage and Ministry*, 86.

[14] Albert J. Ramaker, *Eine kurze Geschichte der Baptisten* (Cleveland, OH: Verlagshaus der deutschen Baptisten, 1906), 129.

[15] The Germans from Volhynia in Russia, for instance, had come in the 1880s and 1890s from a region of dense forests; they preferred the land around Lake Michigan and the thick forests of central Alberta. Cf. Reinhold J. Kerstan, "Historical Factors in the Formation of the Ethnically Oriented North American Baptist General Conference" (PhD diss., Northwestern University, Evanston, IL, 1971), 167.

[16] "Verhandlungen," Bundes-Konferenz (1874), 10.

[17] "Verhandlungen," Bundes-Konferenz (1877), 15. The North American Baptist Seminary was eventually relocated to Sioux Falls, South Dakota, in 1949.

[18] The first conference rejected slaveholding as being opposed to the spirit of the Gospel ("Verhandlungen" [1851], 6).

[19] "Verhandlungen," östlichen Jahres-Konferenz (1859), 7.

[20] "Verhandlungen," östlichen Jahres-Konferenz (1861), 14-15.

[21] Eric Henry Ohlmann, "The American Baptist Mission to German-Americans: A Case Study of Attempted Assimilation" (ThD diss., Graduate Theological Union, Berkeley, CA, 1973).

[22] Ernest K. Pasiciel, "North American Baptist Sociological Survey" (1974). Cf. Pasiciel, "The Interrelationship between Sociocultural Factors and Denominationalism: A

Comparison of the Early and Modern Sociocultural Profiles of the North American Baptist General Conference, 1874-1974" (PhD diss., Baylor University, Waco, TX, 1974).

[23] Will Herberg, *Protestant-Catholic-Jew: An Essay in American Religious Sociology* (Garden City, NY: Doubleday, 1955), 31.

[24] Otto E. Krueger, *In God's Hand: The Story of the North American Baptist General Conference* (Forest Park, IL: Roger Williams Press, 1958), 64.

[25] Kerstan, "Formation of Ethnically Oriented NAB," 223-24.

[26] The conference was to have met in Winnipeg but was relocated to Burlington, Iowa, because of the outbreak of World War II. Significantly, the Northern Conference was the last to make the change to English, in 1953.

[27] Ohlmann, "American Baptist Mission," 201-10; and Link, "North American Baptists," 94-95.

[28] John Binder, "Ministries and Finances of N.A.B. Reviewed," *Baptist Herald* 50 (October 1972): 20; and *N.A.B. Directory*, 1990, 6.

[29] *N.A.B. Directory*, 1990, 5.

[30] "Verhandlungen," Bundeskonferenz (1916), 4. Similar sentiments were still expressed in 1924 by Ramaker, *German Baptists*, 120.

Chapter 6

Church and Community:
Old School Baptists in Ontario, 1818-1901

Paul R. Wilson

The endeavours of the Particular Covenanted Baptist Church in Canada reveal a successful transplant of Calvinism to rural Ontario. Encouraged primarily by religious intolerance and economic hardship in their Scottish homeland, members of this sect first emigrated to southwestern Ontario in 1818. In response to the challenges of settlement and cultural adjustment, these Old School Baptists created an enduring church in 1820 which reflected their understanding of the Scriptures.[1]

Immigration, Settlement, and Cultural Adjustment

Essentially, Old School Baptist emigration to Upper Canada in 1818 lay rooted in the economic and religious situation of the Scottish Highlands. Economic hardship brought on by an elite desire to modernize the Highlands promoted emigration. Concurrently, evangelization of the Highlands heightened religious tensions and opened a running battle between church and sect which served to encourage the exodus of many dissenters.

In the early years of the 19th century, economic conditions in the Scottish Highlands continued to decline. The mercantile modernization policy of government, landholders, and entrepreneurs failed to produce the desired prosperity. Instead, its demand for a total change of lifestyle and livelihood only served to exacerbate the discontent of dispossessed and unemployed tenants.[2] Thus, by the early 19th century, emigration to Upper Canada was increasingly seen by many Highlanders as a means to improve their economic lot.

Coinciding with declining economic conditions was a rise in religious tensions in certain areas of the Scottish Highlands. In the closing years of the 18th century, itinerant dissenting missionaries attracted the attention and disdain of the Church of Scotland as they began to roam the countryside preaching their message of repentance.[3] Usually based in Edinburgh, these missionaries were sent initially by individual churches and later by mission societies. Primarily Congregational (Independent) and Baptist in persuasion, the missionaries produced autonomous churches that held their principles, predominantly in Perthshire and Argyll. It is to the founding and flight of one of these churches that the story now turns.

The origin of the Particular Covenanted Baptist Church in Canada lay in the efforts of Calvinist Baptist missionaries in the Cowal District in the County of Argyll at the beginning of the 19th century, though it is difficult to say with certainty which itinerant minister first taught Old School Baptist doctrine in the region. A lack of evangelical preaching in Cowal encouraged reception of the Calvinistic message proclaimed by these Baptist itinerants. Their emphasis on salvation by faith upon divine election found ready acceptance in the district and soon produced local itinerants willing to contend earnestly for this faith.

Instrumental in the establishment of a Calvinist Baptist Church in Cowal was a layman named Daniel McArthur.[4] Following his conversion to the Old School Baptist sect, McArthur began a preaching ministry in his district which resulted in the founding of Baptist congregations in the predominately Gaelic communities of Strachur (1801), Port Bannatyne (1804), and Dundoon (ca. 1805). For believer's baptism and ordination, McArthur turned to a fellow Baptist in Edinburgh named McFarland, who designated him pastor of his active flock in Cowal District. The ordination of McArthur and the prospect of a Baptist church under his supervision in Cowal opened a running battle between church and sect in the area. The growing Baptist presence threatened to undermine established church power and provoked anger among certain members of the local clergy.

The anger of these Presbyterian clergymen led to an attack on Daniel McArthur. Their calls for his punishment resulted in his seizure, forced service in the British Navy, and imprisonment. Eventually, the persistent efforts of friends resulted in McArthur's removal to Edinburgh. Here he was put on trial for heresy before the Lords of Session and acquitted, while his adversaries were assessed fines totalling £4,000.[5] Subsequently, McArthur emigrated to Thompkins County, New York, about 1812.

Despite such opposition, the Baptist church in Cowal prospered. McArthur's ministry had produced converts willing to accept the risks associated with preaching dissenting doctrine and leading Baptist congregations. The most notable for the present study was Deacon Dugald Campbell of the Knapdale District. In his capacity as deacon, Campbell gained the respect of his brethren and local notoriety as a zealous and able preacher.[6]

The ascendancy of a moderate element within the General Assembly of the Church of Scotland in the first quarter of the 19th century meant that dissenters occasionally gained sympathy and clemency. Still, Nonconformists proclaimed and practised their beliefs under the constant threat of censure and imprisonment. Thought began to turn to other places to live.

By July 1818, Dugald Campbell headed a group of Baptists committed to emigrate to Canada. A letter dated that month indicates they had applied for land grants but they now wanted information about "the encouragement Government gives us on our arrival and the proper steps necessary to be pursued by us to compose[!] that end."[7] Their letter provides partial insight into the plans and motives of the Baptist immigrants and reveals an awareness of the economic opportunities Canada offered. Thus while religious intolerance at home prompted thought of emigration, the prospect of a better economic lot provided the impetus for action.

The actual journey to Upper Canada followed a course which became common for Old School Baptist immigrants. On 28 July 1818, thirty-six families departed for Canada from Tobermory; included in the journey were the five Baptist families of Deacon Dugald Campbell, Alexander Gray, Donald Buchan, Dugald McLarty, and Duncan McCallum. On 1 September, they landed at Pictou, Nova Scotia; and by the 20th, they had arrived in Quebec City. From there, they travelled by lake schooner to Port Glasgow in Aldborough Township, Elgin County, Ontario.[8]

Most purchased land from Col. Thomas Talbot or applied for land grants and settled on lots located on the 12th and 13th concessions in Aldborough.[9] Here succeeding waves of Old School Baptist settlers found an enclave which stood ready to offer hospitality to their co-religionists. By the late 1820s, Scotch Particular Baptists could be found along the Longwoods Road in Ekfrid Township and in Lobo Township near Poplar Hill. Similarly, Dunwich and Orford Townships gained a sufficient number of Old School Baptists to organize regular worship services before the end of the 1840s.[10] Thus, they had followed the general flow of immigration and established residences in the counties of Elgin, Middlesex, and Kent.

While most members of a new immigrant family usually stayed in Aldborough, a delegation would be sent elsewhere to acquire land. The experience of Malcolm Campbell illustrates this process. In 1834, at the age of twenty-two, he came to Canada with his parents, sister Mary, and brothers Donald and Dugald. After the family arrived in Aldborough, their Baptist brethren provided them with food and lodging. Subsequently, Malcolm and James Campbell, son of (now "Elder") Dugald Campbell, were sent to Port Talbot to buy land. They succeeded in purchasing land along the Thames River in Ekfrid Township at a cost of $3 an acre.[11]

With settlement came the challenges inherent to life in early Upper Canada. Harsh climate, dense bush, poor drainage, and heavy clay soil were a few of the formidable environmental obstacles Old School Baptists faced. In addition, the personal tragedy of accidental death or illness touched numerous Baptist households. Despite the difficulties of pioneer life, the hardy Scots persevered and either found better land or gradually made their initial site productive. They constructed personal dwellings with logs until the 1850s; then, most built frame houses. By the early 1880s, brick replaced wood as the material of choice in house construction.[12]

Inadequate roads made travel and the transport of goods extremely difficult. The significant improvements in transportation brought by better methods of road construction and the advance of the railways did not begin to affect any township containing Old School Baptists until the early 1850s.[13] None of the townships which the Old School Baptists had chosen lay near a major centre of population. Thus, their experience in Ontario would remain tied to the rural community.

Many Old School Baptists found adjustment to their new cultural surroundings challenging. Many, speaking only Gaelic, experienced the scorn of English-speaking neighbours and had to struggle to overcome feelings of cultural isolation. An Old School Baptist farmer-poet in Ekfrid Township represented the extent to which racial discrimination and personal sorrow could permeate the life of an immigrant from the Scottish Highlands. After watching a crowd of English-speaking people make sport of an old Gaelic-speaking immigrant in Port Stanley, Campbell expressed his indignation and empathy:

> The voice of the Saxon is hissing around me,
> Like the breath of the adder it sounds in my ear;
> In low mocking speeches they cruelly wound me,
> Ah! old is this arm when their scoffing I bear.
> . . . .
> My dear loved companion, who shared in each danger,
> I've left her asleep 'neath the wild ocean's foam;
> My children I've laid in the grave of a stranger,
> And now I'm alone without friendship or home.
> . . . .
> Have those Saxons forgot how you stood by their banners,
> When the Corsican legions were threatening their strand?
> Shall their weak bleating flocks now save them their manors,
> Should the foe's hostile trumpet be blown o'er the land?
> . . . .
> Thou may'st thrust from thy bosom the young and the hoary,
> But, Britannia, no child that thou ever did'st bear,
> With fond glowing heart will exult in thy glory,
> Or weep in thy shame like the brave mountaineer.[14]

In brief, the Old School Baptist move to Upper Canada involved both simple motives and complex challenges and changes. The combination of economic hardship and religious intolerance in the Highlands of Scotland prompted Baptist emigration. Once in Upper Canada, Old School Baptists established pockets of settlement, offered assistance to their succeeding immigrant brethren, and struggled to overcome the physical obstacles and cultural barriers present in their new homeland.

Church: Faith, Function, Form, and Fellowship

The maintenance of a consistent faith, function, form, and fellowship became the quintessential hallmark of Old School Baptist religious activity in 19th-century Ontario. As with most Ontarians in the 19th century, religion played a central role in the lives of Old School Baptists. Following a brief period of cooperative worship, they established and extended their distinct faith and practice.

Initially, Old School Baptists participated in a cooperative church venture based on ethnic and doctrinal similarities. They worshipped as the first Protestant church in Aldborough Township with Highland Presbyterians who maintained belief in the deterministic elements of Calvinist theology. In 1820, doctrinal differences precipitated a split in the church. Elder Dugald Campbell and his followers withdrew and covenanted among themselves to form the Baptist Church of Christ in Aldborough, later called the Particular Covenanted Baptist Church in Canada.[15]

In 1820, the formative period of their independent development began with the composition of a statement of Old School Baptist faith and function. In their "Articles of Faith," the new church first set out its doctrinal position. Through the use of both a literal and allegorical hermeneutic, these Baptists affirmed their belief in biblical authority, inerrancy and inspiration, the Church, the Trinity, salvation, sanctification, and glorification. Sundry articles addressed temperance, lawsuits, marriage, and the ordinances of baptism and communion. In general, the soteriological articles revealed that in doctrine the Old School Baptists represented a Calvinist extreme in the Baptist theological spectrum.[16]

While most Baptists in Ontario retained their formal allegiance to an inherited Calvinism, the Old School Baptists took a hard line position. The "Articles" spelled out in detail their belief in human total depravity, "absolute predestination," limited atonement, effectual calling, and justification by faith alone.

This distinctly hyper-Calvinistic interpretation of the Scriptures provided the foundation for the creation of a separate Baptist church committed to faith in the absolute sovereignty of God. This uncompromisingly deterministic theology produced a legalistic polity and practice.

The practical application of these convictions in the 19th-century Ontario Baptist setting shows that order served as the expression and guardian of orthodoxy. Thus, in their church activities, Ontario Old School Baptists sought to restore what they understood to be the pattern of the primitive Christian church as reflected in the New Testament.

Church polity followed a carefully ordered traditional Baptist structure. The principles of autonomy and democracy provided the basis for church government. Quarterly business meetings were established to handle matters of church concern. Church members voted on all matters of church business, and every church had the responsibility to govern its own affairs in accordance with the teaching of the Scriptures.[17]

The Scriptures also identified and defined the orderly functioning of spiritual leadership within the church. For the Old School Baptists, God had ordained that men should serve as the church's spiritual leaders in the role of elder or deacon. Elders (which included pastors) were ordained and licensed to preach by a "presbytery" called specifically for this purpose and then dissolved. Elders administered the ordinances and officiated at weddings, funerals, business meetings, and worship services. Deacons served communion and performed certain official functions in the absence of an elder. Through these officers, the spiritual vitality and purity of the congregation received constant attention and scrutiny.

Concern for the orderly administration of church business affairs also led to the creation of lesser church offices such as clerk, treasurer, and auditor. Though leadership tended to be male-dominated, these lesser church offices allowed for participation by women.[18]

Worship followed a simple and prescribed order. The service began and ended with prayer. Following the opening prayer, congregation and minister would join together in the singing of psalms. Hymns were always sung *a cappella*, usually in four-part harmony, from the Scottish Psalter. At the conclusion of the last hymn, the Scripture was read. The service climaxed with "the preaching" which most often emphasized one's need for repentance. This simple worship format characterized Old School Baptist worship in Ontario throughout the 19th century.

Similarly, admission to membership followed an established procedure through which the purity of the church might be safeguarded. First, candidates gave public testimony of "the dealings of God with his or her soul." Next, the church, in the absence of the candidates, voted on their suitability; a unanimous voted was needed for a person to become a member. Third, the accepted candidate underwent baptism by immersion and, finally, received the right hand of fellowship as a sign of formal acceptance into the church body.

The articles also legislated the use of church discipline. Both preachers and members were subject to exclusion for moral "disorder" or persistent heretical views. Permanent exclusion required a two-thirds vote of the membership. Not all sin resulted in the complete withdrawal of fellowship. A member could be admonished or denied fellowship temporarily. Upon "their expression of penitency and pardon" excluded members might also be restored to fellowship. Though the degree and nature of enforcement is difficult to judge at present, it appears that these Scotch Baptists exercised a close watch over the conduct of their members.[19]

More distinctively, Old School Baptist determinism resulted in the rejection of certain evangelistic techniques. Revivalism, with its delivery of a general call for salvation, offended their Calvinist sensibilities. In their view, the Holy Spirit alone called certain men to salvation. The "Articles" stated plainly that "we do not, therefore, believe that the 'general call', or use of general invitations and exhortations, is preaching the gospel." Such tactics intruded on the work of the Spirit; a preacher should preach repentance and leave conviction and calling to the Holy Spirit.

Nevertheless, the Spirit could move a pastor to evangelize and use him effectively:

> In 1827...Elder Dugald Campbell...was greatly impressed by the Spirit of God to blaze a trail through the bush from his home in Aldborough to Lobo for he believed that several families of the same faith were settling there. He was accompanied on his fifty mile journey through the wilderness by Thomas McColl, a young school teacher in Aldborough.... In Lobo they found people of similar belief whom Elder Dugald Campbell organized as a congregation.[20]

Though Spirit-guided pastoral initiative was a legitimate form of evangelism, a thoroughly Calvinistic perspective was sustained. Evangelism was the work of God. Pastors were human instruments bearing a God-given burden and message.

Old School Baptists also saw the hand of God at work in personal invitations extended to their preachers. They believed, for example, that the Holy Spirit had moved Malcolm McIntyre, formerly of Aldborough, then living on the Longwoods Road in Ekfrid Township, to invite Elder Dugald Campbell to preach in 1828. Between three or four dozen residents turned out to hear what, according to one account, "was the first gospel sermon ever preached in Ekfrid Township."[21] Following this first gathering, a congregation formed, confirming that the Spirit had prompted and led the preacher and his auditors. Any itinerant ministry on their part was thereby given a spiritual justification. The elect were gathered and the circle of fellowship in Ontario was expanded.

Changes in the places Particular Covenanted Baptists worshipped best exemplify the development of form among them between 1820 and 1857. Homes provided the first setting for worship and communion. The first communion in Aldborough, for example, was served in the home of Duncan Peterson, who lived three-quarters of a mile from Eagle. Then in the 1830s, the Old School Baptist congregations in Aldborough, Lobo, Ekfrid, Dunwich, and Orford constructed log meeting houses. Their meeting houses changed again in the 1840s and 1850s, with the construction of frame buildings in Aldborough (1844), Dunwich (1852), and Ekfrid (1853).[22] These structures usually were barn frame design and made extensive use of hardwoods like black walnut in their furnishings. Utilitarian in design and function, they provided places of worship that reflected the Old School Baptist ideal of simplicity and order. The utilitarian architectural form was designed to serve church function.

The Old School Baptists did adjust to the predominant culture, however, by partially incorporating Gothic architecture in their church buildings in Ontario after 1880. Though comparatively understated, the buildings they constructed in this period were influenced by this late-Victorian desire to give the sacred a distinctive place in the secular world.[23]

The best example of the change in form is the brick meeting house built at Mayfair, in Ekfrid in 1901. The use of Gothic doors and stained glass Gothic windows combined with the round rose window in the front façade to make this attractive structure reflect the Gothic architectural style in the Protestant churches of late 19th-century Ontario. It is a typical Victorian church building where form followed function and expressed the purpose it served. To the outside eye, Ontario Old School Baptists had displayed a desire to stay within the mainstream of Ontario culture by using the current architectural form for their church buildings.

By the 1850s, the Particular Covenanted Baptist Church in Canada had created its own niche within Ontario's Baptist community. Its hyper-Calvinistic faith distinguished it from most other Baptist churches. In an ordered universe where the decisions of men were divinely predetermined, God's chosen people, the Church, must institute a polity in accordance with the pattern established by the New Testament. This meant, in part, that the fellowship of the elect could be expanded only through means consistent with the sovereign will of God. The Holy Spirit, by 1857, had raised up a strong Old School Baptist church consisting of five local congregations. Also, the changes in the form of Old School Baptist church buildings between 1820 and 1857 represented the blend of religious belief and an emerging set of rural Ontario utilitarian values.

The third stage of church development began in 1857 with the establishment of a connection with American Old School Baptists. In addition to extending the circle of fellowship, this connection allowed the Ontario church to exchange ideas and information with their brethren in the United States. Through this interchange, Old School Baptists in Ontario adopted an entrenchment strategy intended to insure that faith, function, form, and fellowship remained constant in the face of profound social and intellectual change. Thus, in the latter part of the 19th century, they increasingly viewed themselves as protectors of truth in the midst of an ever more irreligious and hostile society.

Fellowship with American Old School Baptists started in Ekfrid. At the June quarterly meeting held at Mayfair in 1857, ministers from the United States accepted the invitation to speak to their Canadian brethren for the first time. The list of visiting preachers included Elder Gilbert Beebe and Elder Hill from Utica, New York, and Elder Meaders from Mississippi. Though the exact number in attendance is indeterminable, the establishment of connections with Old School Baptists in the United States signalled the beginning of a new era in the Canadian church.

The isolation that the Canadian church had experienced since its inception ended. Pastoral exchanges became a regular part of church life. Though local men continued to hold most of the positions of spiritual leadership within Ontario, American pastors like William L. Beebe served the Canadian church. The connection with the American church also expanded the circle of eligible marriage partners for Canadian Old School Baptist youth; for example, Ebenezer McColl married Ella Beebe from Middletown, New York, on 9 September 1879.[24]

Interaction also involved the Canadian church in the American Old School Baptist paper, *The Signs of the Times*. *Signs* constituted an important communication link for the Old School Baptists of the two nations. Here they obtained a sense of identity as well as a source of information and instruction. This magazine provided a powerful organ through which the fundamentals of faith, function, and fellowship were strengthened. Throughout the 19th century, the Canadian church voiced its concerns and struggles and published news of church meetings, marriages, and deaths.

Specifically, *Signs* reiterated the sect's hyper-Calvinistic position and stressed the need for the faithful to remain true to such doctrine. Even obituaries, by implication, challenged the living to doctrinal and practical fidelity. The death notice of Elder Dugald Campbell, for example, reported:

> The man of God made his exit in the full triumph of faith. The doctrine which he preached during his public ministration was that which will stand the ordeal of fire, for it was the doctrine promulgated by Christ himself, and by His Apostles and by all true ambassadors of the Lord Jesus: justification by faith alone, salvation by grace, effectual calling, total depravity, definite atonement, election, predestination and so on, all of which were preached by him in their purity.[25]

At every opportunity these Baptists were challenged to entrench, without reservation or exception, their faith and order.

In addition, *Signs* became a moral guidebook. For some Ontario Old School Baptists, it surpassed the Scriptures as a source of moral instruction. They devoured its contents on a variety of important moral issues or current events.[26] The American Civil War, for example, engendered a spirited debate between Gilbert Beebe and his son, William (pastor in Canada, 1877-81) over the morality of war. This debate illustrates an Old School Baptist awareness of the constant need to make their faith morally relevant.

Relevance did not, however, entail moral accommodation or compromise. Articles in the church paper consistently stressed the importance of maintaining a separate morality and lifestyle. Often, past declarations informed the present moral concerns. The statements concerning temperance and participation in temperance and secret societies generally best exemplify the application of this separatistic and staid moral perspective: "We contend earnestly for the highest form of temperance known to man upon earth, even that temperance which is the fruit of the spirit, and when drunkenness occurs among us church discipline is employed for its correction."[27] This declaration cast temperance in spiritual terms and clearly outlined drunkenness as sin and church discipline as the remedy for such behaviour. Membership in temperance and secret societies was seen to be misguided, even heretical.

> We do not object to habitual drunkards forming and maintaining a temperance society on any ground they choose to govern and restrain themselves. The present fashionable temperance societies of various designations, when employed as a stepping stone to the church, is Arminian sophistry.[28]

In the issue of temperance and society's response to it, Old School Baptists saw an Arminian attempt to deny total depravity and one's inability to choose good over evil. Temperance societies, then, were feeble, misguided, doctrinally unsound, and increasingly secular efforts to merit God's favour.

The Old School Baptist disdain for temperance societies carried over to their view of participation in secret societies generally. Essentially, they considered organizations like the Masons or Orange Lodge as worldly, carnal rivals to the church:

> for those who are called out of the world, and into the kingdom of Christ, which is not of the world, to patronize [secret societies] conflicts with their holy calling to come out of the world, and their pledge to renounce the world, the flesh, and the devil, and be satisfied with the fullness, fatness and goodness of the house of God.[29]

A similar line of reasoning was applied to certain aspects of popular culture. The first editorial of 1880 rebuked other Baptists for worldliness:

> Among the numerous modern inventions of the New Order of Baptists to entice the multitude to fall into their ranks and replenish their coffers…are significant advertisements which from time to time have appeared in our village newspapers, inviting the public to attend various carnal diversions, plays, festivals and amusements, from that of the Melodies of Mother Goose, to oyster, strawberry ice cream, chicken pie and numerous other festivals.[30]

For Old School Baptists, the use of public advertisement and common amusements as methods of evangelism violated the law of God because it mistakenly equated the work of the Spirit with the work of the church and employed worldly means to achieve a spiritual end.

Instead, they celebrated their other-worldly beliefs and practices and sought to entrench them through the implementation of a morality consistent with the past. The establishment of fellowship with American Old School Baptists served to both enhance and accelerate the entrenchment process.

Nonetheless, Ekfrid's Particular Covenanted Baptists represented an anomaly among Ontario Baptists. While other Canadian Baptists sought to find the solution to secularization through unity, these Old School Scots entrenched a separate faith and order. For fellowship, they sought the solace and support of American Baptists who shared their commitment to a hyper-Calvinistic theology. Only in form did Ontario's Old School Baptists partially accommodate to cultural trends.

Community: Involvement and Response

Throughout the 19th century, separated though they were religiously and doctrinally, Old School Baptists in Ontario actively participated in a variety of political, economic, and social activities. In politics, they worked diligently for the adoption of Reformed principles and policies and tended to prefer involvement at the municipal level. In the economic sphere, they displayed initiative, industry, and integrity. Socially, they interacted informally with their community and maintained a strong commitment to education. The response of the larger community to the Old School Baptists included hostility, praise, and indifference.

For these Particular Baptists, religion informed politics. The principles of autonomy and democracy present in their faith and order were applied with equal vigour to the political sphere.

As their first cause, they fought for the separation of church and state. Like many of their fellow Nonconformists in Upper Canada, Old School Baptists considered the privileges afforded the English religious establishment in the *Constitutional Act* of 1791 to be unjust and intolerable. In particular, they objected to the need for their ministers to go before Quarter Sessions and produce proof of ordination and their moral fitness for ministry. They also took offence at the requirement compelling dissenting ministers to take the Oath of Allegiance before they could perform marriages.[31] Government refusal to sanction "Calvinist ministers" served to encourage resistance and resentment in Old School Baptist quarters.

More than any other single political issue in the 19th century, the 1837 Mackenzie Rebellion drew attention to Ontario's Old School Baptists. Essentially, the Rebellion placed them in a difficult position. While they undoubtedly sympathized with the rebels, they were hesitant to take up arms against the state. One observer found the Scotch Baptists under Elder Dugald Campbell "Quakerish in their sentiments as to war, believing it to be contrary to the instruction of our Saviour." Still, they were accused of stirring up sedition. The local Anglican minister reported that the Baptists in Lobo were "greatly tainted with voluntaryism and radicalism." Specifically, he charged that "one of the name of Campbell in Lobo and Proudfoot in London...secretly cools and distracts the minds of our countrymen." While he complained that "petitions were everywhere among them," most called for religious tolerance or better administrative and judicial services. Old School Baptists, like many of their Presbyterian or Regular Baptist neighbours, maintained the view that they should be accorded equal rights and privileges in religion, politics, and education. The Rebellion and the controversy surrounding it brought to the surface certain long-standing grievances that cut across religious lines in the London district. In particular the Rebellion revealed the Old School Baptist loyalty to the principles of democracy and individualism.[32]

Both before and after the Rebellion, Scotch Baptists in Ontario considered involvement in politics part of their Christian duty. While they believed that temporal powers were ordained by God and every Christian should submit to that authority (provided such obedience did not contradict the law of God), submission seldom translated into political passiveness or automatic acceptance of government policy. Legal opposition to unjust governmental decisions was the Christian's right and obligation. Consequently, they spared no energy in their efforts for reform.[33]

The political activities of Malcolm Campbell in Ekfrid Township, for example, reveal a high degree of political involvement at the municipal level. Campbell, a bachelor-farmer, at various times from 1851 to 1868 held the positions of auditor, councillor, Reeve and Deputy Reeve of Ekfrid, and Warden of Middlesex County. In 1867, he contested West Middlesex in the interest of the Reform Party, losing by eighty-eight votes to the Conservative candidate. A later commentator noted that "he was outstanding in his contribution to all that was calculated to advance the moral well-being of the township." The same could be said about many other Baptists of this connection.[34]

Ontario Old School Baptists also valued education highly. They were involved in the creation and staffing of schools in their townships. The McColl family of Aldborough, for example, were devoted to the advance of education. In 1819, Elder Thomas McColl opened a school near Brock's Creek.[35] Numerous other McColls received advanced education and entered the teaching profession. Thomas McColl's nephew, Ebenezer, pursued advanced education at the Fort Edward Institute, in Washington County, New York. After he received his "Grade B" teaching certificate in 1860, Ebenezer began to teach school in the Western Circuit of Elgin County. He taught for nearly fifteen years.[36] Throughout the 19th century, higher education, teaching, and school administration remained areas of priority and involvement for Ontario's Particular Covenanted Baptists.

This commitment represented an extension of the Scottish Enlightenment, not an attempt at proselytization. These Baptists viewed education in purely intellectual and non-sectarian terms.[37] In a further application of their belief in the separation of church and state, they supported the notion of "free schools" devoid of control by the established clergy.[38] As long as Ontario's educational system retained its Judeo-Christian moral base, they steadfastly encouraged the pursuit of knowledge within the public school system.

In the economic sphere, Old School Baptists brought a strong belief in the Protestant work ethic to their activities. The pursuit of excellence dominated their value system. Adults encouraged young people to give their best effort to every venture. The acquisition of expertise, primarily through education, increasingly became associated with the quest for economic success. Regardless of occupation, one must always strive for success. Wealth, though not an end in itself, provided a tangible sign of God's blessing on his people.

Assessment

Local community response to the Old School Baptists varied. In the years before Confederation, open hostility characterized the attitudes of the ignorant or intolerant. For their practice of "closed communion" and their unyielding hyper-Calvinistic theology, the Particular Covenanted Baptists gained the derogatory name of "hardshell Baptists." Still, by the later decades of the century, antiquarians and local historians expressed respect for the accomplishments of early Scottish Baptists.[39]

Entrenchment of religious beliefs and practices did not result in their withdrawal from community activities. Instead, the combination of a Scottish cultural heritage and a rigid Calvinism produced a commitment to participate in most community activities.

Today the extreme form of Calvinism preserved and practised by a relatively few Scots in the 19th century appears odd to a society increasingly dominated by the secular philosophies. Yet, the earnestness, simplicity, industry, and integrity of these Baptists recall values which lay at the core of Ontario life in the last century. By 1901, the Old School Baptist church in Ontario had carved out its niche within the province's religious community. The establishment of links with American Baptists and adoption of an entrenchment strategy to cope with the process of secularization both reflected and shaped their experience. This combination of religious fervour, rural setting, Reformed politics, and the Protestant work ethic imbued them with a strength that has insured the small denomination's survival to the present.

Notes

[1] The nomenclature for the Old School Baptists in Ontario is inconsistent and confusing. Government documents usually employ the general term "Calvinist Baptists" (e.g., *Journals of the House of Assembly of the Province of Upper Canada* [26 January 1931], 27). Other sources variously use the titles of "Primitive," "Old School," "Predestinarian," "Covenanted," and "Scotch" Baptist (e.g., *History of the County of Middlesex* [reprint Belleville, ON: Mika Studio, 1972], 55, 494, 504). In this article, "Old School," "Scotch," and "Particular Covenanted" (the formal name adopted by the Canadian church) are used interchangeably.

[2] J. M. Bumstead, *The People's Clearance* (Edinburgh: Edinburgh University Press, 1982), 29-51.

[3] Donald E. Meek, "Evangelical Missionaries in the Early Nineteenth Century Highlands," *Scottish Studies* 28 (1987): 1.

[4] J. Stewart McColl, "Ekfrid Church Development since the Early 1800s: The Particular Covenanted Baptist Church in Canada," *The Glencoe Transcript*, 23 April 1981, 12, calls him "Daniel;" Meek calls him "Donald" ("Evangelical Missionaries," 23).

[5] "From Log Meeting House to Handsome Edifice—Rise and Advancement of a Worthy Denomination," *Glencoe Transcript*, 14 November 1901, 1.

[6] McColl, "Ekfrid Church," 12.

[7] Secretary of State Correspondence, Number 3, Emigration 1818 North America, Offices; Settlers, 327, National Archives of Canada (NAC).

[8] Aldborough Old Boys' Association (OBA), *The Pioneer Days in Aldborough* (reprint; Aylmer, ON: Aylmer Express, 1984), 24; and McColl, "Ekfrid Church," 12. Cf. *The Quebec Gazette*, 14 September 1818, 2; and *The Quebec Mercury*, 22 September 1818, 298-99.

[9] James Henry Coyne, *The Talbot Papers*, vol. 1 (Ottawa: Royal Society of Canada, 1908-09), 75-80; also, Frances McColl, *Ebenezer McColl: "Friend to the Indians"* (Winnipeg: Hignell Press, 1989), 20.

[10] McColl, "Ekfrid Church," 12.

[11] Donald L. Carroll, *Robert's Bairns* (Aylmer, ON: Aylmer Express, 1983), 353.

[12] Charles M. MacFie, *The Township of Ekfrid, 1821-1949* (Strathroy, ON: Holiday and Ekfrid Township Council, 1949), 21, 26-31; Aldborough OBA, *Pioneer Days*, 12-13; McColl, "Ekfrid Church," 12; Donald Whyte, *A Dictionary of Scottish Immigrants to Canada before Confederation* (Toronto: Ontario Genealogical Society, 1986), passim; Aldborough OBA, *Pioneer Days*, 24; McColl, *Ebenezer McColl*, 23; and James S. Brierley, ed., *A Pioneer History: Elgin County* (reprint: Petrolia, ON: E. Phelps, 1971), 18-19, 63-70.

[13] *Illustrated Historical Atlas of the County of Middlesex* (Sarnia, ON: E. Phelps, 1972), 7.

[14] Humphrey Campbell, "The Highland Exile," Miscellaneous Collection, File 7, Archives of Ontario, .

[15] Aldborough OBA, *Pioneer Days*, 17; and McColl, "Ekfrid Church," 12.

[16] *Articles of Faith Approved of by the Particular Covenanted Baptist Church in Canada* (Middletown, NY: G. Beebe, 1873), 1-5.

[17] *Articles*, 6-8; cf. Fred Landon, *Western Ontario and the American Frontier* (Toronto: Ryerson Press, 1941), 105-106; Stuart Ivison and Fred Rosser, *The Baptists in Upper Canada before 1820* (Toronto: University of Toronto Press, 1956), 6; and John W. Grant, *A Profusion of Spires: Religion in Nineteenth Century Ontario* (Toronto: University of Toronto Press, 1988), 31.

[18] Interview with J. Stewart McColl, 7 November 1989. Access to the church minutes is not permitted at present; an examination of these records would enable one to study the participation of women in official church capacities.

[19] For a modern case of the discipline applied, see *An Official Statement of the Particular Covenanted Baptist Church in Canada Regarding the Disorder of Mr. Alex McColl* (London, ON: Particular Covenanted Baptist Church in Canada, 1983), 1-16.

[20] McColl, "Ekfrid Church," 12.

[21] McColl, "Ekfrid Church," quotes the words of Malcolm McIntyre's son James.

[22] Hugh McColl, *Some Sketches of the Early Highland Pioneers of the County of Middlesex* (Ottawa: Canadian Heritage, 1979), 16; and McColl, "Ekfrid Church," 12.

[23] William Westfall, *Two Worlds: The Protestant Culture of Nineteenth-Century Ontario* (Kingston and Montreal: McGill-Queen's University Press, 1989), 126-58.

[24] *Glencoe Transcript*, 14 November 1901, 1; see also *The Signs of the Times*, passim, espec. 50, no. 22 (15 November 1882), 263; McColl, *Ebenezer McColl*, 41-42, 62, 153; and McColl, "Ekfrid Church," 12.

[25] *The Truth* 1 (January-March, 1983): 20—this is the church paper presently published by the Particular Covenanted Baptist Church in Canada.

[26] Interview with J. Stewart McColl, 13 March 1990.

[27] Elder Thomas McColl, *Signs of the Times* 42, no. 16 (15 August 1874), 35.

[28] McColl, *Signs of the Times* 15 August 1874, 35.

[29] *Signs of the Times* 36, no. 6 (15 March 1868), 20.

[30] *Signs of the Times* 48, no. 1 (1 January 1880), 10.

[31] *Journals of the House of Assembly for the Province of Upper Canada* (14 January 1826), 78; cf. W. R. Riddell, "The Law of Marriage in Upper Canada," *Canadian Historical Review* 2 (1921): 226-48.

[32] George Bevins, letter to John Macaulay, Civil Secretary, 15 December 1838, in Upper Canada Sundries, R.G. 5, A 1, Vol. 211, p. 116392, NAC; Rev. William McKellican, letter to John Macaulay, 8 December 1838, R.G. 5, A 1, vol. 211, p. 116169, NAC; Frank Hunt, *Essays on Elgin County*, ed. George Thorman (St. Thomas, ON: Elgin Historical Society, 1989), 130-31; and Landon, *Western Ontario*, 151-69.

[33] Interview with J. Stewart McColl, 7 November 1989.

[34] MacFie, *The Township of Ekfrid*, 38, 40; and Roderick Lewis, compiler, *History of the Electoral Districts, Legislatures and Ministries of the Province of Ontario, 1867-1968* (Toronto: Queen's Printer, 1968), 220.

[35] MacFie, *Township of Ekfrid*, 31-36; and Aldborough OBA, *Pioneer Days*, 18-19.

[36] McColl, *Ebenezer McColl*, 25, 27, 31.

[37] Interview with J. Stewart McColl, 7 November 1989.

[38] Grant, *Profusion of Spires*, 146.

[39] *Illustrated Historical Atlas of the County of Elgin* (Owen Sound, ON: Richardson, Bond and Wright, 1877), xii. Cf. *Biographical Sketches of Some of the Residents of Elgin County* (Toronto: Stewart Publishing, 1887), vii-xxv.

Chapter 7

The Establishment of the
Canadian Convention of Southern Baptists

G. Richard Blackaby

The emergence of Southern Baptists in Canada in 1953 was an attempt by indigenous Baptist pastors and laymen to identify and develop a distinctively Baptist identity.[1] This "search for identity" did not originate with those Canadians who became interested in Southern Baptists, however, but has characterized Baptists here from their beginnings.[2] The formation of the first association in British North America was an attempt by the heirs of Henry Alline to establish a Baptist position. The open vs. close communion debate represented an attempt to differentiate the Baptist witness from such paedobaptist groups as the Congregationalists and Anglicans. The fundamentalist-modernist controversies of the 1920s centred in part around the difficulty for Baptist schools and institutions to unequivocally set forth a lucid statement of Baptist faith. T. T. Shields argued that: "the term, Baptist, had a certain historical content, that it represented certain Biblical principles, and that if you emptied the word of its significance... they might have the name, and I would retain the principles."[3]

John B. Richards, long-time historian at Northwest Baptist Theological College, Vancouver, British Columbia, saw that Regular Baptists in British Columbia had wrestled with their Baptist identity in their "struggle to maintain sectarianism."[4] Walter E. Ellis suggested recently that the Baptist Union of Western Canada (BUWC) has undergone a re-evaluation of its identity in search of "a place to stand."[5] The effort by Canadians to establish the Canadian Convention of Southern Baptists (CCSB) as a thoroughly Baptist denomination, therefore, was not a unique phenomenon in Canadian Baptist history but lay squarely within the Canadian Baptist tradition itself.

The attempt to use American ingenuity and resources to develop a Canadian Baptist denomination also was not unique in Canadian Baptist history. The New Light movement in Nova Scotia centred in large part among immigrants from New England. The Nova Scotia Baptist Association was based primarily upon the Danbury Association in Massachusetts. The purpose of adopting close communion in 1809 was to "bring the Nova Scotia Baptist Association into harmony with the New England Baptist associations." Until the War of 1812, American Baptist missionaries regularly ministered in churches throughout Upper and Lower Canada.[6]

In 1876, at the opposite end of the country, the first Baptist church established in British Columbia soon affiliated with the Puget Sound Association in the United States and, along with other Canadian Baptist churches, "figured conspicuously" within the American association for the next two decades. Between 1882 and 1897, the American Baptist Home Mission Society (ABHMS) contributed over $12,000 to Canadian churches in British Columbia. When in 1897 the Society withdrew all financial support to Canadian churches, eleven congregations formed the Convention of Baptist Churches of British Columbia. Of these, all but one had received assistance from the ABHMS. "The Baptist tradition, like all others that make up our Canadian stream of life, was imported from elsewhere."[7]

Thus, the desire for a thoroughly Baptist denomination and the willingness to receive American support for this venture both have antecedents in Canadian Baptist history.[8]

Southern Baptist Beginnings in Canada

Southern Baptists in Canada received their initial impetus from Regular Baptists in British Columbia. At the outset of the 1950s, BC Regular Baptists expressed growing dissatisfaction over the powerful, interdenominational parachurch groups which recruited Baptist young people and financial resources for their projects, yet refrained from supporting denominational programs. John Pickford, a Regular Baptist pastor and educator, lambasted the churches of his denomination:

> The naked truth is that we are doing so little, not through lack of funds but through our dissipation of funds. We are being bled white by foolishly responding to the sentimental high pressure appeals of unbaptistic organizations who after getting all they can, turn and disdainfully look down on our emaciated condition and pronounce us "dead."[9]

The *Western Regular Baptist* was the new organ of the Regular Baptist churches in the west. Numerous articles expressing dissatisfaction with the condition of their denomination began to fill its columns. In 1944, BC Regular Baptists had affiliated with the General Association of Regular Baptists (GARB) in the American northwest and created the Pacific Northwest Baptist Fellowship. Pickford noted that many of the Canadian pastors affiliated because they "sought proven methods and tools to do the job of building strong Baptist churches."[10] By the 1950s, however, BC Regular Baptists had become disenchanted with the dispensational flavour of the GARB churches and their tendency to maintain looser denominational ties than the Canadian churches were inclined to cultivate.

Concurrent with BC Regular Baptists' increasing disaffection with their denominational relations was a growing awareness of the rapid growth of Southern Baptists in the northwest. In April 1951, R. E. Milam, the executive secretary of the (Southern) Baptist General Convention of Oregon-Washington (BGCOW), attended a meeting of Regular Baptists at the Northwest Baptist Bible College, Port Coquitlam, British Columbia, and was invited to speak. Milam "captivated his audience with his tremendous vision and energy to see the lost won and New Testament churches established in the Pacific Northwest."[11] As a result of this encounter, the British Columbia Regular Baptist churches (BCRBC) appointed a committee to "assess the Southern Baptist programme to see if it were possible to affiliate with the Baptist General Convention of Oregon-Washington."[12]

In the ensuing months, the *Western Regular Baptist* carried numerous articles on Southern Baptists and their evangelistic and educational techniques. Milam, educational expert John T. Sisemore, and other Southern Baptist leaders were featured frequently at Regular Baptist meetings and clinics. This resulted in growing excitement about the possibilities of the Southern Baptist program for their churches. J. D. Grey, president of the Southern Baptist Convention, addressed the 1952 sessions of the BCRBC. Milam's report at those sessions on Southern Baptist growth in the northwest from seven churches to fifty in the previous five years gave Regular Baptists a glimpse of the "electrifying possibilities of further fellowship with Southern Baptists."[13]

Three months later the Northwest Baptist Bible College announced that it would offer a diploma in Religious Education; to do so it was withdrawing from the Evangelical Teacher Training Association and beginning to use textbooks from the Teacher Training Course of the SBC. Following a Sunday School conference in Vernon, British Columbia, led by Sisemore, the Interior Pastor's Conference passed the following resolution:

> We recognize that the well-integrated Sunday School Program of the Southern Baptist Sunday School Board offers a solution to many of our pressing problems in our task of evangelism in British Columbia; that we instruct our present Sunday School Committee to promote this program among our churches.[14]

Attempts to Affiliate

Regular Baptist leaders disagreed over the extent to which they should work with Southern Baptists. Ross MacPherson, pastor of Emmanuel Baptist Church in Vancouver, urged the denomination to accept all possible assistance that Southern Baptists had to offer. In 1953, the BCRBC executive council could not agree to accept an offer of financial and personnel assistance from the Oregon-Washington convention. Sensing that a united move to affiliate with the Southern Baptists of the northwestern states was no longer possible for the BCRBC, MacPherson led Emmanuel Baptist Church to change its name to Kingcrest Southern Baptist Church and to request acceptance into the BGCOW. In part, their letter of request echoed Pickford's charges of three-and-a-half years earlier:

> Nondenominational missionaries alone are available to us at the present time. They are good people, yet they bring the wrong focus before the church. Many belittle the New Testament church, decry denominationalism, plant financial pipelines into the church and keep local finances drained to promote foreign programs that do not stand the test of the Great Commission.[15]

The BGCOW voted to seat the messengers from Kingcrest, despite reluctance among the convention leadership. Although desiring to assist the Canadian churches, Milam later explained: "I tried my best to discourage MacPherson and others from forcing the issue at Seattle but to no avail.... After our Convention received them with all the SBC leaders present I raised the battle cry in 1954 and for years afterward."[16]

During that same meeting, Percy Lee, a prominent Regular Baptist layman, approached Roland Hood about the possibility that Southern Baptists would sponsor a church in North Vancouver. Hood informed Lee that the Oregon-Washington convention would not initiate new work in Canada but would support the work of churches affiliated with them. Lee joined Kingcrest, therefore; and the church requested a Southern Baptist missionary to come and help establish a new work. Horace Burns was sent and began a Bible study in Lee's home.[17] When Lee's group announced it had purchased a building for a church, however, a storm of controversy broke around Kingcrest.

Leaders of the BUWC in Vancouver sent letters of protest to Porter Routh, the executive secretary of the SBC. As a result, the Home Mission Board (HMB) sent a letter to Hood instructing him that no staff person whose salary was paid in part or in full by them was to work in Canada.[18] Burns immediately resigned his connection with the HMB and continued his ministry in North Vancouver.

In an effort to facilitate greater assistance for work in Canada, Milam made a motion at the 1954 Southern Baptist Convention that the "Home Mission Board, the Sunday School Board and other Southern Baptist agencies be permitted to aid us in this work in Canada in and through churches affiliated with our state convention."[19] Milam's motion passed, and both the HMB and the SSB began to develop policies by which Canadian work could be supported without seeking to align existing Baptist works with that of Southern Baptists.[20]

At the 1955 BCRBC meetings, several resolutions were directed toward Kingcrest, particularly one that called on the member churches to "reaffirm our loyalty to our Convention and its interests and refrain from having sympathy and fellowship with every element that would further divide and hinder us."[21] As a result of the pressure mounting upon Kingcrest, it decided in October 1955 to withdraw from the BCRBC. Four other Regular Baptist churches were by then affiliated with the Oregon-Washington Southern Baptist state convention: Westwood, Edmonton, Alberta; Faith, Saskatoon, Saskatchewan; Whalley, Surrey, British Columbia; and Grace, North Burnaby, British Columbia.

To improve communication and understanding between Baptists in Canada and the SBC, a joint committee was established in 1957. It consisted of the executive secretaries of the HMB, of the SSB, of the SBC, and the Convention president; also included were three from the Canadian Baptist Federation (CBF) and one each from Southern Baptists in Canada, the Baptist General Conference, and the North American Baptist Conference. In a further effort to develop mutual understanding, the HMB appointed W. Bertram King as its liaison in Canada.[22]

Southern Baptists in Canada objected that although the joint committee was providing assistance to churches in the CBF, it was preventing aid from going to Southern Baptist churches here. Jack McKay, pastor of the Edmonton SBC church, claimed that doctrinal loyalty was pre-eminent over national loyalty. He argued that due to the CBF's involvement in the Canadian Council of Churches, Southern Baptist-aligned churches could not support their efforts and, therefore, must receive support from like-minded Baptists in the United States in order to develop a purely Baptist organization.[23]

In response to such feelings by Canadian Southern Baptists, Milam made a motion at the 1958 Southern Baptist Convention that they be seated as messengers. It was objected that this violated Article 2 of the constitution. The following year a motion was presented to amend the article by adding the words "and churches in Canada who cooperate with the Southern Baptist Convention." When its constitutionality was challenged, the motion was withdrawn.[24]

Thus, Canadian members of the Oregon-Washington state convention found themselves in limbo; they were neither members of a Canadian Baptist group nor were they seated at the national convention whose program they promoted. Even before they were formally consigned to such uncertain status, representatives from fifteen Southern Baptist churches in Canada had met in February 1959 to form the Canadian Southern Baptist Pastor's Conference; this was an inspirational fellowship to encourage pastors. During the organizational meeting, the Oregon-Washington convention was requested to support mission work in Canada. That body responded by budgeting $6,000 for Canada; this financial support was continued for over two decades.

In 1962, another attempt was made to affiliate the Canadian churches with the SBC. This time Nolan Kennedy moved that the words "the United States and its territories" be deleted from Article 2 of the constitution so that Canadian churches might directly affiliate. After it had been referred to the SBC Executive Committee, Kennedy withdrew his motion in the interest of Baptist unity during the continental "Baptist Jubilee Advance."[25]

It had become apparent that little assistance would come through official SBC national channels. Canadian Southern Baptists, therefore, began to organize themselves into a more cohesive and functional organization. The first association they organized was the Capilano Association of Vancouver, in 1955. Two years later, the Midwest Baptist Association, encompassing the provinces of Alberta and Saskatchewan, was formed. After another three years, the churches in interior British Columbia established the Plateau Association. The churches of these associations organized the Canadian Southern Baptist Conference in 1963. This structure superseded the Pastor's Conference and was intended to do more than provide fellowship; it was a temporary organization to coordinate mission work throughout western Canada and serve as a forerunner to a full-fledged convention to be linked with the SBC.[26]

On the United States side, a California pastor and member of the HMB, Hazen Simpson, at the 1976 Southern Baptist Convention moved that they "immediately extend encouragement to Southern Baptists dwelling and working in Canada, by financial assistance plus any and all other means of support that we make available to ministry outside the United States." The Foreign Mission Board (FMB) was commissioned to study Simpson's proposal. The following year its study committee recommended that all Southern Baptist boards and agencies be free to respond to requests for assistance from all Baptist groups in Canada.[27]

As a result of the 1977 decision, the HMB began to invest its resources into the Canadian work. Cecil Sims was appointed the Associate Director of Missions for Canada in order to coordinate Home Mission funds in Canada. Numerous Home Mission personnel toured the Canadian churches and offered assistance and encouragement.

During the 1970s, Southern Baptists in Canada experienced rapid growth. The number of churches grew from twenty-three to forty-five in the decade. Faith Baptist Church, Saskatoon, exemplified the concern for missions many of the churches felt. Its Minister of Outreach began in 1974 to start mission churches as far away as Winnipeg.[28] Hamilton, Ontario, was the eastern edge of Southern Baptist work by the end of the seventies. The Canadian Baptist Theological College, opened in Saskatoon in 1973, undertook to train Canadians for ministry in Southern Baptist churches.

As the 1980s commenced, the fledgling work was advancing rapidly. During the decade, they established new associations in Saskatchewan, Manitoba, Ontario, and Quebec; churches and missions grew to total 106.[29]

With the continuing development of the work in Canada, it was inevitable that the question of seating Canadian messengers at the Southern Baptist convention would be raised again. A motion was proposed from the floor in 1983, trying again to amend Article 2, this time to include the words "and Canada."[30] The twenty-one-member Canada Study Committee appointed to examine the motion would provide the most thorough analysis of the Canadian situation made to date by the SBC.

It immediately faced divided opinion: the HMB and the Northwest Baptist Convention (as the BGCOW had renamed itself) favoured seating Canadians, while the FMB was opposed. William Tanner, executive secretary of the HMB, argued: "If we were willing to receive their money in Cooperative Program gifts, which we did, then they had a right to representation."[31] He maintained that while the future goal was the development of an autonomous convention, Southern Baptists in Canada might need to be seated in the SBC temporarily until they developed enough strength to carry out an independent program. He also argued that Southern Baptists in Canada did not become any less indigenous by using Southern Baptist programs or resources to evangelize Canada.[32] Keith Parks, president of the FMB, warned that if Canadians were seated in the convention, the SBC could become a multinational body. Further, the SBC could develop a "Big Brother" image which might offend already existing Baptist groups. He suggested that perhaps an indigenous convention which was "like-minded with Southern Baptists" would be the solution.[33]

The Study Committee decided to recommend the formation of an autonomous Canadian convention with an organizational structure similar, though not identical, to that of a state convention in the United States. The SBC adopted this proposal at its 1984 convention, thus presumably settling the "Canada question."[34]

Canadian Convention of Southern Baptists

The 1984 Canadian conference unanimously concurred in the decision, adding that its acceptance was intended to be "without prejudice to the later possibility of our being seated."[35] It set out immediately to develop a convention structure. It commenced by withholding the "Cooperative Program" money it had been sending to the Portland office of the Northwest Baptist Convention; these funds would finance its own forthcoming convention. The FMB appointed James Teel to serve as its liaison in Canada to assist with student work and the development of theological education in Canada. The HMB increased its investment in providing directors of missions for each of the seven associations as well as funding foreign-language missionaries among immigrants across Canada.

The next year the Canadian Conference enthusiastically adopted a new constitution, transforming itself into the Canadian Convention of Southern Baptists (CCSB). The messengers also approved the Theological Study Committee's motion to adopt Calgary as the site of the future seminary. The FMB would provide the bulk of the funding for the school, including the salaries of six professors by 1990.[36] By the following April the FMB had also arranged for Canadian Southern Baptists to serve as foreign missionaries; the Canadian Convention would pay the salaries and pensions of their missionaries while the FMB would provide training, transportation, housing, insurance, and medical coverage.[37]

The 1986 annual convention proved to be another milestone for the fledgling convention. It elected Allen Schmidt as its first executive director-treasurer. The convention also adopted the constitution for the second and final time. A motion to purchase five acres from the 149-acre seminary site at Cochrane in order to establish the convention office next to the seminary was approved. An annual "Harvest Mission Offering" was initiated to promote the development of the work in Canada. Finally, the convention initiated the Foundation of the Canadian Convention of Southern Baptists in order to receive financial contributions for the convention.[38]

Administratively, the convention continued to grow. Canada became the only country in the world where both the SBC Home and Foreign Mission Boards actively operated. The FMB supplied a liaison, campus ministers, and a seminary president and professors. The HMB supplied funding for language missionaries, including a national director, directors of missions in each of the seven associations, a national director of missions, and indirectly supported an executive director-treasurer.[39] The SSB also contributed funds for executive personnel. As a result, the CCSB's annual budget rose during the eighties from $183,836 to $1,284,603.

Southern Baptist work in Canada expanded culturally, geographically, and numerically. In 1970, the Vancouver Chinese Baptist Church grew to seventy-seven members one year after its founding; this made it the largest church in the Capilano Association. In 1973, the first native Indian church affiliated with Southern Baptists in Canada. In 1976, the first Korean church was organized, in Vancouver. By 1990, ethnic churches represented one-third of the Canadian Convention of Southern Baptists, including Spanish, Korean, Chinese, Laotian, Cambodian, East Indian, native Indian, and Haitian churches. Geographically, the convention advanced beyond its western Canadian confines and developed churches as far east as Montreal.

A significant development within the CCSB was the establishment of Canadian Southern Baptist Seminary. In September 1986, Clinton Ashley, formerly a missionary to Brazil, was called as its first president. The next month work began on the seminary buildings. A library of over 17,000 volumes was developed by the fall of 1987 when the inaugural class of twenty commenced training under two professors. In two years, there were twenty-eight full-time students with six professors. Perhaps most significant was the calling of four students from the first graduating class to churches within the convention. With the placement of Canadian pastors trained in Canada by Southern Baptist professors, the Canadian Convention had reached a new era in its development as a Baptist denomination in Canada.

Southern Baptist Contributions to Canada

If the CCSB is to justify its existence in Canada, it should be able to demonstrate significant contributions to the Canadian religious scene. There are at least four areas in which it appears they have. First, Southern Baptists have upheld a robust view of denominationalism in contrast to powerful ecumenical and anti-denominational forces within Canada. They have steadfastly refused to disperse their resources through interdenominational organizations but rather invested in the development of a homogeneously Baptist organization which used Baptist literature, Baptist programs, Baptist personnel, and Baptist doctrine. At a time when Regular Baptists in British Columbia were permeated with interdenominational forces and the Baptist Union of Western Canada was searching for its "place to stand" within the denominational spectrum, Southern Baptists unapologetically upheld a thoroughly Baptist position.[40]

A second contribution to Canadian Baptist life has been in religious education. The initial impetus for Regular Baptist contacts with Southern Baptists was an interest in their Sunday School, teacher training, and Training Union programs. The SBC offered an integrated educational program which used literature that promoted the local church as well as Baptist emphases. The concern for educating church members continued to characterize Canadian Southern Baptists as late as 1989 when they led all state conventions within the SBC in the percentage of members earning church study course awards. While not discrediting educational successes of other Baptist groups in Canada, Southern Baptists have provided literature and programs which have helped Baptist churches across Canada.

A third contribution to Baptists in Canada has been in evangelism and missions. During the 1950s, Southern Baptists demonstrated that local churches did not have to rely upon home mission funds or administrative initiative before planting new churches. They encouraged churches simply to begin churches. Furthermore, Southern Baptists place paramount importance upon evangelism. Evangelism conferences were frequently held.

Simultaneous revivals were introduced. Southern Baptists promoted the Sunday School as a primary evangelistic tool of the church. Laymen played a vital part in evangelism through the churches and courses were offered to train them to witness. Southern Baptists in the United States also sent numerous pastors to preach revival meetings in Canadian churches at their own expense. The result of this evangelistic emphasis was growth.

In 1982, a Canadian Baptist theological educator suggested that in order to grow, a church needed to have a ratio of baptisms/members as low as 1:10. While studying churches related to the CBF, he noted that in 1978 the ratio in the Maritimes was 1:44. The year before it had been 1:39 in Ontario, 1:30 in the BUWC. That Southern Baptists at that time enjoyed a 1:9.9 ratio, he felt, "augurs for rapid growth."[41] While not a large denomination, Southern Baptists' expansion in Canada from one church in January 1954 to 106 by January 1990 as well as their continued stress on evangelism has challenged other Baptist groups to continue to develop their own evangelistic methods and strategies.

A final contribution made by Southern Baptists in Canada has been their unifying influence. Many Regular Baptists were first attracted to Southern Baptists during the 1950s in part because of their unified efforts in evangelism and in developing their denomination. Despite some early friction and misunderstanding, Southern Baptists have proven to be catalysts for a number of Baptist-wide projects in Canada. During Expo '86 in Vancouver, CCSB churches initiated two Baptist worship services on-site in which all five Baptist groups participated. Not only was this one of the first such efforts in Vancouver, the effect continues in a standing committee consisting of representatives of all Baptist groups to arrange further cooperation; Henry Blackaby of the CCSB serves as its first chairperson.

In July 1989, the executive director of the CCSB proposed a meeting of the executive leaders of each major Baptist group in Canada. They met that December; a second meeting was scheduled for the following year. This was the first such meeting of all five Baptist executives; and it was initiated and led by a Southern Baptist. The formation of the Canadian Southern Baptist Seminary in Cochrane with a well-stocked library and faculty, gives Southern Baptists yet another tool by which to promote joint ventures with other Baptist groups to educate Canadian Baptist ministers.

Conclusion

The history of Southern Baptists in Canada is not a peripheral peculiarity outside the Canadian Baptist mainstream. Rather, the CCSB exemplifies the historic Canadian struggle to provide an untainted Baptist witness amidst overwhelming demographic and ecumenical pressures. Southern Baptists insisted that there were principles sacred to Baptists which transcended any culture and which could never be sacrificed on the altar of ecumenical or national expediency. Southern Baptists, therefore, did not so much bring American ingenuity north of the 49th parallel as Canadian Regular Baptists perceived in the SBC principles which were effectively developing Baptist churches. Neither have Southern Baptists claimed to be Canada's salvation, as if they could evangelize the whole country single-handedly. Southern Baptists did not enter Canada in order to denigrate existing Baptist groups. Rather, Southern Baptists aided Canadians to develop a denomination which they perceived to be wholly Baptist in nature in order to add their efforts to those of existing Baptist bodies that already were engaged in the enormous task of proclaiming the Gospel to Canadians.

Notes

[1] For a more exhaustive study of Southern Baptists in Canada, see G. Richard Blackaby, "Southern Baptists in Their Canadian Context, 1953-1990: An Evaluation of the Validity of the Canadian Convention of Southern Baptists" (PhD diss., Southwestern Baptist Theological Seminary, Fort Worth, TX, 1990).

[2] Jarold K. Zeman used this phrase as a subtitle for the edited papers of a 1979 Baptist symposium: Jarold K. Zeman, ed., *Baptists in Canada: Search for Identity Amidst Diversity* (Burlington, ON: G. R. Welch, 1980), vii-viii; cf. Samuel Mikolaski, "Identity and Mission," in *Baptists in Canada*, ed. Zeman, 1-19.

[3] T. T. Shields, *The Plot that Failed* (Toronto: The Gospel Witness, 1937), 154.

[4] John B. Richards, "Baptists in British Columbia: A Struggle to Maintain Sectarianism" (MA thesis, University of British Columbia, Vancouver, 1964).

[5] Walter E. Ellis, "A Place to Stand," *American Baptist Quarterly* 6 (March 1987): 31-51.

[6] Gordon T. Stewart and George Rawlyk, *A People Highly Favoured of God: The Nova Scotia Yankees and the American Revolution* (Toronto: Macmillan, 1972), 155; Edward Manning Saunders, *History of the Baptists of the Maritime Provinces* (Halifax, NS: John Burgoyne Press, 1902), 86; D. G. Bell, ed., *The Newlight Baptist Journals of James Manning and James Innis*, BHAC, 6 (Hantsport, NS: Lancelot Press, 1984), 26-27; Stuart Ivison and Fred Rosser, *The Baptists in Upper and Lower Canada before 1820* (Toronto: University of Toronto Press, 1956); and Elmer G. Anderson, "The Work of American Baptist Missionaries in Upper Canada to 1820" (BD thesis, McMaster University, Hamilton, ON, 1952).

[7] Stuart Ivison, "Is There a Baptist Tradition?," in *The Churches and the Canadian Experience: A Faith and Order Study of the Christian Tradition*, ed. John Webster Grant (Toronto: Ryerson Press, 1963), 53.

[8] J. C. Baker, *Baptist History of the North Pacific Coast* (Philadelphia: American Baptist Publication Society, 1912), 95; Gordon H. Pousett, "A History of the Convention of Baptist Churches of British Columbia" (MA thesis, Vancouver School of Theology, 1982), 47; and Pousett, "Formative Influences on Baptists in British Columbia, 1876-1918," *Baptist History and Heritage* 15 (April 1980): 16-17.

[9] John H. Pickford, "While Baptists Slumber and Sleep," *Western Regular Baptist (WRB)*, January-March 1950, 4.

[10] John Pickford, *What God Hath Wrought: Sixty Years of God's Goodness in the Fellowship of Regular Baptist Churches of British Columbia* (Vancouver: Baptist Foundation of British Columbia, 1987), 103.

[11] Pickford, *What God Hath Wrought*, 104.

[12] *WRB*, July 1951, 9.

[13] Richards, "Baptists in British Columbia," 115.

[14] *WRB*, January 1953, 13.

[15] Quoted in R. E. Milam, *Win America Now* (Shawnee, OK: Bison Press, 1954), 77-78.

[16] Letter received from R. E. Milam, Portland, OR, 11 January 1989; cf. letter received from Ross MacPherson, Vancouver, BC, 1 October 1988.

[17] Roland Hood, *Southern Baptist Work in Canada*, ed. Allen Schmidt (Portland, OR: Northwest Baptist Convention, 1977), 4.

[18] Hood, *Southern Baptist Work in Canada*, 6.

[19] *Southern Baptist Convention Annual* (1954), 53.

[20] *Baptist Horizon*, November 1954, 1,3-4; and "Action of the Home Mission and Sunday School Boards on Canadian Missions," *Pacific Coast Baptist (PCB)*, 20 January 1955, 1, 4.

[21] "Resolutions," *WRB*, July 1955, 16. Resolutions had been directed against Kingcrest the year before, also—*WRB*, July 1954, 16.

[22] Bertram King, "My Work in Canada," *PCB*, 5 February 1962, 7; and T. B. McDormand, "Reports on Conference with Southern Baptists," *Canadian Baptist*, 15 October 1957, 11, 15.

[23] Jack McKay, "Some Reasons Why Some Canadian Baptist Churches Wish Direct Affiliation with the Southern Baptist Convention," *PCB*, 20 April 1959, 1.

[24] *SBC Annual* (1958), 50, 69, 72; *SBC Annual* (1959), 55, 58-59.

[25] *SBC Annual* (1962), 69-70; *PCB*, 5 February 1963, 3.

[26] George Irvin, "The Purpose, Plan and Future of the Canadian Southern Baptist Conference," *PCB*, 5 March 1963, 2.

[27] *SBC Annual* (1976), 32; *SBC Annual* (1977), 43; and "Foreign Mission Board Recommends Canadian Church Help," *Northwest Baptist Witness (NBW)*, 4 May 1977, 1.

[28] Henry T. Blackaby, *What the Spirit Is Saying to the Churches* (Atlanta, GA: [SBC] Home Mission Board, 1989), 41.

[29] Allen Schmidt, "Looking Up," *Baptist Horizon*, January 1990, 2.

[30] *SBC Annual* (1983), 36.

[31] Letter received from William Tanner, Oklahoma City, OK, 23 June 1989.

[32] Gerald Palmer, "Home Mission Board Study Report," 1983.

[33] Keith Parks, "Report to the Canada Study Committee," 17 October 1983, 1-8.

[34] *SBC Annual* (1984), 54, 219-21.

[35] "Canadians Okay SBC Committee Report," *NBW*, 9 May 1984, 1.

[36] *Northwest Baptist Convention Annual* (1985) 191, 193.

[37] Erich Bridges, "Canadians Launch Overseas Missions," *NBW*, 22 April 1986, 4; and *Canadian Convention of Southern Baptists Annual* (1986), 50-51.

[38] *CCSB Annual* (1986), 18-24; and "Canadian Convention Adopts Constitution, Elects Schmidt," *NBW*, 6 May 1986, 1, 8.

[39] Mike Creswell, "Our Neighbor to the North," *Commission*, January 1987, 10-54; and "Canadian Southern Baptists Have the Best of Three Worlds," *NBW*, 10 March 1987, 1, 4.

[40] Cf. Ellis, "A Place to Stand," 49.

[41] Samuel J. Mikolaski, "Baptists on the March," *CB*, July-August 1982, 4-5; Mikolaski, "Peeking over the Baptist Horizon," *CB*, May 1979, 4-5.

Chapter 8

Fragmented Baptists:
The Poverty and Potential of Baptist Life
in Western Canada

Walter E. Ellis

Since Confederation in 1867, Canadian unity has been precarious. As the deadline for passage of the Meech Lake Accord drew near in 1990 and a Quebec referendum was promised in 1995, the prospect that centrifugal forces may bifurcate the state is now quite thinkable. Regionalism, provincialism, and linguistic, ethnic, economic, and cultural diversity are factors that continue to test severely the will to nationhood, the fabric of Canadian federalism. In part, this is because historically nationalists have been hard-pressed to demonstrate that Canada has a significant and unique contribution to make to the world community. Canada was founded with no messianic vision; hence, the nation totters.

In like manner for Baptists, the vision of a national denomination mobilized to serve Canada and the world has been equally illusive and elusive. In the Canadas during the 1840s, leaders attempted to unify disparate Baptists. Then in 1900, in Winnipeg, the National Baptist Convention of Canada was delivered stillborn. From 1907 through 1911, a commission under the leadership of H. F. Laflamme struggled to prepare a constitution for an all-Canada Baptist Union, only to be defeated by the opposition of a small clique from the Ontario establishment centred at McMaster.

It was not until 1944, under the leadership of Watson Kirkconnell, that Convention Baptists finally formed the Baptist Federation of Canada (CBF). But by then, regional interests were entrenched behind incorporated structures, the fundamentalist-modernist controversy had bifurcated the denomination, and the German and Swedish conferences, oriented to their American counterparts, had terminated or were in process of ending dual affiliation with the Baptist Union of Western Canada (BUWC).

Even when the CBF emerged, it was hardly informed by scriptural warrant or doctrinal injunction. Federation was motivated by pressures to organize nationally which cosmopolitan leaders felt was necessary for Baptists to move with respect in wider religious circles. Kirkconnell and his associates wanted to convert "an unorganized rabble of regional groups"

1940s into a dignified and unified church equal to other Canadian mainline denominations. Their "progress" was consistently undermined by the Baptist idol, the autonomy of the local church. Hence, pragmatic and utilitarian appeals for respectability and efficiency in outreach were used to justify the Federation. In Kirkconnell's words:

> Through consultation and united policy-making and action, [Convention Baptists] may hope to achieve a closer sense of denominational fellowship across Canada and a higher sense of the dignity of the Baptist cause.... By the new integration of our work we may hope to share more effectively in cooperative efforts, both in the Baptist World Alliance [founded in 1905] and in the Canadian Council of Churches.[1]

In short, the first national Baptist entity was born in answer to the concerns of persons George Rawlyk has described as those "expertly trained to impose hegemonic order and control over Canadian society."[2] It was not our Lord's high priestly prayer that his disciples might be one (Jn. 17.11) that triggered the modest accomplishments made by Convention Baptists in 1944 when they created the weak CBF.

In 1953, the Fellowship of Evangelical Baptist Churches in Canada (FEBC) united fundamentalist and conservative Regular and independent Baptists in Ontario and Quebec. But this was accomplished only after Dr. T. T. Shields and his followers were excluded in the battles of the late 1940s over the spread of "non-Baptist" influence among the Regulars. Their counterparts in western Canada, having organized provincial conventions in the late 1920s and early 1930s, soon followed in alliance with the FEBC, making it a truly national body. Again pragmatic appeals for evangelism and efficiency informed the mergers; and doctrinal accommodations, especially in the area of eschatology, necessarily followed.[3]

Growing Canadian nationalism was a factor in recent years in the separation of the Baptist General Conference of Canada (BGCC—originally Swedish) from its parent denomination (BGC) in the United States. But, unlike similar movements among Lutheran and Reformed churches, independence was not motivated by any wider vision for Canadian Baptist unity. The same pragmatism and nationalist impulses produced the recently organized Canadian Convention of Southern Baptists (CCSB). Add to these four major "religious outlets" the more than 110 North American Baptist Conference (NABC—originally German) churches in Canada which maintain their binational ties, the numerous smaller ethnic groups, and countless independent churches; and what emerges is a confused mosaic of Baptist groups—often competitive, sometimes antagonistic—together facing a secularized Canada which espouses a bilingual, multicultural, multifaith agenda as the road to national unity.

Sociological wisdom is that with a national commitment to religious pluralism the "country's dominant religious groups" will seek to diversify in an attempt to meet the consumerism of the religious populace.

This general pattern of diversification can be expected to contribute to the polar tendencies of ecumenism externally and conflict internally. The denominational menu diversification means that over a period of time many of the religious outlets across Canada will look very much the same...[which could lead to] a measure of merging....

    At the same time, *within* denominations,...advocates of different emphases...[might trigger schism].[4]

Elsewhere I have suggested that the BUWC is falling prey to paradenominationalism; that is, in its search for institutional growth and under the influence of transdenominational and parachurch movements, it has succumbed to an all-pervasive evangelical syncretism.[5] Is this also true of other Baptist groups? May there be any clues in the patterns of membership interaction among Baptists and with other religious outlets? This chapter constitutes a preliminary study of the interchange in western Canada of church members among Baptist denominations and between Baptists and other churches.

The Baptist Mosaic in Canada and the West

The 1981 census shows that 696,850 Canadians report a Baptist preference. Of these, 230,000 are affiliated with approximately 2,000 congregations. The majority belong to one of the five bodies previously mentioned. The largest is the BUWC (1,125 churches, 135,000 members, affiliated with the CBF). Second, is the FEBC (475 churches, 56,000 members), historically a product of 1920s schisms related to the fundamentalist-modernist controversies that swept North America. Concentrated in western Canada are the NABC (120 churches, 18,000 members) and the BGCC (75 churches; 6,000 members). Both are now English-speaking and maintain close relations with their parent denominations in the United States. The last of many American incursions into Canada came in the 1950s when, encouraged by disaffected Fellowship Baptists and by funding and personnel from churches affiliated with the Southern Baptist Convention, the independent CCSB eventually emerged (80 churches, 5,000 members). Statistics for smaller ethnic groups, now increasingly Asian and Latin American, and independent churches are unavailable.[6]

Has all this institutional proliferation facilitated denominational growth? The evidence is negative. For example, in 1871, Baptists were 7 percent of the population. They are still the largest "believers' church" denomination in Canada but now a mere 2.9 percent of Canadians. Table 1 compares Baptist strength in the four western provinces over the course of seventy years from 1911 and 1981. In western Canada, where Baptists are most diverse, their relative numbers continue to decline, from 4 percent to

2.67 percent. The churches Reginald W. Bibby designates as "conservative" together hardly approximate the 4 percent reported as Baptist prior to World War I.

Table 1
Baptist Religious Preference: Western Provinces, 1911-81

	Manitoba	Saskatch-ewan	Alberta	British Columbia	Total
1911					
Baptists	14,003	18,371	19,491	17,228	69,093
Tot. pop.	461,394	492,432	374,295	392,480	1,720,601
1981					
Baptists	19,265	16,790	66,375	81,850	184,180
Tot. pop.	1,013,700	956,440	2,213,650	2,713,615	6,897,405

Source: *Census of Canada*, 1921, 1, part 3, 593, 1911 statistics; and *Census of Canada*, 1981, 2, Provincial Series: 93-931-2, Table 5. Used with permission.

Methodology

In an era when "the circulation of the saints" often occurs without communication between congregations, it is difficult to ascertain with certainty the patterns of interaction among churches. However, Baptists generally retain the practice of transfer by exchange of letters. Letter, "Christian experience" (a testimony to faith and report of previous believer's baptism by immersion), or baptism are the usual ways members are accepted. For example, in 1988, the Baptist Union received 661 members by baptism and 1,003 by letter or experience. If one assumes that members received by experience are disbursed in the same pattern as those who came by letter, then the data on letter transfers should be a reliable indicator of denominational interaction.

Questionnaires were sent to 112 Baptist churches (46 BUWC, 20 BGCC, 20 FEBC, and 26 NABC). Only three of twenty FEBC congregations responded, insufficient for analysis. Data grouped to reflect rural, urban, and prairie-coast demographics showed no significant differences from the statistics reported below for BUWC, BGC, and NAB.

The sample was chosen to reflect relative size and regional and demographic differences. Statistics on letter exchanges from 1985-89 were requested along with subjective comments on the denominational backgrounds of members received by Christian experience and baptism. The research design could not probe interaction between most Baptists and paedobaptists since membership in a Baptist church requires what paedobaptists perceive as "rebaptism" and few churches think it important to keep records on the religious backgrounds of converts. What follows then is primarily a study of interaction among believers' church denominations.

The Baptist Union of Western Canada

The BUWC is the largest, oldest, and most ethnically and theologically diverse indigenous Baptist movement operating in western Canada.

Table 2
Baptist Union of Western Canada:
Members Received/Dismissed by Letter, 1985-89[7]

Denomination	Received from		Dismissed to	
	Number	%	Number	%
Baptist Federation (Union)	656	52.05	502	64.19
Baptist General Conference	31	2.44	25	3.19
Fellowship Baptist	51	4.02	27	3.45
North American Baptist	50	3.94	36	4.60
Southern Baptist	38	2.00	9	1.15
Christian and Missionary Alliance	57	4.50	23	2.94
Evangelical Free	11	.87	6	.76
Nazarene	4	.31	1	.13
Pentecostal	26	2.05	8	1.02
Brethren	17	1.37	3	.38
Other	178	14.06	88	11.25
Mennonite Brethren	31	2.44	15	1.91
Mennonite General Conference	5	.40	--	--
Anglican	14	1.10	4	.51
Roman Catholic	17	1.34	--	--
Lutheran	8	.63	--	--
Presbyterian	25	1.97	14	1.79
United Church	44	3.47	21	2.68
Total	1,266	100.0	782	100.0

Note: Number of questionnaires: 46. Number of responses: 35. Percentage of response: 76.08%.

A minority of Union churches practice open membership and accept transfers from churches that practise paedobaptism. Table 2 documents the backgrounds of 1,266 members received and 782 dismissed from 35 churches. Half the persons received and over 60 percent of those dismissed were within the Union. The 5 percent recruited from paedobaptist churches should be adjusted upwards, since data reflect responses from only five open-membership churches.

The data reveal significant interaction with four other Baptist groups (13.4 percent received; 12.4 percent dismissed). Surprisingly, the Union experienced a small net increase from holiness/pentecostal groups, especially the Christian and Missionary Alliance. The Union is holding its own with the small fundamentalist denominations and new charismatic churches, though respondents reported some undocumented movement to the latter.

Given the significant presence of Anabaptists on the prairies and in British Columbia, some suggest that Baptists serve as a way-station on the road to social integration for Mennonites. With only 3 percent interaction between the Union and Anabaptist churches, the thesis cannot be supported.

Union statistics clearly document the "baptistification" of the Christian world and the market-place syndrome.[8] They raise the issue of the apparent unimportance of denominational distinctives presently to the members of evangelical churches, since 36 percent of additions and 25 percent of dismissals were to denominations *outside* the immediate Baptist family.

The Baptist General Conference of Canada

Table 3 contains data from ten BGCC churches. From 1894 until 1947, General Conference churches maintained dual affiliation with the BUWC. However, strains between the then Northern Baptist Convention (now American Baptist Churches in the USA) and the BGC on issues of "Americanization," doctrine, and missions coincided with the schism and formation of the Conservative Baptist Association of America (1947). The BGC took the opportunity and went its separate way. These American controversies resulted in dis-affiliation in Canada as well because some viewed Union Baptists as roughly equivalent to the NBC/ABC.[9]

These data suggest the BGCC churches in western Canada have made a successful transition from their Scandinavian origins. However, their ability to maintain a unique identity among the 65 percent recruited from other evangelical groups may be in question. Less than 35 percent of their additions come from the BGCC. On the other hand, these churches received 30 percent from other Baptist groups and appear to provide acceptable neutral ground for the wider Baptist movement.

Thirteen percent of those received by letter come from FEB

churches; and this interaction can be expected to increase as the two denominations cooperate in the Associated Canadian Theological Schools (ACTS) consortium at Trinity Western University, Langley, British Columbia. However, because 40 percent of transfers come from holiness and other evangelical sects, the BGCC risks becoming an undifferentiated religious outlet and will have to struggle hard to maintain a strong Baptist identity.

Table 3
Baptist General Conference of Canada:
Members Received/Dismissed by Letter, 1985-89

Denomination	Received from		Dismissed to	
	Number	%	Number	%
Baptist General Conference	81	34.76	42	28.96
Baptist Federation (Union)	22	9.44	9	6.21
Fellowship Baptist	30	12.87	14	9.65
North American Baptist	12	5.15	6	4.13
Southern Baptist	5	2.14	2	1.37
Christian and Missionary Alliance	12	5.15	9	6.20
Evangelical Free	5	2.14	2	1.37
Nazarene	2	.85	2	1.37
Pentecostal	5	2.14	3	2.06
Brethren	--	--	2	1.37
Other	49	21.03	42	28.96
Mennonite Brethren	6	2.57	8	5.51
Lutheran	--	--	1	.68
Presbyterian	2	.85	--	--
United Church	2	.85	--	--
Total	233	100.0	145	100.0

Note: Number of questionnaires: 20. Number of responses: 10. Percentage of response: 50%.

The North American Baptist Conference

The first German Baptists in Canada appeared in Ontario in 1851 as products of the missionary enterprise of August Rauschenbusch, the indefatigable church-planter and, later, Rochester Seminary professor. After 1890, German immigration to the prairies gave rise to many new congregations under the continental influence of the General Conference of German

Baptist Churches in North America. Heavily supported by English-speaking Canadian Baptists, these Canadian churches remained in dual affiliation with the BUWC until 1919.

Their first Canadian historian, Edward B. Link, maintains that the "break came on grounds of polity and language, not doctrine."[10] But here, again, decisions were made in the continental context; Baptist alignments in Canada were determined by Baptist politics in the United States.

By 1952, the issue was assimilation; and the need for "bringing the gospel to communities regardless of their ethnic composition" had to be addressed. A conference held in Philadelphia concluded that "assimilation was not the end of an ethnically-rooted denomination."[11] In consequence, the NABC set out to serve the general population while maintaining their institutional identity. Table 4 is a profile of 1,136 members received and dismissed from sixteen closed-membership NABC churches.

Table 4
North American Baptist Conference:
Members Received/Dismissed by Letter, 1985-89

Denomination	Received from		Dismissed to	
	Number	%	Number	%
North American Baptist	302	55.92	250	41.94
Baptist Federation (Union)	29	5.37	34	5.70
Baptist General Conference	10	1.85	36	6.04
Fellowship Baptist	40	7.40	100	16.77
Christian and Missionary Alliance	24	4.44	21	3.52
Evangelical Free	14	2.59	21	3.52
Nazarene	2	.37	2	.32
Pentecostal	4	.74	19	3.18
Brethren	18	3.33	2	.32
Other	67	12.40	73	12.24
Mennonite Brethren	23	4.25	33	5.53
Mennonite General Conference	1	.18	1	.16
Anglican/Catholic	--	--	1	.16
Presbyterian	2	.37	1	.16
United Church	2	.37	1	.16
Total	540	100.0	596	100.0

Note: Number of questionnaires: 25. Number of responses: 13. Percentage of response: 52%.

Respondents reported little contact with paedobaptists. However, the significant interaction with holiness/pentecostal churches is one indication of successful adjustment to the evangelical melting-pot. Cultural accommodation among second-generation German immigrants may account for their loss of 13.5 percent to other Baptist groups. Common ethnicity explains their closer relationship with Mennonites than other Baptists show. In short, if BGCC churches are the more vulnerable to "evangelical" syncretism, then the NABC is most open to interaction with mainline Canadian Baptists and Anabaptists.

Summary and Conclusions

Table 5 is a comparative summary of the data for BUWC, BGCC, and NABC churches, with the denominations identified in previous tables here grouped by theological family. At least in the case of believers' churches, Bibby's optimistic findings related to the perseverance of denominational loyalty in the wider Canadian society may require modification. The proliferation of religious outlets in western Canada combines with religious pluralism to challenge denominational loyalties within the Baptist movement.

It may be argued in support of Bibby that in two groups over half of those received and dismissed remained in churches of their own union and that 65 percent or more of transfers were among Baptists. On the other hand, up to four of ten changed to another denomination. This circulation of evangelicals is exacerbated, and hidden, by large numbers of undocumented erasures from church rolls of vanished members.

Further, worldwide religious movements, such as the charismatic renewal, cross denominational lines, increase tensions within the most dynamic Baptist congregations, contribute to their pluralism, add new potentials for schism or mobility, and offer a plethora of new "outlets" to tempt religious consumers. Must the "baptistification" of the Christian world always walk hand-in-hand with the devaluation of doctrine and prove inimical to denominational unity and stability?

Respondents indicate there is no groundswell of interest to facilitate the development of one strong indigenous Baptist church in Canada. Pragmatic leaders appear quite satisfied and entrenched in the status quo.

At least in the west, and especially in British Columbia, Protestantism appears to operate like two large competing superstores—the one catholic, ecumenical, and liberal; the other decreasingly "baptistified," evangelical, and in the process of structuring a new ecumenical-conservative alliance by means of the Evangelical Fellowship of Canada (EFC).[12] Inside these conglomerates the denominations operate like specialty shops with independent administrations and modest menu diversification. In such a climate, the theological question, "Is it true?" is quickly replaced by the pragmatic question, "Does it work?"

Table 5

Theological Grouping: Members Received/
Dismissed by Letter, 1985-89[13]

Grouping	BUWC		BGCC		NABC	
	No.	%	No.	%	No.	%
Own Convention						
Received	659	52.05	81	34.76	302	55.92
Dismissed	502	64.19	42	28.96	250	41.94
Other Baptist						
Received	170	13.43	69	29.61	79	14.62
Dismissed	97	12.40	31	21.37	170	28.50
Holiness/ Pentecostal						
Received	115	9.08	24	10.30	62	11.48
Dismissed	41	5.24	18	12.41	65	10.90
Fundamental/ Charismatic						
Received	178	14.06	49	21.03	67	12.40
Dismissed	75	11.25	42	28.96	73	12.24
Anabaptist						
Received	36	2.84	6	2.57	24	4.44
Dismissed	15	1.91	8	5.51	34	5.70
Paedobaptist						
Received	108	8.53	4	1.71	6	1.11
Dismissed	39	4.98	1	.68	4	.67

These trends are lamentable to persons who appreciate the continuing relevance of the biblical and theological debates that gave rise to the historic Protestant denominations. Religious syncretism can be countered by intentional training in the theology, history, and polity which taken together comprise the denominational distinctives of the Baptists. The challenge for pastors and leaders in the realm of Christian education is both an imperative and a priority.

Meanwhile, Baptists appear to be moving towards new, if limited, pragmatic rather than confessional alignments. The FEBC and BGCC cooperate in the ACTS consortium with the Evangelical Free Church of Canada

(EFCC) in ministerial education in continuity with the fundamentalist impulse. The BUWC remains locked into an unequal alliance with transdenominationalist "new evangelicals" and Brethren at Regent College but, happily, are in renewed dialogue with the NABC seminary in Edmonton. Financial pressures encourage wider "evangelical" cooperation in the western religious culture. The new alliances are often forged pragmatically by adoption of statements of doctrine that exhibit a minimalist theology—for example, the statement of faith of Regent College or the EFC. The "Basis of Agreement" for ACTS left intact the statements of faith of the EFCC (*sic*), the BGCC, and the FEBC but added a "Parallel Accord." Included among the seven principles was the simplism that "'infallible', 'verbal', 'plenary', and 'inerrant' have always had the same intention when used to affirm the authority of Scripture."[14] Care must be taken to ensure that the new generation of leaders, trained in environments of evangelical syncretism by non-Canadian scholars, are not robbed of their Baptist heritage and a sense of their Canadian identity.

The sense of cultural alienation which encourages evangelical pragmatism and doctrinal accommodation was analyzed by a respected Baptist educator in a recent conversation:

> If you have a nominally Christian environment, then one can be comfortable with a comparatively narrow denominational focus. However, with the prevailing secularism, one sees oneself as a "self-conscious minority"; and this makes historical differences in theology [of] more minor [importance].[15]

Clearly, for some Baptists, this "self-consciousness" increases the importance of theology and moves them towards a more sectarian position on the sociological "church-sect" continuum.

A third option deserves exploration. The times make possible renewed dialogue among Baptists and Anabaptists. In this wider forum, many historic, ethnic, and theological differences among Baptists might be addressed on neutral ground. The time has clearly come for Baptist leaders who would be statespersons to abandon their Meech Lake separatist mentality and move toward a made-in-Canada Baptist/Anabaptist alliance of conviction rather than convenience. The threefold framework for renewal is available—the Bible, the prayer of Jesus for unity, and the historic Anabaptist and Baptist confessions of faith.

More than once, Baptists in Canada have missed the opportunity to build a vibrant national denomination. It has been said that to learn from history one must learn to forgive the past. Baptists must.

Notes

[1] Quoted in J. R. C. Perkin, "Kirkconnell and National Federation," *Canadian Baptist* 135, no. 2 (February 1989): 59, 62. See Walter E. Ellis, "Organizational and Educational Policy of Baptists in Western Canada 1873-1939" (BD thesis, McMaster Divinity College, Hamilton, ON, 1962), 25-29.

[2] G. A. Rawlyk, "A. L. McCrimmon, H. P. Whidden, T. T. Shields, Christian Higher Education, and McMaster University," in *Canadian Baptists and Christian Higher Education*, ed. G. A. Rawlyk (Kingston, ON: McGill-Queen's University Press, 1988), 35.

[3] Leslie K. Tarr, *This Dominion, His Dominion* (Willowdale, ON: Fellowship of Evangelical Baptists in Canada, 1968).

[4] Reginald W. Bibby, *Fragmented Gods: The Poverty and Potential of Religion in Canada* (Toronto: Irwin, 1987), 239.

[5] Walter E. Ellis, "A Place to Stand: Contemporary History of the Baptist Union of Western Canada," *American Baptist Quarterly* 6 (1987): 31-51.

[6] Jarold K. Zeman, "Baptists in Canada," in *Dictionary of Christianity in America*, ed. Daniel G. Reid et al. (Downers Grove, IL: InterVarsity Press, 1990), 115-16.

[7] Statistics in BUWC yearbooks utilize only "baptism" and "other." "Other" includes persons received by letter and statement of Christian experience. In 1988, sixteen responding churches showed 137 received by letter, while their "other" statistics reported 198. Assuming similar patterns throughout the denomination, 69.2 percent of "other" additions are by letter, 30.8 percent by Christian experience.

[8] Martin E. Marty, "Baptistification Takes Over," *Christianity Today*, 2 September 1983, 33-34; and Bibby, *Fragmented Gods*.

[9] The *American Baptist Quarterly* 6 (September 1987) is completely given over to explaining BGC relations with the ABC. For the "ethnocentricity and xenophobia" that informed the Social Darwinism of the late 19th century, see William H. Brackney, "Baptist General Conference," *ABQ* 6 (1987): 149-55.

[10] Edward B. Link, "North American (German) Baptists," in *Baptists in Canada*, ed. Jarold K. Zeman (Burlington, ON: G. R. Welch, 980), 96.

[11] Link, "North American Baptists," 100.

[12] The BUWC, the BGCC, and the NABC are members of EFC. FEBC continues to eschew all ecumenical alliances, even conservative ones. The United Baptist Convention of the Atlantic Provinces recently voted not to affiliate but to strengthen the CBF; salvation from evangelical syncretism may yet come from the east.

[13] Three of twenty FEB churches responded, listing 119 additions, 112 deletions. Data is not representative enough for analysis; but here are the figures: received from—FEBC, 41 (34%); other Baptist, 38 (32%); holiness/pentecostal, 13 (11%); other, 10 (8%); Anabaptist, 4 (3%); paedobaptist, 13 (11%); dismissed to—FEBC, 45 (40%); other Baptist, 20 (19%); holiness/pentecostal, 11 (10%); other, 29 (26%); Anabaptist, 3 (2.5%); paedobaptist, 4 (3.5%).

[14] "Catalogue," Associated Canadian Theological Schools at Trinity Western University 1988-1989 (Langley, BC: ACTS, 1988), 8.

[15] Personal conversation, 6 April 1989.

Chapter 9

"Baptist Unity in the Midst of Evangelical Diversity:" Canadian Baptists and the 19th-Century Evangelical Debate over Christian Unity

Philip G. A. Griffin-Allwood

As Canada's Baptists entered the 19th century, they were divided into a variety of denominations with two primary means of transcongregating— associations and societies.[1] Separating them were issues of faith and order. In the Maritimes were Regular Baptists, Free Christian Baptists, African Baptists, and minor denominations such as the Freewill Baptists and the Free and Sovereign Grace Baptists. In the Canadas were Regular Baptists, Particular Baptists, Free Communion Baptists, Freewill Baptists, representatives of both sides of the Scotch Baptist schism, Carson Baptists, Sinclair Baptists, adherents to the independent immersionism of the Haldane brothers of Scotland, and members of the Christian Connexion. All these groups had varying regional strength.[2]

As the same churches entered the 20th century, they found themselves uniting in regional conventions. While at the beginning of the century Baptists transcongregated into associations and societies, at the end their form of interchurch government was described as "federation."

One means of describing the change is to use the typology formed during the evangelical debate about the nature of Christian unity or union. The forum for the debate was the regional and international meetings of the Evangelical Alliance, which had been formed in 1846 "for the purpose of promoting Christian Union."[3]

The Evangelical Debate over Christian Unity

The Evangelical Alliance was an expression of the changes wrought as a result of the Great Awakening and the Evangelical Revival. Writing in 1855, George Fysch described that transformation:

> In the bosom of those large Reformation Churches, which, during the last century, had nearly all fallen asleep, a revival has taken place, separating the true disciples of Christ from the multitude who remain

indifferent and worldly. This revival is wonderful for its unity of principle and its diversity of forms. Everywhere it rallies around those great truths which are the foundation of the Christian's hope and the aliment of his spiritual life. From its commencement it was understood that the Gospel must be sent to the heathen. More slowly it was felt that this awakening should be directed to another purpose—that of proclaiming and developing the unity of life in the midst of diversity of forms....[4]

While the Alliance itself disclaimed any status as an organization of organizations or denominations, it was a forum for discussion of Christian unity. Frequently at international and regional gatherings in the last half of the 19th century, the program included a session on "Christian Union." Philip Schaff summarized the discussion in an address to the Evangelical Alliance for the United States in 1893. He identified "three kinds of union": individual, federal or confederate, and organic or corporate.[5]

Individual union was defined as "a voluntary association of Christians of different churches and nationalities for a common purpose." Schaff illustrated his definition with the Bible Societies, Tract Societies, Sunday-School Unions, Young Men's and Young Women's Christian Associations, Evangelical Alliances, and Christian Endeavour Societies.

Federal or confederate union was described as

a voluntary association of different churches in their official capacity, each retaining its freedom and independence in the management of its internal affairs, but all recognizing one another as sisters with equal rights, and co-operating in general enterprises, such as the spread of the gospel at home and abroad, the defense of the faith against infidelity, the elevation of the poor and neglected classes of society, works of philanthropy and charity, and moral reform.

The strength of federal union was that it combined "the general sovereignty with the intrinsic independence." Federation was viewed as a means of uniting denominations which differed in "interpretation, or in the rigidity of subscription [to creeds], or in the number of minor differences of government and discipline, or in methods of church work."

Organic or corporate union for Schaff would place "all the churches under one government." His prime example of organic union was the Roman Catholic Church. At the same conference, Anglican Bishop A. Cleveland Coxe of Buffalo argued for organic union along the lines of the Lambeth Quadrilateral and the historic episcopate.[6]

Underlying the discussion within the Evangelical Alliance was the assumption that union meant "Unity in principle, diversity only in manifestation:—Unity in essential truth, diversity in the external development of that Truth." Schaff believed that "diversity in unity is the law of God's physical and moral universe."[7]

Canadian Baptists and the Evangelical Alliance

The proposal for the creation of the international Evangelical Alliance circulated following the Conference on Christian Union held in Liverpool, England, in October 1845. In Canada West, the Toronto Association for Christian Union was formed in April 1846. In Canada East, the Canada Evangelical Alliance was organized in January 1846. A Christian Union was formed in Saint John, New Brunswick, by 1848.

The secretary for the Toronto Association was Robert A. Fyfe, whose greatest contribution to Canadian Baptist life would come as editor of the *Canadian Baptist* and Principal of Woodstock College. One of the three secretaries of the Canada Evangelical Alliance was Baptist educator J. M. Cramp, who after the collapse of Montreal College became President of Acadia College. The Saint John union included a number of Baptist ministers.

These organizations were short-lived but Canadian Baptist consciousness of evangelicalism did not die. Benjamin Davies, writing in 1856 for a British audience, described Baptists in the Canadas as divided into "evangelical Baptists" and "Regular Baptists...the more strict among them refusing communion even to baptists [*sic*], unless of exactly the same faith and order with them." There were "however, many who desire to promote Baptist unity in the midst of evangelical diversity."[8]

The Evangelical Alliance experienced its greatest period of vigour following the 1873 international meeting in New York. As a result, the Dominion Evangelical Alliance was formed in 1874 with Canadian Baptists present. At the Canadian meeting, addresses defined unity as organized around doctrinal consensus that created "a truly broad and evangelical platform" which recognized the "relative rights [of] all those various creeds of Christendom." Important for achieving cooperative unity was the assumption that "the visible church catholic [was] constituted of denominations of Christians."[9]

Canadian Baptist Organization

Baptists, in general, as they entered the 19th century were divided between adherents of the associational and the societal principles. As the Committee of Nine noted in their 1848 report to the American Baptist Missionary Union, care must be taken not to "confound our *voluntary* organizations with our *ecclesiastical.*"[10] Baptist societies represented the individual form of church union, while their associations were organic unions concerned about faith and order.

Corporate Union in Associations

In the early 19th century, there were two traditions about the role of associations in North America. Associations following the Philadelphia tradition exercised a great deal of control over local congregations. Benjamin Griffith's 1749 "Essay on the Power and Duty of an Association of Churches" stated that

> an association of the delegates of confederate churches may doctrinally declare any person or party in a church, who are defective in principles or disorderly in practice, to be censurable, when the affair comes under their cognizance, and—without exceeding the bounds of their power and duty—to advise the church that such belong unto, how to deal with such.[11]

The Philadelphia Association's *Discipline* of 1743 assumed that messengers and delegates assembled together to consider "matters of differences in point of doctrine" could "declare and determine the mind of the Holy Ghost revealed in Scripture concerning things in difference, and may decree the observation of things that are true and necessary." Churches were expected "to receive" the "determinations" but were not to be coerced into accepting them. The *Discipline* of 1798 declared that "the associated body may exclude any church that may act an unworthy part."[12]

This principle of "confederation" went beyond federation as understood by Schaff, for it resulted in the practice of giving a matter under debate to a "presbytery" of ministers. Their decision was not to be put to a vote but was to be accepted, based on their "superior skillfulness."[13]

There was a reaction against this practice as Separate Baptists in New England were incorporated into the Regular Baptists through the organization of the Warren Association. Separate Baptists rejected any assignment of authority to a "presbytery" for resolution of difficulties. They joined the newly organized Warren Association only when the plan was changed to affirm: "That such an association is consistent with the independency and power of particular churches, because it pretends to be no other than an *advisory council* utterly disclaiming superiority, jurisdiction, coercive right and infallibility."[14]

Both associational traditions made their way into Canada. In the Maritimes, former Allinite congregations produced by the Nova Scotia Great Awakening turned the Association of Baptist and Congregationalists into a Regular Baptist association in 1800 by adopting a plan of organization "agreeable to that of the Danbury Association in New England." The plan reflects the modifications made in associational life when the Warren Association was organized. Maritime associations, though, retained the right to "dissolve its connection with any church which, after proper examination, shall be judged by the Association to have departed essentially from the Baptist faith and practice."[15]

In Canada West, the influence of the Philadelphia tradition was felt. For example, the "Plan" of the New York Association, to which the Niagara church belonged, acknowledged the independence of the "particular churches" but considered it their "duty to disown such churches, received by them, which may have essentially departed from the faith." The constitution of the Western Association provided for similar practice in Canada West.[16]

Another organic union was the conference structure used by the Free Christian Baptists in New Brunswick and Nova Scotia. The union in Nova Scotia with the Freewill Baptists in 1866 moderated the authority of that conference. The New Brunswick conference experimented unsatisfactorily with societies for home and foreign missions from 1864 until 1887.[17]

Individual Union in Societies and Conventions

Societies, the individual form of church union, were formed early in the life of British North America. Societies were organizations parallel to associations. However, a society consisted not of churches, like associations, but of members that contributed financially. The first society formed was the Massachusetts Baptist Missionary Society in 1802. Its object was "to furnish occasional preaching, and to promote the knowledge of evangelistic truth in the new settlements within these United States; or further, if circumstances render it proper."[18]

The General Missionary Convention of the Baptist Denomination in the United States of America for Foreign Missions was organized in 1814 by "delegates from Missionary Societies, and other religious Bodies of the Baptist denomination." The triennial convention was to consist of delegates from missionary societies and "other religious bodies of the Baptist Denomination" that contributed financially to the Convention. Missionaries for appointment were to be "in full communion with some regular Church of our Denomination." No mention was made of associations.[19]

In 1815, the Baptist Association of Nova Scotia and New Brunswick meeting in Cornwallis voted that "the Association [is] considered as a Missionary Society, and with them is left the whole management of the Mission business." The New Brunswick Baptist Domestic Missionary Society was organized in 1829. During the 1820s, missionary societies were organized in churches throughout the Maritimes. In 1832, the Nova Scotia Baptist Association resolved itself into a society to promote home and foreign missions.[20]

Five years later, the New Brunswick association urged its churches to consider the role that its churches could play in foreign missions. In the next year, the Nova Scotia association invited the New Brunswick Baptists to help fund a foreign missionary and to form a united society for that purpose. An interassociation committee was created in 1841. In addition to home and foreign missions, Maritime Regular Baptists were engaged in education, assistance to infirm ministers, Bible Society, and Sabbath schools. All had their own fundraising societies which sent a multitude of fundraisers into the churches. Consequently, at the Nova Scotia Association meeting in 1842 it was resolved:

> That the great body of the Baptist Denomination, now convened at Wilmot, form itself into a Society, to be called the Associated Society of Baptists of Nova Scotia, and that for the practical working of which there be Branch societies formed in each church, for the furtherance of the cause of Education, Foreign and Domestic Missions, Sabbath Schools, and for the support of superannuated ministers and their families.[21]

Local societies were appointed in some churches, and field agents promoted the cause, but they were not as successful in raising funds as had been hoped. Therefore, the Baptist Convention of Nova Scotia, New Brunswick, and Prince Edward Island was founded on 21 September 1846. Its constitution stated:

> That the objects of the Convention shall be, to advance the interests of the Baptist Denomination, and of the cause of God, generally; to maintain the religious and charitable Institutions hereinafter mentioned; to procure correct information relative to the Baptist body, and to advise and carry out such measures as may, with the Divine blessing, tend to advance the interests of the Baptist Denomination, and the cause of God, generally.[22]

Membership was open to any individual or church who contributed a minimum of ten shillings annually or a Local Union Society that collected at least five pounds annually. Individual membership categories of Life Member and Life Director were available for large contributions; delegates were also to be appointed by missionary and educational boards. There were no direct lines of accountability to the associations, although the associations were expected to submit annual statistical reports to the convention.

In the Canadas, the first society was the Baptist Missionary Convention of Upper Canada (BMCUC), which was organized in 1833, due to the efforts of the Eastern, Western, and Haldimand associations. The concern of the convention was "the destitute of the province." Membership in the convention was open to individuals who paid one dollar; and life membership was available for those paying a larger sum. Provision was made for the organization of auxiliary societies. The convention "for want of concert and energy, soon became extinct," according to a report in the New York *Gospel Witness*.[23]

By 1836, the work and treasury of the BMCUC was assumed by the Board of the Missionary Society of the Eastern Upper Canada Baptist Association. In that year, the Western Association united with the Eastern Association to organize the Upper Canada Baptist Missionary Society. This society was an auxiliary of the American Baptist Home Missionary Society, which supported seven missionaries in Upper Canada.

British Baptist concern about the Canadas was raised after the publication of F. A. Cox and J. Hoby's report of their North American tour in 1836 which contained a recommendation of assistance for Baptists in the Canadas.[24] John Gilmour went to Britain in 1836 to collect mission funds; and, as result of his tour, the Baptist Canadian Missionary Society was organized in the City of London Tavern. After Gilmour's return to Lower Canada, at the annual meeting of the Ottawa association, the Canada Baptist Missionary Society was organized as a cooperative organization with the British society. The object of the society was "the moral and religious cultivation of the Canadas, by aiding the establishment and support of a Collegiate Institution for the education of pious young men for the ministry, and the employment of missionaries in those provinces, and such other means as may be deemed suitable."[25]

Initial hopes of cooperation between the two societies in Canada and in England failed due to disagreement over the definition of "Baptist" as a consequence of the Canada Baptist Missionary Society uniting a variety of Baptist denominations: Scotch Baptists, British Particular Baptists, and American Free Communion Baptists.

The failure of the Regular Baptist Union (discussed below) to attract significant support resulted in the creation in 1851 of the Regular Baptist Missionary Society (RBMS). Its "design" was "to promote the preaching of the Gospel and disseminate the Word of God in the Province of Canada." The society restricted its supporters by ratifying the declaration of the special convention of Regular Baptists held on 1 September 1853, which affirmed Regular Baptist adherence to strict closed communion and administration of ordinances by "regularly ordained" ministers. It was renamed, in 1854, the "Baptist Convention of Canada" and, after five years, the "Baptist Missionary Convention of Canada West."[26]

In April 1858, a meeting was held in Montreal to organize "a Society for Missionary and other purposes, in connection with the Baptist denomination east of Kingston." The object of the convention was "the promotion of the Gospel in Central and Eastern Canada, by employing Evangelists, aiding feeble churches, circulating religious publications, and by other suitable means."[27]

A "General Convention of the Baptists of Canada" was held in 1860 at Woodstock, Canada West, "to collect as far as possible, the brethren from all parts of the province, in fraternal sympathy and co-operation, in sustaining and promoting the great interests of the denomination." The only continuing organization that resulted from the meeting was a "Baptist Ministerial Education Society."[28]

The auxiliary of the American Baptist Missionary Union (formed in 1867) was reorganized as the Regular Baptist Foreign Missionary Society of Canada in 1870 with the object "to preach Christ and Him crucified, in all the world, but especially in India."[29]

Usually specific in their focus of ministry, these individual unions, conventions, and societies were composed of voluntary members—persons, sometimes churches, and local societies—who maintained their connection by small annual or substantial lifetime contributions.

Union on a Broader Scale

A federal or corporate union, uniting "the general sovereignty with the intrinsic independence", was founded among Canadian Baptists early in the 19th century. The Ottawa Baptist Association was organized in 1836 for "the promotion of united exertion in whatever may best advance the cause of Christ in general, especially Home Missionary operations."[30]

Its constitution was modelled on that of the Baptist Union of Great Britain and Ireland; it was to consist of "Churches composed of Baptized Believers." The fourth article stated:

> In all the proceedings of the Association, no bond of any kind shall be considered as entered into, or acknowledged, by which any one Church is bound to conform to the usages of the rest; but it is a principle distinctly understood and recognized, that every separate Church has, and ought to retain, within itself, the power and authority to exercise all Church discipline, rule, and government, and to put in execution the laws of Christ necessary to its own edification, according to its own views, independently of any other Church or Churches whatsoever.[31]

Another early Baptist federation was among the Free Communion Baptists. Their general meeting commenced in 1803.

> The conference licensed and ordained ministers at the request of the churches of which they were members, and attended to such matters of general interest as came before them. They disclaimed any power to revoke the decisions of individual churches. Councils, with advisory powers, were also appointed deliberate in matters of difficulty.[32]

Their first church was organized in Canada West after American Baptist immigrants invited Thomas Tolman to preach in the London District in 1820. Eleven churches and the "Free Communion Baptist Conference of Canada" were organized under his leadership. In 1829, a meeting was held between the Free Communion Baptists and the Free Will Baptists. Formal union did not result but the meeting resolved to cooperate fully because differences were negligible compared with their agreement on the work to be done.[33]

The first attempt to create a federal union for the Canadas occurred in 1843 when the Canada Baptist Union was formed in Paris, Canada West. It was an attempt to imitate the organization of the Ottawa Baptist Association on a larger scale. The Union was of ministers, churches, and associations and adopted objectives almost identical to that of the Baptist Union of Great Britain and Ireland. With respect to "unity of exertion," they included the object to "especially watch over our religious rights and privileges,—to secure their permanence and promote their extension." The second article of the constitution was similar to the Ottawa association's declaration of autonomy and authority of the local church. The union failed to achieve its goals due to objections by adherents of the Regular Baptist "organic union" definition of faith and order. The Western and Grand River associations, advocates of the Strict/Regular Baptist principle of "Strict Communion," were not represented at the annual meeting in 1847; and in 1848, the Union annual meeting drew a sparse attendance.[34]

Another attempt at a federal union occurred in 1848; these two associations and the Eastern, Haldimand, and Labours Associations had passed resolutions "to meet conjointly on the 6th of September, 1848, to take measures to effect a Union of the Strict Communion Baptists of Canada." The delegates considered themselves to be a "conjoint committee from the several Associations of Baptist Churches." The stated "design" of the Regular Baptist Union was

> to unite the Regular Baptists of this Province as a distinct body of Professing Christians, in the support of Missions, and dissemination of the word of God, at home and abroad—the advancement of Ministerial Education, and the increase of Gospel labourers—the establishment and improvement of sabbath schools—the support of a Depot of denominational and other Evangelical publications, with the necessary agents for their extensive diffusion—the publication of a weekly paper as the organ of the denomination, and the adoption of all necessary measures for the defense of religious liberty, and the promotion of the voluntary principle in religion.[35]

The Union, though, had an organic definition for cooperation; and membership in the Union was open to churches that supported a Strict definition for a Regular Baptist church. When the plan failed to attract significant support, the RBMS mentioned above was created to accomplish some of the Union's purposes as an individual society.

Responding to the Regular Baptist Union's failure to be inclusive, the inactive Canada Baptist Union reorganized in 1855 in Toronto. The assembly declared:

> Inasmuch as united evangelical operations among the Baptists in Canada, which were commenced in the year 1836 and carried on for above twelve years, have been suspended for some time past, owing chiefly to the fact that many of their brethren who now call themselves by the name of "the Regular Baptist Denomination in Canada" have refused to co-operate in missionary and educational institutions on the old basis of the Union, and inasmuch as a solemn conviction of duty urges to united action, therefore it is resolved:
> That the brethren now assembled form themselves into a Union, to be known as the Canada Baptist Union, adopting the following as the Articles of their Constitution and agreement.
> 1. That the ministers and Brethren now present and such as shall hereafter be admitted, together with all such churches as may send representatives as hereinafter provided, constitute the Canada Baptist Union.
> 2. That this Union, shall be composed of such ministers and brethren or churches of the Baptist denomination as agree in holding the sentiments commonly called Evangelical.[36]

This revived Union never obtained a great deal of strength, functioning only into the 1860s. Its primary medium of expression was its periodicals *The Union Baptist* in 1856 and later *The Christian Freeman* from 1860.

The move to federation as the dominant form of unity began in the 1870s, at the time when the Evangelical Alliance was experiencing its period of greatest vigour. The Baptist Union of Canada was formed by an Act of the Dominion Parliament in 1879 in response to actions by the two regional conventions in Ontario and Quebec. It did not achieve the desired cooperation between the two conventions because of the conflicting legal natures of the respective provincial organizations. A meeting of representatives of churches from the two Ontario/Quebec conventions was called for October 1882 to reorganize the Union. The Union was to consist of "members of regular Baptist churches in Canada" representing churches and denominational agencies and societies.[37]

The experience of cooperation in the Union brought a change in attitude toward operation of separate conventions. To facilitate cooperation, the western convention renamed itself the "Regular Baptist Home Missionary Society of Ontario" in 1885; individual memberships were eliminated, making the society a union of churches and associations. After the idea of federation had been proposed at the 1886 meeting of the Canada Baptist Union, the eastern convention the following year proposed union of the conventions. In response, the Ontario convention passed the resolution: "Whereas this question of Union has been carefully considered, both by the

Society in the East and by us, therefore, resolved that we do now receive the Eastern Society into union with us", thus uniting the two conventions. The 1888 convention of the united societies adopted a new constitution that united all the previously incorporated organizations. The Baptist Convention of Ontario and Quebec was a union of all the different societies and agencies. By constitution, it was a convention of "Regular Baptist Churches" (though the term was undefined) and their associations.[38]

In the Maritimes, the constitution of the convention was revised in 1879. The name was changed to the "Baptist Convention of the Maritime Provinces" and the stated object was "to maintain the educational and missionary operations of the body, and to advance the general interests of the denomination." Membership consisted of the associations, churches belonging to the associations that contributed financially to the convention, and ordained ministers. Individuals who had made a minimum of a fifty dollar contribution to the convention before the revision were allowed to continue as members, as were life directors who had contributed one hundred dollars. But no more individual memberships were permitted. The convention appointed two boards, one for home mission and one for foreign mission.[39]

This laid the basis for admission of the Free Baptists into the convention in 1905 and 1906. When the union of 1905 took place, a federal polity was adopted for all the Maritime Baptists.

> The voluntary principle underlies the whole church polity of the New Testament. Each church is independent, but the churches are interdependent. All the power the more general bodies have over the less general and the individual churches, is to advise and to enforce advice with the strongest moral motives. In case a church, of the churches composing a less general body, depart from the belief and practice of the denomination, it shall be the right of the more general body to withdraw fellowship.[40]

The influence of federal unity was to be felt as the churches in western Canada formed transcongregational structures. The Red River Association was organized in 1880; and the Regular Baptist Missionary Convention of Manitoba and the Northwest, in 1882. These two groups merged to form the Baptist Convention of Manitoba and the North-West in 1884. Their constitution expresses the federal nature of their unity:

> ART. III.-The object of this Convention shall be to promote the general efficiency of our churches: preserve a watch-care over them; receive annual reports and present the same. Also to promote and maintain Home Missions throughout Manitoba and the North-West, as well as any other department of denominational work that will tend to the furtherance of the cause of Christ throughout the world.
> ART. IV.-This Convention shall recognize the organized co-operation of the churches of the "One Lord, one faith, one baptism," for the

more efficient execution of the Divine Commission of our Great Head is clearly a scriptural obligation, while, at the same time, the supremacy of the churches is strongly adhered to. The approved record of the decisions of the Convention may be considered morally and principally binding on the local congregations represented.[41]

The convention, unlike its two predecessors which were unions of individuals and churches, was composed of churches. In 1906 and 1907, this convention and that of British Columbia established a joint Superintendency of Home Missions. In separate sessions the two conventions voted in 1907 to unite. A union meeting was held in Moose Jaw on 19-20 November of that year to create the Baptist Convention of Western Canada. In 1909, the convention was renamed the "Baptist Union of Western Canada" and reorganized as a union of provincial conventions; it would not become a union of churches until 1938.[42]

Conclusion

As Canadian Baptists entered the 20th century, they were cooperating regionally in "federal union" structures. The multitude of Baptist denominations had become one, although the early decades of the century would prove that their unity was tenuous. As evangelicalism fractured into ecumenism and fundamentalism, Canadian Baptists, too, would divide over faith and order issues. Proponents of organic union could not be comfortable with the diversity preserved in federal unity.

Notes

[1] Eugene M. Thompson et al., "The Status of Transcongregational Polity," in *Canadian Baptist History and Polity*, ed. Murray J. S. Ford (Hamilton, ON: McMaster University Divinity College, 1983), 93-107.

[2] See Philip G. A. Griffin-Allwood, "The Canadianization of Baptists: From Denominations to Denomination, 1760-1912" (PhD diss., Southern Baptist Theological Seminary, Louisville, KY, 1986), 69-127, 148-95; cf. Joseph Ash, "Reminiscences...or History of the Rise and Progress of Our Cause in Canada," *Christian Worker*, 1882 and 1883.

[3] *Evangelical Alliance: Report of the Proceedings of the Conference Held at Freemasons' Hall, London, from August 19th to September 2nd Inclusive, 1846* (London: Partridge and Oakey, 1847), 44, 202; and Philip Schaff and S. Irenaeus Prime, eds., *History, Essays, Orations, and Other Documents of the Sixth General Conference of the Evangelical Alliance* (London: Sampson Low, Marston, Low, and Searle, 1874), 174n.

[4] George Fysch, "Historical Account of the Evangelical Alliance," in *The Religious Condition of Christendom: Second Part* (London: Office of the Evangelical Alliance, 1857), 7.

[5] Philip Schaff, "The Reunion of Christendom," in *Christianity Practically Applied*, ed. Philip Schaff (New York: Baker and Taylor, 1894), 315-27. Not everyone shared

Schaff's distinctions; for example, the Philadelphia Baptist Association, which defined itself as a confederation, meets Schaff's definition for organic; see Winthrop S. Hudson, ed., "Documents on the Association of Churches," *Foundations* 4 (1961): 334-39. The union between the Free Christian Baptists and Regular Baptists in the Maritimes was federal but they used the phrase "organic union" (*Baptist Year Book of the Maritime Provinces of Canada* [1887], 41). Cf. James McCosh, "The Federation of Churches," in *Christianity Practically Applied*, ed. Schaff, 230-33.

⁶ Schaff, "Reunion of Christendom," 316; and A. Cleveland Coxe, "Organic Union: Its Reasons and Prospects" in *Christianity Practically Applied*, ed. Schaff, 221-29.

⁷ *Evangelical Alliance: 1846*, 364; and Philip Schaff, "Discord and Concord of Christendom, or Denominational Variety and Christian Unity," in *The Religious Condition of Christendom*, ed. Lewis Borrett White (London: Office of the Evangelical Alliance, 1885), 142.

⁸ Davies, *Baptist Magazine* 48 (1856), 425—this supplies the phrase in the present chapter title.

⁹ Philip Schaff, "The Doctrinal Consensus of Evangelical Christendom," *Evangelical Alliance Extra* [*Montreal Daily Witness*], October 1874, 9-11; cf. "The Doctrinal Basis of the United States Evangelical Alliance," in *History, Essays, Orations, and Documents*, ed. Schaff and Prime, 760. For the development of the consensus, see *Evangelical Alliance: 1846*; and R. L. Dabney, "The Scriptural Idea of the Visible Church Catholic as Constituted of Denominations of Christians," *Evangelical Alliance Extra* (1874), 13-18. Within the Canadian context, the most significant address of the Montreal Conference was G. M. Grant, "The Church of Canada—Can Such a Thing Be?" *Evangelical Alliance Extra*, 1874, 40-55.

¹⁰ Quoted in Winthrop S. Hudson, *Baptists in Transition: Individualism and Christian Responsibility* (Valley Forge, PA: Judson, 1979), 105.

¹¹ Hudson, *Baptists in Transition*, 337. Griffith's essay was approved unanimously by the Association. See also Robert T. Handy, "The Philadelphia Tradition," in Winthrop S. Hudson, ed., *Baptist Concepts of the Church* (Philadelphia: Judson, 1959), 47.

¹² Hudson, *Baptist Concepts*, 334, 339.

¹³ William G. McLoughlin, *New England Dissent 1630-1833*, vol. 1 (Cambridge, MA: Harvard University Press, 1971), 506.

¹⁴ Quoted by McLoughlin, *New England Dissent*, 507, n.31, 502-11. For a discussion of the change in influence of ecclesial councils, see Philip G. A. [Griffin-]Allwood, "'Joseph Howe Is Their Devil': Controversies among Regular Baptist in Halifax, 1827-1868," in *Repent and Believe: The Baptist Experience in Maritime Canada*, ed. Barry M. Moody, BHAC, 2 (Hantsport, NS: Lancelot Press, 1980), 75-87.

¹⁵ The reference to the Danbury Association reflects a description of the annual meeting of the Danbury Association that appeared in the *Massachusetts Baptist Missionary Magazine* prior to the meeting of the Nova Scotia Baptists: "Declaration of the Association" (1797, Baptist Collection, Acadia University Archives [AUA], Wolfville, NS); and "Minutes of the Association held at the Baptist Meeting House in Granville, June the 23rd and 24th, 1800" (AUA). See Winthrop S. Hudson, "The Interrelationships of Baptists in Canada and the United States," *Foundations* 23 (1980), 40. The Maritime plan verbally echoes that of the Danbury Association; cf. "Constitution and Bye-Laws of the Association" in S. T. Rand, *An Historical Sketch of the Nova Scotia Baptist Association* (1849), 8-11; and "Minutes of the Nova Scotia Western Baptist Association" (1879), 34.

¹⁶ Griffin-Allwood, "Canadianization," 157-58; and "Minutes of the New York Association," 1791, 6. To see how this transcongregational polity differed from that adopted in New England, compare the "Plan of the [Warren] Association" in Reuben Aldridge Guild, *Life, Times, and Correspondence of James Manning* (Boston: Gould and Lincoln, 1864), 78-80, with "The plan or constitution of the regular Baptist Associations"

in John Asplund, *The Annual Register of the Baptist Denomination in North-America* (1791; reprint Lafayette, TN: Church History and Research Archives, 1979), 54-56. See also "Minutes of the 6th Annual Meeting of the Western Baptist Association," 1835, 6.

[17] See Griffin-Allwood, "Canadianization," 98-114, 128-36; and Joseph Macleod, "A Sketch of the History of the Free Baptists of New Brunswick," in *History of the Baptists of the Maritime Provinces*, by E. M. Saunders (Halifax: Press of John Burgoyne, 1902), 429-30.

[18] William H. Brackney, ed., *Baptist Life and Thought, 1600-1980: A Source Book* (Valley Forge, PA: Judson, 1983), 157-58.

[19] Brackney, *Baptist Life*, 170-71.

[20] "Minutes of the Nova Scotia and New Brunswick Baptist Association," 1814, 4. See M. Allen Gibson, *Along the King's Highway* (Lunenburg: Progress Enterprise, 1964), 15-16; Saunders, *History of the Baptists*, 226-28; and J. M. Cramp, "The Baptists of Nova Scotia (1760-1860)," a collated and indexed photocopy of an edited scrapbook of a column which appeared in the *Christian Messenger*, 18 January 1860 to 23 September 1863, 226, AUA.

[21] Cramp, "Baptists of Nova Scotia," 277. See George E. Levy, *The Baptists of the Maritime Provinces 1753-1946* (Saint John, NB: Barnes-Hopkins, 1946), 137-38; and I. E. Bill, *Fifty Years with the Baptists of the Maritime Provinces* (Saint John: Barnes and Co, 1888), 99.

[22] Levy, *Baptists of Maritimes*, 329; Cramp, "Baptists of Nova Scotia," 251, 277-79; and Bill, *Fifty Years*, 590.

[23] A. H. Newman, "Sketch of the Baptists of Ontario and Quebec to 1851," *Baptist Year Book (Historical Number) for Ontario, Quebec, Manitoba, and the North-West Territories and British Columbia* (1900), 77-78. Cf. *Annual Report of the Baptist Missionary Convention of Upper Canada* (1833 and 1834), Microfilm No. 6, Canadian Baptist Archives, Hamilton, Ontario (CBA).

[24] F. A. Cox and J. Hoby, *The Baptists in America* (New York: Leavitt, Lord, 1836), 214-29. See *Baptist Magazine* [London] 27 (February 1835): 54, and 28 (December 1836): 540-42.

[25] *Baptist Magazine* 28 (December 1836): 541; 29 (August 1837): 354.

[26] "Minutes of the Regular Baptist Missionary Society, 1851," TS, Microfilm No. 6, 2, CBA; "Minutes of the Regular Baptist Missionary Society, 1853," TS, Microfilm No. 6, 4, CBA. See J. U. MacIntosh, "Some of the Labours and Disputes of Open and Close Communion Baptists in Ontario and Quebec" (BD thesis, McMaster University, Hamilton, ON, 1936), 66.

[27] "Minutes of the Canada Baptist Convention East," 1858, Microfilm No. 6, 3, CBA.

[28] *Canadian Baptist* 6 (16 August 1860): 2; (6 September 1860): 2; (18 October 1860): 2.

[29] J. G. Brown, "History of the Foreign Mission Work of the Baptists of Ontario and Quebec, 1866-1900," *BYB* (1900), 151-58. The name of the convention was changed after Confederation when the name of the province also changed; the "Regular" had been dropped in 1869—*CB*, 15 (29 April 1869), 2.

[30] *Baptist Magazine*, 28 (October 1836): 448.

[31] "Minutes of the Ottawa Baptist Association," 1859, 3.

[32] A. D. Williams, "History of the Free Communion Baptists," in *History of all the Religious Denominations in the United States*, ed. John Winebrenner (Harrisburg, PA: John Winebrenner, 1848), 82-83.

[33] David Marks, *Memoirs of the Life of David Marks, Minister of the Gospel*, ed. Marilla Marks (Dover, NH: Free-Will Baptist Printing Establishment, 1846), 210.

[34] *Annual Report of the Canada Baptist Union* (1844), Microfilm No. 6, 1-7, CBA; and *Annual Report of the Canada Baptist Union* (1845), 1. Newman, "Sketch of Baptists," 95; cf. J. E. Wells, *Life and Labours of Robert Alex. Fyfe, D.D., Founder and for Many Years Principal of the Canadian Literary Institute, Now Woodstock College* (Toronto: W. J. Gage, n.d.), 194-205.

[35] *Annual Report of the Regular Baptist Union* (1848), Microfilm No. 6, 1, 10, CBA.

[36] *Canada Baptist Union* (1855), 4-5, Microfilm No. 6, 3, CBA. The first nine articles are the founding consensus of the Evangelical Alliance—see *Evangelical Alliance: 1846*, 189.

[37] *BYB*, Ontario, Quebec and Manitoba (1881), 9-10; *BYB*, Ontario, Quebec and Manitoba (1882), 15-16; and *BYB*, Ontario, Quebec and Manitoba (1883), 4-5.

[38] *BYB*, Ontario, Quebec and Manitoba (1886), 32-34; *BYB*, Ontario, Quebec and Manitoba (1887), 14, 20-21; *BYB*, Ontario, Quebec and Manitoba (1888), 15, 26-30.

[39] "Constitution," in *BYB*, Maritime Provinces of Canada (1879), 5-6; cf. 46-47; and "Minutes of the Baptist Convention of Nova Scotia, New Brunswick and Prince Edward Island," 1879, 19.

[40] *Free Baptist Year Book* (1905), 33.

[41] Art. III-IV, *BYB*, Ontario, Quebec and Manitoba (1885), 82. See Margaret E. Thompson, *The Baptist Story in Western Canada* (Calgary: Baptist Union of Western Canada, 1974), 93-100.

[42] E. R. Fitch, *The Baptists of Canada* (Toronto: Standard, 1911), 254, 254-55; *The Western Year Book* (1907), 5-12; (1909), 9-14; and W. C. Smalley, "Baptist Work in Western Canada," in Davis C. Woolley, ed., *Baptist Advance* (Nashville: Broadman Press, 1964), 180.

Chapter 10

Baptist Unity

Harry A. Renfree

The bewhiskered byword depicting the supposed dialogue between two Baptists and a three-opinion outcome really has more to do with freedom of thought than with rigid self-determination in action. Although, to be sure, Baptist expression of the Christian faith appears in a considerable variety of shapes and sizes, historically unity has transcended isolation.

Internationally, in this final decade of the 20th century, most who claim the name are partners in the Baptist World Alliance. Nationally, however, there is still significant room for improvement—a situation which cries for solution in a Canada which is assessed at less than "Christian" by the United Nations.

British Baptists

The original English Spitalfield offshoot of what is generally considered to be the founding Baptist church in Amsterdam, Holland, was soon joined by four other General (Arminian) Baptist churches. "From the beginning," writes respected British Baptist historian W. T. Whitley, "Baptists were not 'Independents'; they always sought for fellowship between different churches, and they were very successful in arranging for permanent organization."[1] By 1626, the five congregations were involved in joint consultation and action.

There was similar interconnection among the early British Particular (Calvinist) Baptists as they developed alongside. As the numbers of their churches increased, a pattern of associations appeared; one interesting aspect of this appearance in the 1640s was their corporate involvement financially and then personally in the support of Oliver Cromwell's New Model Army.[2]

In 1644, a grouping of these churches issued the historic Confession of Faith of the London Particular Baptists, "reckoned one of the noblest of all Baptist confessions":

> We do therefore here subscribe it, some of each body in the name,
> and by appointment of seven congregations, who though we be

139

distinct in respect of our particular bodies, for conveniency sake, being as many as can well meet together in one place, yet are all one in communion, holding Jesus Christ to be our head and Lord.[3]

From these two strands, General and Particular, the present Baptist Union of Great Britain and Ireland developed with its continuing unity.

German Baptists

Although Anabaptism, which undoubtedly influenced initial Baptist thought, originated and showed its strength on the continent, it was not until the 19th century that work which could be designated Baptist was begun there. John Smyth's 17th-century Amsterdam congregation had been composed of expatriate Englishmen.

In 1823, German-born Johann Gerhard Oncken, who had been living in the United Kingdom, returned to his homeland as a missionary of the British Continental Society. He lost that sponsorship eleven years later when he embraced Baptist principles. Appointed its German agent by the Baptist Triennial Convention of the United States, Oncken led in the establishment of twenty-six churches by 1845. Four years later these had become forty-one, which immediately demonstrated their unity by linking in the Union of the Associated Churches of Baptized Christians in Germany and Denmark—a number of churches having been planted across the border.[4]

Swedish, Norwegian, and Russian Baptists

Similar unity was evident from the first in both Sweden and Norway. Work which was begun in the former in 1848 resulted in a number of churches and unity in a conference formed nine years later. By 1861, that conference embraced 125 churches and nearly 5,000 members.

In adjacent Norway, a more limited growth was similarly consolidated. With the first church planted in 1860, there were fourteen by 1877, combined in the Norwegian Baptist Conference.

Russian Baptists, who stemmed from home Bible study groups and the missionary efforts of a German Baptist in the 1860s, coalesced by 1884 in the Russian Baptist Union.[5]

Baptists in Early America

Progress toward unity was obviously slower in the New World where, much earlier than in continental Europe, Baptist outreach first developed almost on an ad hoc basis. Even then, however, there was a disposition to unify. As early as 1688, according to a recent American Baptist historian writing on the centre of early Baptist growth in the Middle Colonies (between New England and the South): "a joint meeting of several churches occurred at Lower Dublin for the purpose of administering baptism, of ordaining ministers, and of providing inspirational preaching."[6]

In New England, persecution and state-enforced regulation by the Standing Order inhibited growth; but by 1707, the Philadelphia Association of five churches (which had previously been meeting together irregularly) was formed. From the outset churches in New Jersey were part of the Association. Later, all churches within travelling distance joined, these including congregations in southern New York and Virginia.[7]

As the Baptist movement stretched southward, initially tentative increase became rapid after the First Great Awakening. Although many of the developing churches, north and south, took the name "Separate Baptists" because of their origins out of New Light Congregationalism, they did not remain separate from the Regular Baptists. In 1787, a major merger was concluded with the formation, on the basis of the Philadelphia Confession, of the United Baptist Churches of Christ in Virginia.[8]

Through the early 1800s, three societies of national stature developed—the General Missionary Convention of the Baptist Denomination in the United States of America (1814), the Baptist General Tract Society (1824), and the American Baptist Home Mission Society (1832). "Baptists north and south co-operated effectively together in the work represented by these three societies in these early years."[9]

Although in 1845, stemming from cultural and distance pressures as well as the question of slavery, a division occurred, the resulting northern and southern bodies gradually established regional unities which, with some exceptions, have held strongly until the present. This has been particularly true of the Southern Baptists, who immediately chose a "convention" structure rather than a coterie of societies. That convention now embraces half the Baptists in the United States and is still growing.[10]

Blacks, who were a strong component of southern churches before the Civil War, began to form their own churches after the conflict because "the Negroes were now free and many of them, if for no other reason than to put their freedom to the test, were anxious to separate themselves from the churches of their former masters." That separation did not retard their own unity, for two major conventions developed, with a present membership totalling about ten million, both bodies being active partners in the Baptist World Alliance. These and all other major Baptist bodies in the United States cooperate through the North American Baptist Fellowship of the

Alliance and the Baptist Joint Committee on Public Affairs, a strong voice in the nation's capital.[11]

The Baptist experience in Canada has been more checkered.

The Canadian Baptist Experience

Atlantic Canada

In Atlantic Canada, where Baptist work north of the 49th parallel was inaugurated, the story has been one of integration from the outset. George Levy, Baptist historian of those parts, writes: "A cardinal feature of Baptist history in the Maritime Provinces has been the repeated manifestation of a spirit of unity," for "not once in the history of either the Baptist or Free Baptist denomination was a major enterprise irretrievably defeated by the spirit of disunity."[12]

The initial grouping of some nine churches in Nova Scotia and New Brunswick, the first of which had been established in 1763, occurred as the century turned; meeting in Lower Granville, Nova Scotia, these formed themselves into the Nova Scotia Baptist Association in 1800. "The move was designed to correct unfortunate disintegrating tendencies within the churches, and to preserve the fruits of the work so far accomplished."[13] Among the principles adopted at the historic gathering, it was noted:

> Such a combination of Churches is not only prudent but useful, as has been proved by the experience of many years in England and America. Some of its most obvious benefits are—union and communion among the several Churches,—maintaining more effectively the faith once delivered to the saints,—obtaining advice and counsel in cases of doubt and difficulty, and assistance in distress,—and in general being better able to promote the cause of God.[14]

Upper and Lower Canada

While Baptist origins in Upper and Lower Canada trailed those in the Maritimes by about thirty years, their first association, while small, developed only two years behind their more easterly compatriots. In 1802, three churches grouped near the Bay of Quinte on the north shore of Lake Ontario formed the Thurlow Association, fulfilling the goal of at least one of the congregations, Haldimand, which at its inception five years earlier had covenanted as "brethren and sisters assembled for the purpose of obtaining fellowship with sister churches."[15]

By 1846, Baptists in far eastern Canada had become a full-fledged Convention of Nova Scotia, New Brunswick, and Prince Edward Island, made up of 169 churches and 14,177 members. Such a development was more protracted in the central provinces, but progress toward unity became marked by the 1850s when the Regular Baptist Missionary Convention of Canada West and the Canada Baptist Missionary Convention East were formed. In 1888, the two merged to become the Baptist Convention of Ontario and Quebec, with an 1890 total of 388 churches and a membership approximating 33,000.[16]

Western Canada

Baptist advance into Western Canada was tardy due largely to the societal structure among Baptists in the Upper and Lower Canadas until the late 19th century. The desire to relate closely to one another, however, was most evident right from the foundings of the initial, scattered churches. First Baptist Church, Winnipeg, formed in 1875, was the "mother" church of the prairies—then termed Manitoba and the North-West. Three recently established churches joined Winnipeg in setting up the Red River Association just five years later, and in two more years the Regular Baptist Missionary Convention of Manitoba and the North-West was forged—by then ten churches being involved.

Out on the West Coast, cut off from the prairies by the then impenetrable Rockies, a somewhat different pattern emerged as almost immediate fraternal relationships were sought. Instituted in 1876—a year after First Baptist, Winnipeg—First Baptist, Victoria, at once joined the Puget Sound Association of adjacent Washington when the Regular Baptist Missionary Convention of Ontario was unable to provide a meaningful connection. By 1894, eight British Columbia churches were incorporated within the Northwest Convention (of Washington and British Columbia) which had succeeded the Puget Sound Association.

When a severe recession in the United States caused the American Baptist Home Mission Society, with which the Northwest Convention was affiliated, to discontinue any sustaining or outreach funds to the British Columbia churches in the mid-1890s, those congregations decided in 1897 to form their own British Columbia Convention. This decision thus resulted in two parallel conventions in Canada's west.

Representing 186 churches and 10,196 members, the two linked in the Baptist Convention of Western Canada in 1907, which changed its designation to "Union" two years later.[17]

About the same time, the Maritime Convention and the Free Baptist bodies which had grown up alongside the "Regular" churches also merged, becoming the United Baptist Convention of the Maritime Provinces,

"Maritime" later giving way to "Atlantic" when Baptist churches were established in Newfoundland.

French Canadian Baptists

Markedly among the churches which grew under the aegis of the Grande Ligne Mission, fervour for unity was conspicuous from the first. The Mission, founded in 1836 by Henrietta Feller and Louis Roussy, was itself a strong integrating force; and in 1868, just three months after Mme. Feller's death, the nine then-organized churches formed L'Union des Églises Baptistes de Langue Française, "to cultivate the spirit of union and peace by mutual relationships...to progress in godliness and to cultivate, individually, the missionary spirit."[18]

The Grande Ligne Mission was indeed an early advocate of an all-Canada Baptist alliance, its board in 1908 expressing readiness "to commit the election of its Board to the Dominion Convention."[19]

After many years as an association affiliated with the Baptist Convention of Ontario and Quebec, the work of Grande Ligne as a mission was phased out; and in 1966, the French Canadian churches formed themselves into the present "L'Union des Églises Baptistes Françaises au Canada."

The All-Canada Baptist Vision

Because of distances, regional concerns, and small memberships in proportion to the general population (except for the Atlantic provinces), all-Canada linking of Baptists took a good deal longer than the above-mentioned sectional movements to unity. The first yearnings in that direction were expressed back in 1846 when a letter was received by the Nova Scotia Association from the Canada Baptist Union (one of the earlier attempts at consolidation in the central provinces) stating "the desirableness of a closer union between all the Baptists of British North America being effected and manifested." That association was at the time engaged in discussions which brought about the Maritime Convention the same year, so a committee appointed by the association responded that it was "highly desirable to form a closer union between the Baptists of British North America."[20]

At the time the first Canadian provinces confederated in 1867, Robert A. Fyfe reported to the Missionary Convention of Ontario that he had corresponded with "some of the leading Baptists of the Lower Provinces [the Maritimes] who desired to know whether the Baptists of the Dominion of Canada could not be brought into closer cooperation in regard to matters of general denominational interest and importance." The minutes of the

Ontario Convention record the naming of a committee to correspond "with any committee named by them."[21]

The Canada Baptist Missionary Convention East (Quebec and Ontario east of Kingston) the same year considered "closer intercourse" with their brethren and sisters on the shores of the Atlantic, sending them a fraternal address. In 1868, Fyfe, who visited the Maritime Convention that year, returned to Ontario with a fraternal address to his home society, resulting in paired motions the next year, both supporting the principle of Baptist union and seeking "more frequent and intimate personal intercourse."[22] Yet the dream was not then realized. Complete union did not take place in Ontario and Quebec until 1888 and wider consolidation in Canada was delayed much longer.

A major step to national unity was taken with the formation in 1911 of the Canadian Baptist Foreign Mission Board (later Canadian Baptist Overseas Mission Board, and now Canadian Baptist International Ministries [CBIM]) as the overseas arm of the Ontario-Quebec and Maritime Conventions and the Baptist Union of Western Canada (BUWC). At the time, even greater consolidation was envisaged. An all-Canada Baptist conference was convened in Winnipeg in 1900; and in 1908, a "Baptist Union of Canada" was fashioned. This fell by the wayside; but the now widely recognized CBIM, which did develop, has provided a significant long-term mutual venture for the cooperating conventions/unions.

The greater unity sought finally was achieved in 1944, although in the intervening years the ranks had been thinned by internal pressures. The Baptist Federation of Canada was formed that year, its designation later changed to the Canadian Baptist Federation. Intended to be the national arm of two conventions and two unions (the Union of French Baptist Churches since 1970), the CBF was a "federal" affiliation. It was mandated "to express the common judgment of the constituent churches and organizations on matters of national, international and interdenominational importance."[23]

Increasingly, the Federation accomplished these tasks well, becoming a strong vehicle for unity among those Canadian Baptists now within its constituency, over 125,000 baptized members plus many adherents. Yet in 1995, the CBF as the cooperative domestic agency for the four regional bodies was disbanded and only its foreign services preserved as "Baptist International Ministries."

Other Baptists in the Canadian Mosaic

Additionally, Canadian Baptists who are not in this stream have demonstrated their own pilgrimages to unity. Jarold K. Zeman has pointed to the Canadian "mosaic," noting that "as a nation Canada does not subscribe to the 'melting pot' theory of linguistic and cultural assimilation of immigrants" and that the churches developed by new arrivals have tended initially to attract members among their compatriots.[24]

The North American Baptist Conference

Among the most vibrant of these Baptist congregations are those originally of German background, whch have coalesced under the aegis of the expanding North American Baptist Conference (NABC). Tracing the origins of this conference which straddles the Canadian-American border, their long-time denominational editor states that they "are firmly embedded in 'the great invasion of Teutonic people' that swept over North America after the beginning of the nineteenth century," numbering an estimated two million.[25]

Canadian numbers, particularly of Baptists, were at first quite small until augmented by a large influx of German-speaking immigrants in the 1920s and again in the wake of World War II. Especially noteworthy in this regard was the work of the German Baptist (later, North American Baptist) Immigration and Colonization Society. Just in the period covered by the years 1951 to 1965, over 6,000 immigrants were assisted by the society.[26]

The early German-speaking churches in western Canada were planted through joint assistance of Canadian Baptists and German Baptists of the Unites States and, until 1919, maintained dual affiliation. Mainly due to "polity and language" concerns, the German-Canadian churches at that time opted for the single transborder connection.[27] Relations with the BUWC have remained consistently warm, and in recent years the conduct of a number of reciprocal interests point the way to greater cooperation among all Canadian Baptists.

While a number of their Ontario churches chose to link with the BCOQ, the overall growth of the Canadian segment of the NABC has been marked by estimable growth and notable internal unity. The component in Canada, some 20,000 members, is now over twenty-five percent of the denominational total. Not only has new immigration been a substantial factor, but their strong outreach "proved that North American Baptists could enter the cosmopolitan community and effectively begin churches."[28]

This assimilation of other ethnic groups, including Anglo-Saxon, has not been a one-way street, however. Almost fifty years ago, at the centennial of the German Baptists of North America, the overall conference recorded that during the 100-year period about 12,500 letters of dismission had been granted to churches of "the English Baptist fellowship."[29] The interchange continues on both sides of the border.

The Baptist General Conference

The Swedish-oriented churches of the Baptist General Conference (BGC) followed a similar pattern. In the United States, these congregations had a close relationship with the American Baptist Home Mission Society and the American Baptist Publication Society before the Northern Baptist Convention (now American Baptist Churches) was formed. Reorganization of the Conference, with its own boards and agencies, took place in 1945, there being thirteen district conferences in the United States and two in Canada within the overall General Conference.[30]

The Canadian part of the experience was similar. Through Alexander Grant, pastor in the 1890s of western Canada's initial Baptist church in Winnipeg, Swedish work was launched in that city. A decade later there were eleven churches and about twenty-five preaching points.

In 1905, the then Swedish General Conference of America became interested in Canadian outreach and, after the BUWC was formed in 1907, the Swedish-Canadian churches were dually aligned with the Union and the American conference. This situation obtained until 1948, when the Canadian Central Conference decided on a single American affiliation. The Alberta Conference followed a year later.[31]

A Serious Break in Relationships

Undoubtedly, the most serious break in Canadian Baptist relationships occurred in the mid-1920s; and Baptist witness has been thereby blemished for the intervening sixty-plus years. It is hardly the purpose of this chapter to attempt a description of the causes of the rift or to impute any blame. The effect was that the BCOQ lost a seventh of its churches and membership and the BC Convention, a third of its membership and one-fourth of its congregations. The Maritimes were virtually untouched; the prairie provinces, marginally. But the movement toward national Baptist unity suffered severely.

Such encounters are traumatic both for those who leave and those who stay. Kenneth R. Davis has documented the continued grappling for unity among those who parted, particularly in the years 1953-65. He focusses on "the unitive forces behind, and the struggle for, a national fundamentalistic evangelical Baptist Fellowship in Canada." Such unity was attained in 1965, and "the establishment of a Canada-wide Fellowship of Evangelical Baptist Churches (FEBC) was a significant ecumenical achievement by fundamentalistic evangelical Baptists in Canada."[32]

It remains for that achievement to encompass all Canadian Baptists—including Southern Baptists who began work north of the border in the early 1950s and have now formed a Canadian Convention (CCSB).[33]

In the Post-Christian Era

Baptist ecumenism is a laudable goal, surely, in the Canada facing the 21st century, a Canada which is increasingly indifferent, even hostile, to the faith Baptists proclaim. If there were questions when the concept of the "post-Christian era" was first suggested many decades ago, none remains in the final decade of the 1900s. By and large, our nation is secular.

The Gideons of Canada's third-largest city have been denied the long-held prerogative of distributing the Scriptures in the schools. An obvious anti-Christian bias is increasingly discernible in both the print and broadcast media. This is demonstrably true in British Columbia, where the province's premier in this year of writing is most frequently criticized not so much for his politics as for his "Christian morality." The former minister of health in the same government has been widely ridiculed because of a "leaked" letter he wrote, daring to favour the reservation of sexual activity to marriage and mature adulthood. Pondering over the changed attitudes in Canadian society, the publisher of a popular regional secular magazine remarked that on Good Friday recently he had scanned both AM and FM radio channels in vain for any "religious music" at 11:00 in the morning. "Radio programming reflects how profoundly we've changed."[34]

For good or ill, the churches are losing their heretofore strong influence on Canadian society and culture. Is the salt losing its savour? In some instances the unfortunate but all-too-obvious answer is "yes." To change the figure and alter somewhat the focus, all too often the trumpet has given "an uncertain sound" and many are confused. How may we account for some of the lapses and particularly the lifestyles of a few of television's high-profile evangelistic superstars? The person on the street simply writes them off as hypocrites and, with them, a host of others who are undeserving of the opprobrium. The whole Christian church is tarred with the same brush.

Or how may we account for the "Christian" uncertainties concerning the wholesale dispatch of the unborn or the validity of "alternative sexual lifestyles"? From some theological perspectives a portion of the Church is even seen as apostate. All these leave the lookers-on bewildered but more than ever satisfied with their own mode of living.

Of that living in our day and generation, Charles Colson has recently written:

> We live in a new dark age. Having elevated the individual as the measure of all things, modern men and women are guided solely by

their own passions; they have nothing above themselves to respect or obey, no principles to live or die for. Personal advancement, personal feeling and personal autonomy are the only shrines at which they worship. The reigning God of relativism and the rampant egoism it fosters coarsen character, destroy any notion of community, weaken civility, promote intolerance and threaten the disintegration of those very institutions necessary to the survival and success of ordered liberty.[35]

Christians, including Baptists, must confront this deteriorating spiritual condition with reduced forces. As church historian Jarold K. Zeman has underlined, Baptists in Canada declined from 4.8% of the population in the 1923 census to 2.9% in 1981. The total number, including children, of "census Baptists" (all who name the name) reached 696,850 in 1981; but that was a drop of almost two-fifths in proportion to the burgeoning population.[36]

To face the future in such a Canada, it would seem most compelling to consider once again the concern for Baptist unity. It may be strongly submitted that the questions which caused division early in this present century are much less relevant as it draws to a close. Theologically, the poles are being moved very close together.

Widely respected theologian Clark H. Pinnock holds a similar position. Prefacing a plea to his fellow Canadian Baptists for "the recovery of the power and experiential vitality of the gospel," he writes:

It seems to many that the struggle for doctrinal identity among Baptists has been practically won. The Baptist Union of Western Canada joining the Evangelical Fellowship of Canada, the Baptist Convention of Ontario and Quebec adopting a confessional statement, the changed orientation of Acadia Divinity College and the increasing role of Ontario Theological Seminary and Regent College/Carey Hall in training for ministry—these and other developments suggest that Baptists are clarifying, if not recovering, their theological identity as doctrinal evangelicals.[37]

There are a number of readily discernible movements toward Canadian Baptist unity. For many years, NABs have joined with those of the BUWC and other bodies in an annual conference for ministers and their spouses at Banff, Alberta, currently drawing over 400.

Even as this is written, conversations are going on between the NABC and the BUWC involving their seminaries—Edmonton Baptist Seminary and Carey Theological College (Vancouver)—looking to possible engagement in cooperative theological education at both centres.

Again at this time, an outreach to Ethiopia by the Sharing Way, the world relief agency of the CBF, is being administered on location by Wally Eshenaur of the Baptist General Conference mission.[38]

For well into a second decade, a Baptist Joint Committee on Canadian Public Life has involved working representatives of the BGC, the NABC, the CCSB, the FEBC, and the CBF (represented by the BUWC) in western Canada. These face church-state and social issues in the nation and province, meeting frequently with MLAs.

The magazine *Christian Week* recently reported the merging of two Calgary Baptist churches—South Calgary Community Church (NAB) and Faith Baptist (CCSB): "The enlarged church will remain affiliated with the North American Baptists while contributing to the Southern Baptist mission fund." Writers Legge and Jantz, the latter the editor of the transdenominational paper, comment that "the move may carry an important message to Baptists in Canada." The same article also points to further evidence of this trend to unity, reporting that Rev. Allen Schmidt, executive director of the CCSB, had helped initiate a meeting in December 1989 of representatives of the CBF, the FEBC, the NABC, the CCSB, and the BGCC. Their objective: to make a concerted effort to work more closely together. Commenting on these developments, Dr. Roy Bell, Carey Hall faculty member and program chairman of the Baptist World Alliance, feels that "there's something in the air," adding that the banding together of the two churches "is an indication that we must not let the past dominate the present and the future."[39]

While "one swallow alone does not make the summer" (Cervantes), nor do two nor three, "there is a sound of going in the tops of the mulberry trees" (2 Chron. 14.15 KJV). Might it be a signal to go forward?

In addition to doctrinal restoration and the initial signs of a movement toward closer cooperation, it might be suggested that most, if not all, of the long-held grounds for separateness are less substantial than they once were. Even the ethnic factor among Baptists has largely faded. The membership of the once mainly Anglo-Saxon and Celtic churches has become increasingly broadly based. As pointed out above, the NABs and BGCs have entered the urban community and effectively begun ethnically nondescript churches. Many of the erstwhile barriers among Baptists have disappeared, including the personality differences which frequently entered the past picture.

The opportunities for measured steps toward an increasing unity and the forming of a common front toward the obvious coming tests of the new century are many. One possible avenue might well be an expansion of the CBF—which is a true federation of partner conventions/unions and not an all-encompassing body. Its flexible constitution is open to welcoming Baptist bodies beyond those who make up its present membership, and with no need to change their current structures. Indeed, one of the Federation's objectives, spelled out in its constitution, is "to foster cooperative relationships with other bodies of similar faith and order."

Canadian Baptists, whatever our stripe, for some time have cultivated interchurch fellowship with those of other theological rootage rather than with our fellow Baptists. This is neither to decry the affinities among all Christians nor to appeal for ecumenical synthesis. It is simply to recognize that more recently we seem to be rediscovering that "the ties that bind" easily first encircle those of "kindred mind."

Historically, Baptists have generally and freely chosen the unity expressed in the 1644 London Confession quoted above: "all one in Communion, holding Jesus Christ to be our head and Lord." Resisting further alienation within our community, cooperating and uniting Canadian Baptists may be better fitted to confront the threatening issues of the imminent 21st century.

Notes

[1] W. T. Whitley, *A History of British Baptists* (London: Griffin, 1923), 53; cf. A. C. Underwood, *A History of the English Baptists* (London: The Baptist Union Publication Dept., 1947), 51.

[2] Whitley, *British Baptists*, 90.

[3] William L. Lumpkin, ed., *Baptist Confessions of Faith*, rev. ed. (Valley Forge, PA: Judson Press, 1969), 155. See William L. Lumpkin, "Baptist Confessions of Faith" in *Baptist Advance*, ed. Davis C. Woolley (Nashville, TN: Broadman Press, 1964), 9.

[4] Robert G. Torbet, *A History of the Baptists* (Valley Forge, PA: Judson Press, 1963), 173-74.

[5] Torbet, *History of the Baptists*, 176-78, 181.

[6] Torbet, *History of the Baptists*, 208-209, 211.

[7] Henry C. Vedder, *A Short History of the Baptists* (Philadelphia: American Baptist Publication Society, 1907), 305-06.

[8] Vedder, *Short History of Baptists*, 305-306.

[9] Robert A. Baker, "Southern Baptist Convention," in *Baptist Advance*, ed. Woolley, 261.

[10] Claude L. Howe, Jr., "A Portrait of Baptists in America Today," *Baptist History and Heritage* 24, no. 3 (July 1989): 51.

[11] William Warren Sweet, *The Baptists*, Story of Religion in America (New York: Harper and Row, 1950), 329; and Cyril E. Bryant and Ruby J. Burke, eds., *Official Report of the Fourteenth Congress of the Baptist World Alliance* (Nashville: Broadman Press, 1981), 313.

[12] George E. Levy, *The Baptists in the Maritime Provinces, 1763-1946* (Saint John, NB: Barnes-Hopkins, 1946), 267.

[13] Levy, *Baptists in the Maritime Provinces*, 69.

[14] I. E. Bill, *Fifty Years with the Baptist Ministers and Churches of the Maritime Provinces of Canada* (Saint John, NB: Barnes, 1880), 36.

[15] Stuart Ivison and Fred Rosser, *The Baptists in Upper and Lower Canada before 1820* (Toronto: University of Toronto Press, 1956), 85.

[16] W. E. Norton, "Ontario and Quebec," in *The Baptists of Canada*, ed. E. R. Fitch (Toronto: Standard, 1911), 155.

[17] Margaret E. Thompson, *The Baptist Story in Western Canada* (Calgary: The Baptist Union of Western Canada, 1974), 137.

[18] W. Nelson Thomson, "Witness in French Canada," in *Baptists in Canada*, ed. Jarold K. Zeman (Burlington, ON: G. R. Welch, 1980), 50.

[19] *Baptist Year Book*, Ontario and Quebec (1908), 180.

[20] "Minutes of the Nova Scotia Baptist Association," 22-24 June 1846.

[21] "Minutes of the Baptist Missionary Convention of Ontario, 1867," *Canadian Baptist Register* (*CBR*; 1868), 17.

[22] "Minutes of the Canada Baptist Missionary Convention, East, 1867," *CBR* (1868), 49-50.; "Minutes of the Baptist Missionary Convention of Ontario, 1868," *CBR* (1869), 7-8; and "Minutes of the Baptist Missionary Convention of Ontario, 1869," *CBR* (1870), 12-13.

[23] "Report of All-Canada Committee," *BYB*, BCOQ (1943-44), 76, 78.

[24] Jarold K. Zeman, "Baptists in Canada and Cooperative Christianity," *Foundations* 15 (July-September 1972): 214.

[25] Martin L. Leuschner, "North American Baptist General Conference," in *Baptist Advance*, ed. Woolley, 227.

[26] William J. H. Sturhahn, *They Came from east and west...*[*sic*] (Winnipeg: North American Baptist Immigration and Colonization Society, 1976), 21, 299.

[27] Edward B. Link, "North American (German) Baptists," in *Baptists in Canada*, ed. Zeman, 96.

[28] Link, "North American Baptists," 100.

[29] Frank Kaiser, "Widening Horizons," in *These Glorious Years*, ed. Herman von Berge et al. (Cleveland: Roger Williams Press, 1943), 236.

[30] Torbet, *History of Baptists*, 476.

[31] Harry A. Renfree, *Heritage and Horizon* (Mississauga, ON: Canadian Baptist Federation, 1988), 287-88.

[32] Kenneth R. Davis, "The Struggle for a United Evangelical Baptist Fellowship, 1953-1965," in *Baptists in Canada*, ed. Zeman, 237, 258.

[33] See G. Richard Blackaby, "The Establishment of the Canadian Convention of Southern Baptists," ch. 7 in this volume.

[34] Ted Byfield, "Letter from the Publisher," *British Columbia Report*, 23 April 1990, 52.

[35] Charles Colson with Ellen Santilli Vaughn, "Living in the New Dark Ages," *Christianity Today*, 20 October 1989, 30, excerpted from their book of the same title.

[36] Jarold K. Zeman, *Costly Vision: The Baptist Pilgrimage in Canada* (Burlington, ON: G. R. Welch, 1988), x.

[37] Clark H. Pinnock, "Baptists and the 'Latter Rain,'" in *Costly Vision*, ed. Zeman, 267.

[38] "Prayer Calendar," Canadian Baptist Federation, January-March 1990, 4.

[39] Gordon Legge and Harold Jantz, "Baptist Churches Join Hands in Unusual Union," *Christian Week* (6 March 1990): 1, 4.

PART THREE
People and Their Contributions

Chapter 11

Samuel Stearns Day:
First Canadian-Born Baptist Missionary

Judith Colwell

The founder of American and Canadian missions in the Telegu-speaking part of India was Samuel Stearns Day. Written histories covering his period of labour (1836-53) range from three to five pages.[1] They are dominated by descriptions of the decision processes of the American Baptist Missionary Union around the viability of the mission to the Telegus. Almost all contain, within those same few pages, the six-verse poem entitled "The Lone Star" (see Appendix 1). This poem, written by Dr. S. F. Smith, is credited with clinching the Union decision to maintain the mission. However, after all is read, Samuel Day—the founder, the missionary, the person—remains, unjustly and inexplicably, a shadowy and somewhat ineffectual figure. His diaries, notes, journals, and letters provide an extensive though long-ignored reservoir from which to redress this imbalance.[2]

Biographical Sketch

Background

Samuel Stearns Day was born in Bastard Township, County of Leeds, District of Johnstown, in Upper Canada (Ontario) on Friday, 13 May 1808. He was the ninth child and fifth son of Jeremiah and Submit Day. On the occasion of his birthday each year, Samuel wrote a review of the past year in his life. Included among some of his memories is the information that he first went to Sunday School in 1818 to a Mr. Tew in Plum Hollow.

On his birthday in 1825 at age seventeen, he wrote his autobiography on two narrow scraps of paper. One pithy statement covers his first years: "Born—1808—parents—early training—convictions for sin when about 10 yrs. Foolish and giddy until 1820 when Arch[ibal]d Wait taught school."

He analyzes his spiritual condition at points over the next four years as follows:

1821. When three men & a boy drowned very serious then—
1822. Went to a Sunday school—no good—about '22 or when 14 years old. Read "Swiftness of Time" went out and fell on my face in prayer—Soon forgot—That Autumn Broke D. T.s leg. Then resolved, and practised for months.
1824 or 16 [years old].—Gone all astray dancing sinning.

In June 1825, he was "sitting and reading a tract on [the] Excel-l[enc]y of religion in the young—All was peace—I praised God...." He was baptized in July by Elder Abel Stevens at the "Branch" Church (later known as the Leeds church).

Almost at once the new convert was confronted with controversy in the church. The first issue was whether Abel Stevens, Jr., should be ordained. Samuel dwelt long on the issue. In May 1826, the church agreed to call a council. Apparently, the council was equally uncertain because the younger Stevens was not ordained until 10 June 1833.[3]

A council also was called to decide whether the Leeds branch was a church in "gospel order." They determined that it was not and that its baptisms were not valid. Samuel then had to choose whether he would be baptized again. Others were but he thought that rebaptism was unnecessary. Therefore, he was effectively cut off from the fellowship of the church.

He ceased farming and began his career as a teacher at the Stone School House (1827-28). Since the ruling of the council, he had been struggling with an inner call to the ministry. In April 1828, he submitted to the ruling that his baptism had been irregular; he was rebaptized and received into the church fellowship.[4] He reported in his diary that as he came up out of the water, he was certain that God was calling him to the ministry.

The next fall and winter he again taught, first at the Brick School House and latterly at the Stone School House. From May to October 1830, he went to the Potsdam Academy, St. Lawrence County, New York State.[5] Just before he left the Academy, he and another student organized about ten students into a prayer group "for the welfare of religion in the academy."

Back in Bastard, he again taught school for the winter. In March, he talked to his father about attending the seminary in Hamilton, New York. His father agreed that if he felt it his duty to go, the means would be provided. On 30 April, the church at Bastard granted him a letter to enter ministerial training; four weeks later, Samuel arrived in Hamilton to begin his studies. The executive committee of the college examined him relative to his call to ministry, and he was admitted as a student.

Missionary "Call"

Day's initial idea had been to offer himself as a missionary to the Native Indians of Canada; but by the autumn of his first year at Hamilton, foreign

Day's Ontario and New York

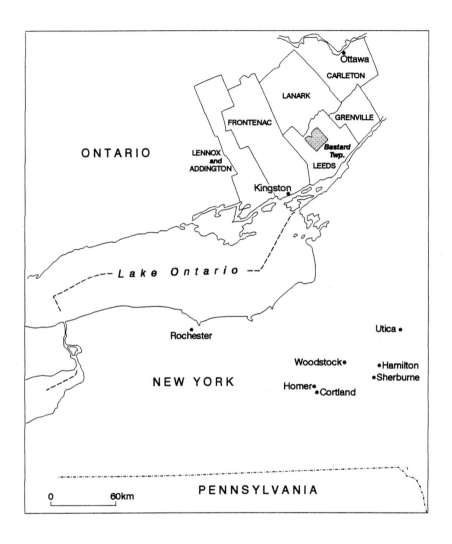

mission seemed to be his calling. He told his diary: "In the Autumn of 1831. A deliberate and prayerful examination of the claims upon me of the heathen of the eastern world led me to decide in *their favour instead* of the Aborigines of America; and this led me also to change my purposes regarding the course of my studies in the Seminary." Again, Samuel was an enterprising organizer of his fellow students. In October 1831, he was one of five who formed an association "for the purpose of more effectually concentrating our efforts to obtain knowledge of missionary operations in the whole world and also for the mutual instruction and help of those here who anticipate entering the field of foreign missions when their course of study terminates in the Institution."

On a return trip to Bastard in 1833, his home church granted him a licence to preach. Over the next two years, he attained a "highly respectable standing in his class." When he was appointed a missionary to India, in August 1835, he ceased his studies.

Three weeks after leaving Hamilton, he married Roenna Clark of Homer, New York. The day following (24 August) he was ordained to the Baptist ministry at Cortland Village, Cortland County, New York. The newlyweds attended the ordination of Mr. E. L. Abbott at Woodstock the next day and proceeded to visit Samuel's family at Bastard, where they remained for nine days. On 23 September, the Days and the Abbotts left on the ship *Louvre* from Boston bound for India and mission work among the Telegus under the American Baptist Foreign Mission Society (ABFMS).

Missionary to India

Upon arrival in Calcutta on 5 February 1836, Mr. Abbott decided to go to Burma. The Days proceeded, alone, to Vizagapatam; they arrived there on 9 March. Language studies were begun without delay. Samuel was immediately active in missionary effort. He went out on trips with London Missionary Society missionaries. One town visited was Chicacole. This place appeared to him to be "the place to commence operations of the American Baptist Mission."

On 6 June 1836, the first of their seven children was born. They named the boy after the American Baptist Foreign Mission Board agent in India, Howard Malcom. Samuel reported in his diary that he did not take Telegu lessons the next day. Two months later the family moved to Chicacole where Samuel began to work among the native people. "Immediately one school was begun for such lads as usually attend schools among themselves, and this within a week had about 40 scholars." Two other schools were established: one for lower caste students; the other an English school.

December 24 and 25 were landmark days for the new missionary.

The local judge granted him permission to perform the rite of marriage for those converted to Christianity; and he, consequently, conducted "the first Christian native marriage that ever took place in Chicacole." After the wedding, the Day family also ate in a native's house for the first time.

From the time of their arrival in India, the Days waited for the company and counsel of Mr. Malcom. Despite the initiative he had already taken, Samuel and his family were not free to choose where they would settle as missionaries; Mr. Malcom was to assign them. In March 1837, Malcom finally met with Samuel and ordered them to Madras. Samuel Day was to work among the English people in Madras and with a branch of the Maulmein church located there. His work among the Telegu people was to be incidental. He was the only Baptist missionary south of Orissa.

He supplemented his Madras duties with tours to other areas. One was to Bellary, about 320 miles north of Madras. At Bellary, twenty-two were baptized in 1838. Among the converts were no Telegus. A Baptist church was founded in Madras on 24 August 1838 with fifteen members (not including the Days). Samuel preached there weekly. Again, there were no Telegus.[6]

Although he appeared successful in his work, he was not happy. He still felt a compulsion to serve the Telegu-speaking people. He developed proficiency in the language both "to read it and speak it with ease." In February 1840, the family moved to the village of Nellore, 110 miles north of Madras, into the midst of millions of Telegu people.

Among his other duties in Madras had been work with the American Baptist Tract Society and the Madras Auxiliary Bible Society. Samuel was treasurer of the Tract Society by 1842 and had served on the subcommittee for revising Matthew in "Teloogoo" since April 1837. He and Rev. Stephen Van Husen, who arrived in Nellore in March 1840, were actively trying to get the Bible Society to produce a more accurate translation of the New Testament. "One version," he reported, "does a palpable error regarding the ordinance of Baptism, and the other version containing unnecessarily a number of untranslated words." The two missionaries wanted to amend and rewrite it and requested copyright information. There is no record of whether they succeeded. However, Samuel did write an *History of Christ in Telegu*, "wholly in the words of the four gospels." This 232-page book was published only years later.[7]

In August 1843, three native converts were baptized at Nellore and on 12 October a church was organized.[8] By the autumn of 1845, both Roenna and Samuel were very ill. Forced to abandon the mission and the country, they sailed for America on 3 December.[9]

Throughout 1846 to 1848, Samuel's health improved greatly. Roenna still was not well. The American Baptists were questioning whether the Telegu mission should be kept or abandoned. On the proviso that Samuel

Day would return to the field, he was promised: "We, the Baptists of America, will not desert you."[10] But in order for him to go, Roenna and the children would have to remain in America. By June, he had acceded to the Board's request provided "that in case my wife's health be restored...she be allowed to join me, and bring one or two of the children if we should think best."[11] The Board agreed; and on 10 October 1848, Samuel Day set sail for a five-year term at Nellore. Accompanying him were a new missionary couple, Rev. and Mrs. Lyman Jewett.

They arrived in India in February 1849 and found the fledgling church that he had abandoned in 1845 largely scattered and the remaining Christians in need of retraining. Language skills needed to be renewed or, in the case of the Jewetts, begun. Samuel undertook to learn Hindustani in addition to polishing his once fluent Telegu. He also set in motion an effort to adapt Telegu music to notes and, hence, for Christian hymnody. His missionary efforts had hitherto been to the Hindu people. On 2 July 1849, he began to work among the Mohammedans in Nellore.

Periodic illnesses plagued him, as did great loneliness; finally, on 7 May 1853, he wrote to Roenna that within two months he must return home on the advice of his physicians. He arrived home later that year.

Final Years

Once his health was recovered, he spent the years 1855-59 as a missionary agent for the American Baptist Missionary Union (ABMU). In this capacity, he frequently travelled over much of the northern United States as well as in Canada to raise funds for the missions in India. Over those years, he earned a total of $600 from the ABMU; but he had to write letters frequently pleading for the monies due him. He also had been working in a school and preaching wherever he had opportunity. In April 1861, he learned that the ABMU was discontinuing even the small allowances he had been receiving for his upkeep. The following years were difficult. There were numerous absences from home as he struggled to financially care for his family. Interim pastorates, which usually lasted only months, became one means of providing shelter for him and Roenna; the churches often allowed the temporary pastor the use of their parsonage. By this time the six living children were grown and living and working in other areas.

Samuel Day was very ill for most of the last year of his life. He died of heart failure on Sunday, 17 September 1871 at Homer, New York.

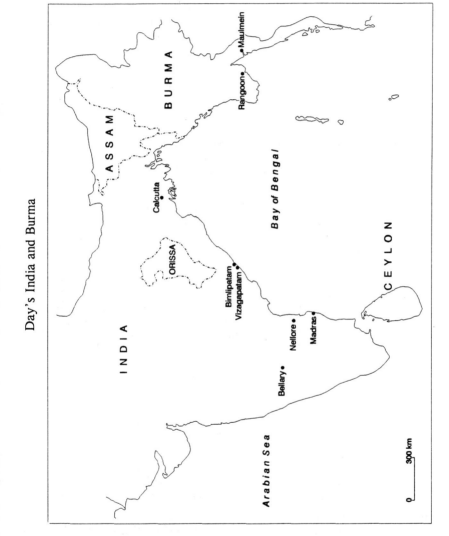

Day's India and Burma

The Nature of the Man

Samuel's diaries belie his self-description of having a frivolous nature. He wrote daily from 1826 to 1834 of his feelings in regard to his relationship to God. Though he lived and wrote 150 years ago, his thoughts echo the reality of many faith journeys of today. He summed up his pattern of religious thought on 7 December 1831: "Sometimes I think I enjoy the influence of the Holy Ghost in a small degree; again, I almost doubt the reality of my professed trust in God." Often he described himself as "cold" or "dark" in faith (May 1826); and far less often was his mind "calm" and "praising" (9 July 1831). His earliest descriptive writing in this vein is in his autobiography written in 1825. He recalled:

> 1824. That Autumn attention arrested—delighted in going to meetings but no clear impressions—felt my sins a burden, but no thoughts of being religious—a work of grace in Plum Hollow— Went in winter to see a Baptism—now mind arrested solemnly— Inquired about my own soul—convictions for sin increased. Began to seek Religion as it was called. Prayed; still found my heart all wrong like a cage of unclean birds—
> 1825. Spring Became Miserable—wretched—*lost.*—Sought the Lord— Prayed night & day—expected soon to die and go to hell—thought it was too late. No mercy for such a wretch.
> Others talked with me—all to no purpose seemingly. I respected them and honored religion, but was shut out from it—Hell was before my eyes by day and by night—awake or asleep.... Go away into the Barn—fields—Swamp—woods—fall on my face—weep—groan— pray—sometimes a little relief—others none—My disease was nothing better but grew until May about the 10th went to a cov[enant] meeting of the Baptist all cut down—would have given my life for one half hour, or one minute of such peace and joy as the Lord's.

He struggled for perfection in his faith throughout his life and repeatedly recorded his want of more control over his personal habits. One supposes also that he expected as much of all who were around him. He was offended by laughter in a home where he boarded and with the men at Hamilton for skipping rope for exercise. Any frivolity or joy seemed to mean lack of faith. However, he did admit to having a tough time eating what he should and even mentioned eating a great supply of his favourite treat, apples, in one day.

He was physically ill much of the time and seemed susceptible to any illness about. Much that was wrong seemed to be with his digestive system. Another diary kept by J. E. Maxwell in the same period would indicate that this was not unusual.[12] Day created potions for himself and had three- to four-day bouts of constipation. "Took an emetic of Ipecac—and about noon a purge (of 6 gr Cal. 12 gr Rhub.)" (16 June 1849). This particular trait was evident throughout his life.

He was reticent about his personal relationships in the early diaries. He missed his family in Bastard but wrote little. He visited relatives in Sherburne, near Hamilton, but wrote about the church life in their vicinity rather than about them. He did record one incident which profoundly influenced him, and which might explain why he seldom mentioned friends: on 7 November 1832, he was accused in Sherburne of defiling his neighbour's bed. He claimed it was a false accusation by only two or three people; and the issue was dropped. Before he was married in 1835, he never wrote, in English, about Roenna in his diaries.[13]

Samuel put much store in his dreams. He interpreted them as teaching instruments or as guidance into new ventures. On 26 March 1834, before he had actually presented himself as a candidate for foreign missionary service, he recorded a dream in which he had heard from the Board of Foreign missions—"for I thought I had presented myself as a candidate for missionary labors"—and that he would be sailing in June. His "mind was affected by the dream all day." Thereafter, foreign missions were frequent topics for his writings.

Dreams also led him to actively pursue work among the "Mahometans" in Nellore.

> I remember a very singular incident in my experience during the past 10 or 12 years. A *dream*...it was spoken of with my wife a number of times, and occasioned, to say the least, some curiosity in our minds— After we had been in the country that is India a few months I one night dreamed of being among my friends in America—but in a state of preparation to depart as a missionary to *Persia*! The *sensation* was as though I were going among the followers of Mahomet.

Missionary Method

Future generations of missionaries imitated the style and method of executing mission among the Telegu people that Samuel Day established. Some patterns were those of earlier missions like that of William Carey in Serampore; but with no guidance, with no fellow missionary, he had to judge the situation and find means of dealing with it alone.[14]

Education

The most evident need in all India was education. Wherever Samuel and Roenna Day were located schools were established. Even as a student at Hamilton, Samuel had worked at establishing Sunday School as a program distinct from Bible classes. He had tried a school in April 1832, three miles south of Hamilton in "a very degraded neighborhood." The residents were opposed, especially bitter against tracts. Undaunted, he returned in May but finally had to settle his school at the nearby Bell schoolhouse.

Upon arrival in August 1836 at Chicacole, his first undertaking was the beginning of a native school. Within a week, he had forty scholars. He also set up an English school which he turned over to a Captain Richardson, "as it is not considered a *mission school*." He fully understood the idea of the caste system but reported that on 17 November he accepted two pariahs into the school.

> I have received them—Do not know as the teacher will allow them to come into the school. There is such prejudice concerning *Caste* among this people that the higher Castes will not even instruct this Caste. However I am resolved to know no distinction in the school. I shall make no enquiry, but place these lads in school without remarks as though they were of the same grade as the rest of the lads.
> 18th. The two who came yesterday remain and appear well; nothing is yet said against them remaining.

By 12 December, there were enough pariahs of the mat-maker class to form a separate school.

In Madras and in Nellore, he again established schools. The Board, however, felt that they were an inappropriate use of funds and of missionary time. So Samuel improvised. He sought donors within the Christian community in Nellore (1844) "for pecuniary assistance that might prevent the necessity of dismissing the free schools, or making other retrenchments which would seriously injure the prosperity of this Mission." He again appealed to the same local people for aid in 1845, since "the Board of Missions [are] not...yet recovered from their Financial embarrassment." By then, there were seven schools with 150 children.

Tracts and Trips

The basic method of mission was the giving of tracts. This was accompanied by sermons, long conversations, and the indirect approach— e.g., teaching at open school windows so that any villagers who wished could listen. Often there were more than twenty-five people listening at the doors and windows who later came requesting tracts to read.

Another established pattern was that of attending the religious festivals. When people did not go on up to the shrines or asked the missionaries for reading material, he and his companions—native preachers and Van Husen or, later, Jewett—went among them. One special annual site was on a hillside at Janavardoo. The natives had heard stories that when the mission at Nellore was built, infants were sacrificed to put their skulls in the walls. This story had been concocted by the native gardener to keep people from taking a short-cut across the compound lawns! The tale caused some distrust and Samuel was stoned at Janavardoo on 7 May 1843.

An ongoing problem with the giving out of tracts was that the American Mission had no printing press. Samuel saw this as lack of support for India. Since the mission in Assam was begun within months of the Telegu mission and had received people, press equipment, and funding that India was not given, he accused the Union of favouritism.[15]

From the time of his arrival in Madras (1837) until he left India in 1853, he periodically wrote of loneliness, of need for more hands for the work: "My heart is not yet faint though heavy, nor do my hands yet flag though trembling, but how long before they will who can tell—I *hope* never"[16] He also appealed for a "Teloogoo [*sic*] press for tracts, scriptures, and books for schools &c."[17]

He also made trips to neighbouring and far-flung towns and villages. One trip took him far north to Bimlipatam; he also returned to assist the failing church at Madras and its branch at Bellary.

Paternalism

Samuel Day was probably as guilty as any other missionary of his era for instilling the notion that new Christians could not be trusted to find and follow indigenous leadership. He was not surprised upon his return to India to find that the mission was no longer visible; on the other hand, he *was* pleased that the converts he left were, by-and-large, still practising the faith and were leaders in the community. He was upset with Jewett when the newcomer presumed, during his first months in India, that Day had misrepresented the state of the mission by reporting that the few he had left in 1845 were faithful. In particular, Samuel was proud of the adopted daughter he had left in India, Elisabeth:

> Br. & Sis. Jewett *saw* dear Elisabeth...in Madras; heard the high commendations bestowed on her by every one that spoke of her—saw how great confidence the Hunts and the Scudders placed in her...but Br. & Sist. J. know not what pains, teaching, praying and patience *one such one* has cost; nor does it seem to them a matter of special interest that a young female disciple should have *such* a *standing* in the esteem of the Christian friends. Comparisons in their minds are made from standards found among the *best* members of the churches in America.

He also, it seems, decided that the Christians in his care, while he was in their midst, should accede to his leadership—both in their personal ministry and in their family decisions. This is illustrated by his dealings with the native teacher and Christian, Zachariah, in 1842. Zachariah had determined on his own responsibility to go to Arnu on a mission in January.

Day gave him written instructions: He would be funded by a Mr. Vansomer and was not to regard himself as an agent of the Baptist mission. Zachariah found a place for himself there and wanted to stay in Arnu. Day opposed this and felt he should move on. He wrote reminding him of the missionary's better judgment: "Remember Dear Br., when you have plainly informed us of the state of affairs at Arnu, and of your own views and feelings, and we have advised you what we think as your duty, if you go directly contrary to our advice we cannot answer to God for what you do." Meanwhile, something had happened to Zachariah's wife; and Day regrets that the Indian now was "sheltering a 'harlot'." Subsequently, when he wished to take his children home from the school on a Saturday, Day would not let them leave. He decreed that if they were taken, they would not be allowed back. Van Husen, his partner at the time, intervened, arguing that Zachariah had a right to remove his children if he chose.

Relationship to Partner Missionaries

In a climate that fostered short tempers, amid a mass of people with a different culture, language, and faith, it was inevitable that frictions between missionaries would become evident. To the vagaries already listed it is necessary to add that during the first term in Nellore (1840-45), two family units tried to live together in one house for three years. It is a testimony to the characters of Samuel and Roenna Day and Stephen Van Husen and his wife that no quarrels or household difficulties were cited.

Two issues with Van Husen did arise. The first, in 1843, was centred around responsibility for the buildings that had been constructed for Day and, later, for the Van Husens on the other side of town. His partner charged that Day engineered the entire project without consulting him and that he should be solely responsible if the Board refused to cover the costs. The quarrel lasted for days and Van Husen never did give in and sign his name to Day's report. Samuel sent his report a month late. Included in it was a letter transferring the mission buildings and property to the ABMU. Samuel's diary concluded the matter: "I will try to humble myself and esteem myself least of all—and I do now resolve that so far as lieth in me, I will freely sacrifice my own rights, feelings, and wishes and even judgment to the cause of peace and harmony among us as missionaries. O God help me."

The second problem with Van Husen was more serious. Samuel had to cope with a slowly advancing mental breakdown in Stephen. He worked with Mrs. Van Husen during much of 1844-45 in covering her husband's lapses from reality and, finally, made the decision to send him back to North America.

There were some initial personality differences in Samuel's second posting (1848-53). The years with Lyman and Mrs. Jewett also were under one roof. It was hard for Samuel to have someone else running his home. The early days were trying as well because Jewett quickly decided that the mission to the Telegus in Nellore should be abandoned and that he could better serve as a missionary in Burma. The new missionary and his wife found it difficult to take instructions from Samuel. But when he stopped making suggestions to make their life a little easier, they resented his lack of leadership. Samuel, in turn, resented their lack of concern for the mission. A long discussion with Mrs. Jewett in July 1849 marked the turning point; and by the autumn, Samuel became more confident that he and the Jewetts could support each other.

Assessment

A citation in his obituary well summarizes Samuel Stearns Day's contributions to his world and helps our understanding of his place in the annals of Baptist history and mission enterprises:

> It is as a missionary of the Cross that br. Day is, and ought to be most widely and truthfully known. In that noble, arduous work, he was a pioneer.... Alone among a strange people...[he] labored long and faithfully in laying foundations upon which others have builded, sowing good seed from which they were permitted to gather some precious fruit....
>
> As an example of consecration, giving himself and all that he had to the mission; of strong faith, waving not in purpose, nor ceasing in effort when other and strong hearts failed, and strong hands were turned to other fields, his name justly deserves an honorable place in the list of missionary heroes.[18]

When the sources of a biography are the letters and diaries of the subject, there is a temptation to record only the virtue he saw in himself. His commitment to issues he believed in is commendable. This is evidenced in a refusal to give up educating the people he had gone to serve, in declining to cease the enterprise when the world seemed against him and when funds and needed companionship were far away, and in persevering when native converts were but five after eighteen years in the mission. But Samuel also wrote his share of complaints about himself no less than about others—particularly in relation to the mission field and fellow missionaries. He emerges as a quite human person who struggled successfully to do what was right in exceptional circumstances and consistently demonstrated a persevering faith.

Appendix 1

"The Lone Star"[19]

Shine on, "Lone Star"! Thy radiance bright
    Shall spread o'er all the eastern sky;
Morn breaks apace from gloom and night;
    Shine on, and bless the pilgrim's eye.

Shine on, "Lone Star"! I would not dim
    The light that gleams with dubious ray;
The lonely star of Bethlehem,
    Led on a bright and glorious day.

Shine on, "Lone Star"! in grief and tears,
    And sad reverses oft baptized;
Shine on amid thy sister spheres;
    Lone stars in heaven are not despised.

Shine on, "Lone Star"! Who lifts his hand
    To dash to earth so bright a gem,
A new "lost pleiad" from the band
    That sparkles in night's diadem?

Shine on, "Lone Star"! The days draw near
    When none shall shine more fair than thou;
Thou, born and nursed in doubt and fear
    Wilt glitter on Immanuel's brow.

Shine on, "Lone Star"! till earth redeemed,
    In dust shall bid its idols fall;
And thousands, where thy radiance beamed,
    Still "crown the Saviour Lord of all."

Appendix 2

The Parental Day Family

Jeremiah Day (1771-1843) married Submit Stearns (d. 4 August 1829)

Children

Betsy (died)
Luke Freeman—served as clerk at Bastard for many years
John Russel (died)
David Vincent and
Jonathan Benson (twins)
Polly Relief (Knowlton)
Rebecca (died)
Sally D. (Alford)
Samuel Stearns (13 May 1808-17 September 1871)—missionary to India
Laura Submit (Bogert)
Nancy Susanna (Holladay)
Sophia (died)

The Samuel Stearns Day Family

Samuel Stearns Day married Roenna Clark (12 October 1809-17 May 1881)
at Homer Village, NY, 23 August 1835

Children

Howard Malcom (6 June 1836-6 July 1902): studied at Shurtleff College,
    Upper Alton, IL (1865); became a pastor
Samuel Clark (11 January 1838-?): captain in the Army during Civil War
Mary Marilla (9 November 1839-14 December 1915): missionary to India
    and
Martha Sophia (twins) (9 November 1839-?): teacher, Wilson Industrial
    School (1865-?)
Ellen Roenna (7 August 1841-?)
William (20-22 August 1843)
James Bacon (15 April 1845-?): dentist

Notes

[1] For example, the following books and pamphlets: Dana M. Albaugh, *Between Two Centuries* (Philadelphia: Judson Press, 1935), 91-93, 102-105; John Craig, *Forty Years Among the Telugus* (Toronto: John Craig, 1908), 12-15; G. W. Hervey, *The Story of Baptist Missions in Foreign Lands* (St. Louis: C. R. Barns, 1892), 735-39; M. L. Orchard and K. S. McLaurin, *The Enterprise* (Toronto: Canadian Baptist Foreign Mission Board, [1924]), 128-31; D. Downie, *A Historical Sketch of the American Baptist Telugu Mission* (Madras: Gantz Brothers, 1879), 2-4; and W. S. McKenzie, *"The Lone Star," A Sketch of the Teloogoo Mission* (Boston: American Baptist Missionary Union, 1893), 4-6.

[2] The diaries, notes, journals, and letters are contained in the "Samuel Stearns Day Collection" (Accession Number 143), Southern Baptist Historical Commission, Nashville, Tennessee. The collection contains 1,358 items in ten boxes covering five linear feet. All quotations and information about Samuel Stearns Day, unless otherwise cited, are from these diaries, notes, journals, and letters. Grandchildren of Samuel Day—Dr. James S. Day, Jr., Spartanburg, SC, and Lt. Col. Malcom Day, Palatka, FL—gave the materials to the Southern Baptist Historical Collections in September 1965.

[3] "History of the Baptist Denomination in the Township of Bastard 1796 to 1934," 4-page MS, Canadian Baptist Archives, McMaster Divinity College, Hamilton, ON (CBA).

[4] Minutes of the Bastard Church (Philipsville, ON), CBA.

[5] Potsdam Academy was a preparatory school for the Hamilton (NY) Literary and Theological Institution. From 1820-39, HLTI offered theology only; from 1839-46, theology and arts. After 1842, HLTI was known as Madison University; the theology department later became Colgate Theological Seminary and finally merged with Rochester Theological Seminary to form Colgate-Rochester Divinity School, Rochester, NY.

[6] Annual Report, *Baptist Missionary Magazine (BMM)* 20, no. 6 (June 1840): 145.

[7] Thomas S. Shenston, *Teloogoo Mission Scrap Book* (Brantford: The Expositor, 1888), 31.

[8] Annual Report, *BMM* 24, no. 7 (July 1844): 214.

[9] *BMM* 16, no. 5 (May 1846): 132.

[10] *BMM* 18, no. 7 (July 1848): 203.

[11] Samuel Stearns Day to S. Peck, Foreign Secretary of the American Baptist Board of Foreign Missions, 13 June 1848, Microfilm FM45-FM46, American Baptist Historical Society (ABHS).

[12] Diary covering 1834-35, attributed to John Eglinton Maxwell, ABHS. Maxwell also has frequent illnesses, usually involving the digestive tract. His potions are not always the same as those Samuel Day uses but his attitude toward and fear of sickness are very like the Canadian Baptist missionary's.

[13] Samuel writes occasionally in an idiosyncratic shorthand. Two complete books in the collection are entirely in this script. Other diaries and some letters also contain shorthand paragraphs. Some members of his family could read the symbols as could a friend in Kitley. Samuel says he wrote some notes in shorthand to Reuben Tupper(?) in Kitley "and thus gave vent to some of my feelings" (Box 6, file 4). The information is closed, however, because several stenographers who have been consulted could not decipher Samuel's version.

[14] Hervey, *Baptist Mission*, chaps. 4 and 5.

[15] Day correspondence with ABMU, Microfilm FM45-FM46, ABHS.

[16] Day to ABMU, 6 January 1838.

[17] Day to ABMU, 30 June 1837.

[18] *BMM* 52, no. 1 (January 1872): 22-4.

[19] Shenston, *Teloogoo Scrap Book*, 28.

Chapter 12

Three Faces of Baptist Fundamentalism in Canada: Aberhart, Maxwell, and Shields

David R. Elliott

Fundamentalists usually depicted themselves as representatives of theological orthodoxy, set against the foes of modernism and infidelity. Yet, upon closer examination we discover that what was paraded as fundamentalism was often a cloak for other activities: seizing power and empire building, or the introduction of theological ideas which had more in common with medieval heresies than with theological conservatism.[1] This was especially the case among Baptist fundamentalists due to the loose ecclesiastical structure of the denomination. This chapter examines the ideas and careers of three separatist fundamentalists—William Aberhart, L. E. Maxwell, and T. T. Shields—who created quite different expressions of Baptist fundamentalism in Canada.

Many of those who described themselves as fundamentalists were often "new men or women." By this is meant that they did not have the same education, social status, or denominational roots as did ministers who remained and worked within the denominational structure. In other words, the average separatist fundamentalist leader had quite a different social background, education, and viewpoint from conventional ministers. Many of the fundamentalist leaders had been raised in homes where organized religion had not been important. One only need think of some of the big names in fundamentalism: D. L. Moody, Billy Sunday, C. I. Scofield, Harry Rimmer, and even Jerry Falwell. When they were converted late in their teens or early adulthood, their religious experience was often informed by ideas that were extradenominational, for example, Plymouth Brethren dispensationalism, British-Israelism, Keswick holiness, or various shades of pentecostalism. These ideas have been described as an "intellectual underworld."[2] Not only did many of the fundamentalist leaders lack a religious upbringing, but they sometimes came from dysfunctional families where alcoholism, neglect, and abuse were common. Because of their economic backgrounds they were often denied access to higher education and sought out substitutes: correspondence courses and Bible colleges. Thus, without the influence of a stable, denominationally centred home life and a traditional theological education, separatist fundamentalists tended to have quite different theologies, eschatologies, worship forms, and ecclesiologies.

While not discounting the validity of their conversions, the newly acquired faith of these future fundamentalists provided them with a means for upward social mobility. They were highly talented and creative individuals. They soon formed independent religious institutions which were very separatistic and autocratic.

I

William Aberhart (1878-1943) was an independent Baptist radio evangelist who became the premier of Alberta from 1935 to 1943. He had been raised on a farm in southwestern Ontario. His father was an illiterate and sometimes sadistic alcoholic who eventually died from a drinking accident.[3] In the census of 1871, his father had given "Lutheran" as his religious affiliation and his mother claimed "Scots Presbyterian;" but neither parent attended church. As a child Aberhart attended the local Presbyterian Sunday School. Some time after a conversion experience, he decided to become a Presbyterian minister; but he lacked the financial resources to pursue that end. Instead, he chose a career as a school teacher and, in 1905, became the principal of Central School in Brantford, Ontario.

While in Brantford, Aberhart became exposed to the "Prophetic Conference" movement and took a Bible correspondence course offered by C. I. Scofield. Dispensationalism became Aberhart's hermeneutical system and D. L. Moody was his theological model. In 1907, as a Presbyterian elder, Aberhart began supply-preaching and teaching Bible classes where apocalyptic themes prevailed.

Aberhart once again considered entering the Presbyterian ministry and began taking a correspondence BA degree from Queen's University. He also received special permission from the General Assembly to take an accelerated divinity program at Knox College once he had his degree completed at Queen's.

In 1910, Aberhart moved to Calgary to assume a new teaching position. He continued his hobby of supply-preaching in a variety of Presbyterian, Methodist, and Baptist churches. But it was not long before his theology ran afoul of ministers at St. Andrew's and Grace Presbyterian churches. So in 1912, he left the Presbyterian Church and dropped his plans for formal theological education.

Aberhart then joined the Methodists, teaching classes at Wesley and Trinity Methodist churches. But by 1916, he had broken with the Methodists and had assumed the leadership of Westbourne Baptist Church, a small mission under the trusteeship of First Baptist Church. There

Aberhart gathered his religious followers, who had floated with him through the succession of earlier Bible classes. The Baptist trustees were unhappy with Aberhart's role in that church because of his theological ideas, his autocratic methods, and the fact that he was not a Baptist. When the trustees and the Home Mission Board ordered Aberhart to leave, Aberhart and the deacons of Westbourne decided to defy them. The power struggle almost became a court case. After the trustees locked Aberhart out of the building, he and the deacons broke off the locks.

Aberhart's theology took another turn in 1920 when he became associated with Harvey McAlister, who brought pentecostalism to Calgary. Aberhart accepted McAlister's ideas of the "Jesus only" baptismal formula and a restored order of apostles. Aberhart was baptized by Rev. James Desson of Heath Baptist Church, who agreed to use the "Jesus only" formula which Aberhart believed was dispensationally correct. Westbourne Baptist Church then went through a "charismatic" phase with the laying on of hands, seeking of divine gifts, speaking in tongues, and divine healing. Rebaptism was practised on those who had been baptized with the Trinitarian formula.

At Westbourne Baptist Church, Aberhart created the Calgary Prophetic Bible Conference, a transdenominational group whose executive came to represent the deacon's board of Westbourne. One of its dominant theological features, besides dispensationalism, was British-Israelism. Aberhart's prophetic interpretations, described by Rev. H. H. Bingham of First Baptist Church as "pathetic," stressed the manifest destiny of Great Britain in future world affairs.

In 1925, Aberhart's Prophetic Conference started to broadcast its meetings over radio station CFCN, then the most powerful station in Alberta. Aberhart used the radio to spread fundamentalism and attack modernism. When T. T. Shields came to Calgary that year, Aberhart hosted his meetings. Aberhart's influence was broadened in 1926 when he created a Radio Sunday School which supplied religious lessons to children scattered across western Canada and the northwestern United States. At its height, the Radio Sunday School had over 9,000 subscribers.

During this time, Aberhart continued to earn his living as a high school principal. He controlled Westbourne Baptist Church as its "apostle" (bishop); but many of the pastoral duties were conducted by Rev. E. G. Hansell, who had recently graduated from the Bible Institute of Los Angeles. When Hansell split from Aberhart in 1926 and took a number of dissidents with him, Westbourne Baptist Church no longer had any connection with the Baptist Union of Western Canada and considered joining with Shields's Regular Baptists. But the two men could not work together; their personalities and ideas clashed too much.

The Calgary Prophetic Bible Institute (CPBI) was built in 1927. It would house Westbourne Baptist Church and the part-time Bible College he had been operating since 1925. Westbourne received the short end of the deal because of the high rent CPBI charged and the church's inability to attract a minister who would abide Aberhart's autocratic control and theological ideas. In 1929, sixty percent of the congregation, including most of the deacons and members of the Prophetic Conference executive, bolted from Aberhart and returned to their old church building and joined the Regular Baptists (later, the Fellowship of Evangelical Baptists [FEBC]).

From among his remaining followers, mostly younger people who did not have deep Baptist roots, Aberhart organized the independent Bible Institute Baptist Church. His peculiar beliefs on baptism, apostleship, premillennialism, and the infallibility of the King James Version became dogma. Aberhart traced his apostolic roots back through the medieval Paulicians and Albigensians, who had a marked dualism in their theology. Their neo-Manichaeism dominated Aberhart's thinking.

CPBI's main purpose was to further the cause of fundamentalism and to promote evangelism in the rural areas. Aberhart had little interest in foreign missions, probably because he could find few mission boards which would meet his theological approval or would accept his graduates. Instead, his students often established branches of the Bible Institute Baptist Church, mainly in Alberta.

When the Great Depression occurred, Aberhart was forced to rethink his earlier otherworldliness. In 1932, he was converted to the economic theories of Social Credit and began preaching a quasi-Social Gospel. In 1935, his Social Credit Party won the provincial election in a landslide victory; and he became premier. He held that position until his death in 1943. While in office, he continued his religious broadcasts and his role as apostle of the Bible Institute Baptist Church and dean of CPBI.

Although Aberhart's theology was broadened by political life, he had little to do with other Baptists. Shields attacked Aberhart's theology and economic views as lunacy. The old wounds from Aberhart's fights with the BUWC had not healed; when his branch church at Innisfail found itself evicted by court order from a building owned by the Baptist Union, Aberhart, who was also the attorney general, coached his followers in defying the court order.

Today CPBI and its successor, Berean Bible College/Foothills Christian College, are no longer in existence. The churches which Aberhart founded continue under the name of the "Gospel Missionary Association" (GMA). The GMA had eleven member churches, in 1987—ten in Alberta, one in the Yukon.[4] The group has not grown due to its doctrinal peculiarity and theological isolation. Currently, its churches individually are discussing mergers with the FEBC and the Baptist General Conference in Canada.

II

One of the best-known Bible institutes in North America exists at Three Hills, Alberta. Its success was largely due to the personality and drive of its principal, *L. E. Maxwell.*[5]

Leslie E. Maxwell (1895-1984) was born on a farm in Kansas and raised in the atmosphere of a pool hall where his father was a part owner. Maxwell described his parents as being irreligious. As a youth he had no career plans but a maternal aunt who was an evangelical Christian got him out of his milieu by securing a job for him in a Kansas City bank. She also took him to the Presbyterian Church where he eventually made a commitment to Christ.

During World War I, Maxwell fought as a corporal in France. Upon his discharge, he desired to attend Moody Bible Institute in Chicago but could not afford to. A Baptist minister pointed him to Midland Bible Institute in Kansas City operated by Rev. William Coat Stevens, a Presbyterian minister who had taught at A. B. Simpson's college at Nyack, New York.

Like Simpson, Stevens was an advocate of Keswick holiness and the idea that divine healing was part of the atonement. The method of Bible study that Stevens taught was very introspective and had little to do with the context of Scripture. After studying with Stevens for three years, Maxwell graduated, was ordained by a Southern Baptist church, and then accepted a position teaching Bible in the small hamlet of Three Hills, Alberta.

Maxwell arrived at Three Hills in 1922; he had eight students, mostly related to the Kirk family, who had requested help from Maxwell's teacher Stevens. After the first year, Maxwell was approached by Bonnie Doon Baptist Church in Edmonton. The congregation wanted him to become their minister, but the BUWC requested that he take more education at the University of Alberta. Maxwell turned down the offer/requirement and remained at Three Hills to establish Prairie Bible Institute (PBI). There he stayed until his death in 1984. Although ordained as a Baptist, Maxwell resisted any denominational control and remained an independent.

PBI was marked by its emphasis on missions and Keswick holiness. By 1976, the school had graduated about 1,800 foreign missionaries and some 1,200 home missionaries.[6] While Maxwell was in charge, the atmosphere of the school was extremely otherworldly. It had cultural aspects of a military camp, a monastery, and a Hutterite colony. Staff members, including Maxwell, did not receive a salary but were provided with room and board and a small honorarium. The unmarried sexes were strictly segregated, puritanical dress codes were enforced, and students were encouraged to live a "crucified" life. In the Bible Institute and the associated high school the writings of the eccentric 17th-century Roman Catholic mystic Madame Guyon were used as texts.[7]

Maxwell's involvement in the fundamentalist-modernist controversy was limited. In his *Prairie Pastor* magazine editorials and his books, Maxwell lambasted worldliness but did not address the wider theological controversies at their height. The main object of his later attack was the United Church of Canada.

Maxwell's main controversy was with Aberhart. Although Maxwell had supplied the pulpit at Westbourne Baptist Church on some occasions for Aberhart, he could not accept Aberhart's theological peculiarities, particularly his British-Israelism and the ultradispensationalism which Maxwell believed caused antinomianism. For his part, Aberhart rejected Maxwell's Keswick holiness. When Aberhart moved into the political arena, a war of words between them flew over the airwaves. Maxwell compared Aberhart to Lot, sitting in the gate of Sodom. Aberhart likened Maxwell to the priest and the Levite leaving the wounded man in the ditch. Maxwell claimed that Aberhart's doctrine of eternal security was "straight out of hell." Maxwell's colleague, J. Fergus Kirk, denounced the candidate for premier for turning from the gospel to socialism and communism.[8]

Maxwell had been trained in dispensationalism but had come to reject many of its tenets. He regarded himself as a partial dispensationalist.[9] He held to a pretribulation rapture eschatology; but he rejected the dichotomies which Scofield and others created. Maxwell objected to their idea that there are two systems of salvation in the Bible: works for Jews and faith for Gentiles. He believed that grace was the operative word in both testaments and that faith and works could not be separated. He claimed that dispensationalism had created a spirit of worldliness through its antinomianism. Like Calvin, he felt that the Old Testament laws did not save a person but were necessary in order to live a righteous life.[10]

With such ideas, not surprisingly, Maxwell was a strong Sabbatarian. This may have been influenced by his use of Seventh-Day Adventist literature. Maxwell demanded strict observance of Sunday as a day of rest. His colleague Kirk, a theonomist, went even further, suggesting that Christians should also observe the Jewish sabbath. Although it was not Maxwell's intent, an atmosphere of legalism pervaded PBI and its graduates.[11]

Maxwell's international influence grew rapidly during the post-war period. A strong percentage of Maxwell's students came from the United States. They learned of his school by word of mouth, through his books which Eerdmans and Moody Press published and sold by the hundreds of thousands, and from his yearly recruiting tours. Those who graduated from PBI were funnelled into "faith" foreign mission organizations.

While the numbers of Maxwell's students were impressive, the quality of their education was another matter. In analyzing the impact of Maxwell's mysticism upon his students, Ian Rennie, a conservative Presbyterian theologian and church historian, has noted that such "very heavy, introspective and morbid preoccupation with how they [could] crucify themselves" had profound psychological effects. Rennie, in a counselling context, found graduates, particularly those who had not become foreign missionaries, suffering from intense guilt, with no sense of identity, no sense of self-worth, unable to relate to the opposite sex in an integrated way, suspicious of other Christians who had different views, and unable to cope with the secular world. This situation was more pronounced after World War II among those who had taken all of their education at PBI.[12]

After Maxwell died in 1984, many of the rigid social rules and emphases began to change. Educational standards have been raised and the staff placed on salary. Yet the future of the institution is in question as the financial support base decreases.

III

The most militant fundamentalist in North America during the first half of this century was *T. T. Shields* of Toronto.[13] Thomas Todhunter Shields (1873-1955) was born in Bristol, England, into a family whose forebears on both sides for several generations had been Anglican ministers. Shields's father was somewhat of a theological maverick. He started his career as an Anglican minister, then switched to the Primitive Methodists and, finally, joined the Baptists.

After his conversion during his teens, Shields decided to follow in his father's footsteps. Without any university, seminary, or even Bible college training, he began to preach. His only theological education was what he had received from his father. He was also influenced by the books of Spurgeon, the famous Baptist schismatic.

After serving a number of Baptist churches in Ontario, Shields was sought by Toronto's Jarvis Street Baptist Church, then the largest and most prestigious Baptist church in the country. In 1910, he accepted the call and remained there for forty-five years. Shields's first decade at Jarvis Street Baptist Church saw his quick rise to prominence within the Baptist Convention of Ontario and Quebec (BCOQ). He had a great command of the English language; and, in spite of his lack of formal theological education, he has been classed among Canada's finest Baptist pulpiteers. Shields was granted honorary doctorates by Temple and McMaster Universities.[14]

By the end of World War I, Shields had become known as a staunch fundamentalist. He appears to have been influenced in that direction by visits he made to England during the war. While there, he was able to fulfil his childhood ambition of preaching in Spurgeon's Tabernacle, supplying the pulpit for several months during the absence of its minister, the American fundamentalist A. C. Dixon, an editor of the *Fundamentals*.

In 1919, Shields began a campaign to impose his views on McMaster University, the BCOQ, the *Canadian Baptist*, and Jarvis Street Baptist Church. When Professor Matthews was about to retire from McMaster, Shields wrote the chancellor expressing his unhappiness with what Matthews had been teaching; unless an orthodox replacement were found, Shields would not give his wholehearted support to the university.[15]

Controversy erupted at Jarvis Street Baptist Church after Shields preached a sermon in February 1921 entitled, "The Christian Attitude Towards Amusements." In it, he condemned theatre and cinema attendance, card-playing, and dancing. He called for the immediate resignations of those Sunday School teachers and deacons who desired to persist in those activities.[16] A number of resignations took place and that incident set in motion the schism which occurred the following year when dissidents left and formed Park Baptist Church.

As time went on, Shields demanded far more powers than traditionally belonged to a Baptist minister. He reorganized the church's finances and got rid of committees. He fired choir directors. He threatened to resign if he did not get his own way. He closed down the women's groups because he opposed "petticoat politics."

Shields's conflict was primarily ecclesiastical. He wanted to impose strict discipline and doctrine upon a denomination which had been known for its personal liberty, the right of each individual Christian to interpret the Bible as one saw fit. He wanted to introduce a creed to which all Baptist ministers had to subscribe. Moreover, he demanded that Canadian Baptists abide by the "Regular Baptist" position of closed membership and closed communion. Anything less was "modernism," no matter that even his hero Spurgeon had not practised restricted communion.[17] Shields spread these views through the *Gospel Witness* magazine which he founded in 1922.

Shields was not a typical fundamentalist. He rejected dispensationalism and premillennialism. He fought pentecostalism, faith healing, and the Keswick movement. He had no use for sensational evangelists such as Oswald J. Smith, a competitor in Toronto.[18]

In 1923, Shields was one of the founders of the Baptist Bible Union, which sought to impose fundamentalism and restricted membership on all Baptist churches on the continent. They staged rump conventions before the sessions of the Canadian, Northern, and Southern Baptist conventions. A year later, Shields organized Toronto Baptist Seminary, which operated out of Jarvis Street Baptist Church. It was to compete with the theological faculty at McMaster. Because of Shields's disruptive activities, his maligning of denominational officials, and his organization of a rival mission board, he and his supporters were read out of the BCOQ in 1927. He then established his own denomination, the "Regular Baptists." Some seventy-six Baptist churches left the Convention and joined Shields's new denomination.

Besides his seminary at Jarvis Street Baptist Church, Shields influenced the Baptist Bible Union to take over a Baptist-owned university in Des Moines, Iowa. This was to take the place of McMaster. Shields became its acting president and commuted on a weekly basis from Toronto. But due to repeated faculty controversies and student riots over Shields's leadership, the state was forced to close the institution in 1929.[19]

Controversy was never very far from Shields. A major schism occurred in the Regular Baptist Convention of Ontario and Quebec in 1931 over Shields's dictatorial control over the denomination. Dissidents left and created the Fellowship of Independent Baptist Churches.

Shields had little to offer to people suffering from the Great Depression. He saw it as a judgment of God and rejected the panaceas of socialism, the New Deal, and Social Credit. Politically, Shields was a conservative, although he was not a party member. He praised the heavy-handed measures taken against the "On-to-Ottawa" trekkers by R. B. Bennett in 1935 and Mitch Hepburn's use of special police against the striking Oshawa auto workers in 1937. Shields even expressed enthusiasm for the leadership of Hitler and Mussolini; but that enthusiasm waned after the "Night of the Long Knives" in 1934 and the rape of Ethiopia in 1935.

Shields became heavily involved in Ontario politics beginning in 1934. He had voted for Hepburn's Liberal party because of the Conservatives' liquor policies. However, when Hepburn became even more liberal and introduced beverage rooms, Shields proclaimed another crusade which he said would continue until Hepburn was removed from office. Later, when Hepburn extended funding to separate schools, Shields perceived an international Roman Catholic conspiracy. Shields's statements on Roman Catholicism became increasingly paranoid. He saw the Vatican behind the Spanish Civil War and Mussolini's invasion of Ethiopia. He claimed that both Hitler and Canada's justice minister, Ernest Lapointe, were taking their orders from the Vatican.

Shields's anti-Roman Catholicism became his dominant theme during World War II. His attacks on Hepburn, George Drew, Mackenzie King, Quebec, and the Roman Catholic Church became so outrageous that Shields was condemned in parliamentary debates. In 1941, he formed the Canadian Protestant League to fight Roman Catholic influence in Canada.[20] With the help of the Orange Lodge, his Protestant Party contested the Ontario provincial election in 1945.

Shields intruded into the affairs of the Presbyterian Church when he supported the defrocked Presbyterian minister Perry Rockwood of Truro, Nove Scotia. In 1947, he condemned the Presbyterian hierarchy for modernism and raised money so that Rockwood could build a new church.[21] About the same time, Shields linked up with another Presbyterian renegade,

Carl McIntyre. In 1948, they formed the International Council of Christian Churches to oppose the World Council of Churches, which they believed was soft on modernism, Roman Catholicism, and communism.

All these "anti-"crusades took a heavy toll upon Jarvis Street Baptist Church and the Regular Baptist denomination. In 1949, Shields fired the dean of Toronto Baptist Seminary, W. Gordon Brown, who then formed another institution, Central Baptist Seminary. At the annual convention of the Regular Baptists in 1949, Shields was deposed as president of the denomination. He withdrew and formed another denomination, the Conservative Regular Baptist Association of Canada. Shields continued to preach at Jarvis Street Baptist Church until 1954. He remained the power behind the pulpit until his death the next year. Carl McIntyre conducted the funeral.

Over the years, Shields had attracted many followers to his causes because of his powerful personality; but they did not stay with him for long. Few people could work closely with him. His autocratic behaviour alienated them. He had the potential of becoming one of Canada's greatest Baptist ministers; his 1923 sermon, "Other Little Ships," demonstrated that potential.[22] But after he had sunk himself in the modernist-fundamentalist controversy, his pastoral ministry was weakened. Louis Fowler, a 1925 theological student at McMaster, recently defected from Aberhart's organization in Calgary, noted that a sense of worship was lacking in Shields's meetings.[23]

Shields had a mean spirit. He maligned and defamed the character of almost everyone who crossed his path, many times only on the basis of inaccurate newspaper stories. He seldom apologized for his actions. He was a religious anarchist, accepting the authority of no one. His extreme individualism led to paranoia. He saw conspiracies behind others' failures and mistakes, never giving them the benefit of the doubt. Professor Marshall of McMaster, while under attack by Shields's paper, the *Gospel Witness*, said, "in...so far as I have read it, I found very little of the gospel, and very little witness except false witness."[24]

Yet, of his fundamentalist contemporaries, Shields was the most theologically astute. His critiques of the *Scofield Reference Bible* and dispensationalism were most penetrating and pre-dated the better-known works of Oswald T. Allis and Clarence Bass.[25] Shields had rejected most of the other aspects of the intellectual underworld of fundamentalism as well, except for its neo-Manichaean world view.

In all of Shields's causes, there was an element of truth; but his intemperate language quickly distorted the issues. What is certain is that Shields was attempting to change Baptist tradition by imposing a creedal structure. Shields was temperamentally unsuited for the Baptist ministry. His calls for local church autonomy were not consistent. He wanted that for himself but not for others. Shields really desired a confessional church; yet he was not prepared to accept the Westminster Confession, a creed with which he had much in common, nor to cooperate except on his own terms. Shields's campaigns against "modernism" split the Baptist community in Canada and the United States so badly that fellowship has not yet been fully restored. His tirades against McMaster University still prejudice even some mainline Baptists against it. His activities created Baptist sects in Canada. In 1953, two of the groups which had broken with Shields, the Fellowship of Independent Baptist Churches and the Regular Baptists of Ontario and Quebec, united to form the FEBC; this organization's numbers were increased in 1965 when the Regular Baptist Convention of Western Canada also joined. The Conservative Regular Baptist Association of Canada, which remained with Shields, contains only ten churches.

Critics in various quarters felt that Shields would have been satisfied only by being a pope. Shields suggested as much in 1932 when he commented on Pius XI's encyclical calling for Christian unity. "I am not aware that this Encyclical was marked 'R.S.V.P.', and yet such an invitation certainly merits some reply.... I was thinking, Brother Brown, that if certain allegations were true, I might have entitled my address this evening, 'The Word of One Pope to Another.'"[26]

These three Baptist fundamentalists in Canada demonstrate the prima donna nature of fundamentalism and how little it had to do with Baptist theology and polity. It was a movement which misused the Baptist concept of ecclesiastical autonomy to exercise power and introduce theological ideas—dispensationalism, pentecostalism, Keswick holiness, and British-Israelism—which were not part of the established creeds of Christendom.

Notes

[1] The theme of the medieval roots of fundamentalism has been developed in David R. Elliott, "Studies of Eight Canadian Fundamentalists" (PhD diss., University of British Columbia, 1989), chap. 2.

[2] John Maynard Keynes used the term "intellectual underworld" to describe heretical ideas in economics; I have applied the term to the theological periphery. See Elliott, "Eight Fundamentalists," chap. 2.

[3] For Aberhart's career and theology, see David R. Elliott and Iris Miller, *Bible Bill: A Biography of William Aberhart* (Edmonton: Reidmore Books, 1987).

[4] Interview with Rev. George Francisco, Calgary, AB, 11 July 1987.

[5] A biography of L. E. Maxwell is yet to be published; the closest thing is an authorized history of Prairie Bible Institute: Phillip Keller, *Expendable: The Story of Prairie Bible Institute* (Three Hills: Prairie Press, 1972). See also Elliott, "Eight Fundamentalists," chap. 10.

[6] Interview with L. E. Maxwell, Three Hills, AB, 22 December 1976.

[7] See George Balsama, "Madame Guyon, Heterodox...," *Church History* 42 (1973): 350-65.

182   Memory and Hope

[8] L. E. Maxwell, "Mr. Lot and His Government Job," *Prairie Pastor*, March/April 1938; Aberhart's CFCN broadcasts, 21 and 28 April 1935, W. Norman Smith Papers, file 82, Glenbow-Alberta Archives, Calgary; interview with Mrs. Evelyn Street, Calgary, 1973; and J. Fergus Kirk, "Social Credit and the Word of God," mimeographed, 1935.

[9] Interview with L. E. Maxwell, Three Hills, AB, 16 April 1979.

[10] L. E. Maxwell, *Crowded to Christ* (Grand Rapids, MI: Wm. B. Eerdmans, 1950), 333, 230-31, 248-49, 325, 349.

[11] *Prairie Pastor*, August 1939, 3; Maxwell, *Crowded to Christ*, 340-52; and J. F. Kirk, *Who Must Keep the Sabbath?* (Three Hills, AB: J. F. Kirk, n.d.), 23.

[12] Ian Rennie, "The Doctrine of Man in the Bible Belt," lecture, Calgary, 1977(?) (copy from Regent College, Vancouver, BC).

[13] See Elliott, "Eight Fundamentalists," chap. 7.

[14] G. Gerald Harrop, "The Era of the 'Great Preacher' among Canadian Baptists: A Comparative Study of W. A. Cameron, John J. MacNeil, and T. T. Shields as Preachers," *Foundations* 23, no. 1 (1980): 58.

[15] T. T. Shields, letter to A. L. McCrimmon, 3 May 1919; reprinted in *Gospel Witness*, 15 October 1925, 4-7.

[16] *Gospel Witness*, 19 August 1922, 1-7.

[17] See A. C. Underwood, *A History of the English Baptists* (London: The Carey Kingsgate Press, 1947), 205.

[18] T. T. Shields, "The Plague of Religious Quackery," *Gospel Witness*, 2 October 1930, 6-14.

[19] George S. May, "Des Moines University and Dr. T.T. Shields," *Iowa Journal of History* 54 (1956): 193-232.

[20] Donald A. Wicks, "T. T. Shields and the Canadian Protestant League" (MA thesis, University of Guelph, ON, 1971).

[21] *Gospel Witness*, 13 March 1947, 1-4.

[22] T. T. Shields, *Other Little Ships* (Toronto: Hunter-Rose, 1935).

[23] Louis Fowler, "Jarvis Street," *McMaster Monthly* (November 1925); reprinted in *Gospel Witness*, 3 December 1925, 8-11.

[24] *Toronto Star*, 2 February 1926; reprinted in *Gospel Witness*, 4 February 1926, 11.

[25] Oswald T. Allis, *Prophecy and the Church* (Nutley, NJ: Presbyterian and Reformed Publishing, 1945); and Clarence B. Bass, *Backgrounds to Dispensationalism: Its Historical Genesis and Ecclesiastical Implications* (Grand Rapids, MI: Baker Book House, 1960).

[26] T. T. Shields, "The Pope's Encyclical," *Gospel Witness*, 3 January 1932, 5. Cf. *Toronto Star*, 21 April 1947; reprinted in *Gospel Witness*, 24 April 1947, 4.

Chapter 13

The Irony of Fundamentalism:
T. T. Shields and the Person of Christ

Mark Parent

Clark Pinnock, on the issue of differing views of biblical authority within the Believers' Church tradition, rather grudgingly confesses:

> There have been disturbing shifts on the conservative side too, which must not go unnoticed lest we leave a badly distorted impression. Undoubtedly, the most serious weakness here is the significant shift in the list of preferred tests of orthodoxy from, what do you think of Jesus? to, what do you think of the Bible?[1]

To write about North American fundamentalism is to write about a movement which most scholars feel is primarily defined by its attitude towards, and interpretation of, the Bible. Morris Ashcraft, a Southern Baptist theologian, expresses this common scholarly interpretation:

> It seems to me that fundamentalist theology is a theology of one major doctrine—the inerrancy of the biblical autographs. Whether we encounter it during the period of 1880-1925 among the older fundamentalists or in 1980 among the Neo-Evangelicals, the first point on which all others depend is the inerrant Bible in its original manuscripts.[2]

From his study of North American fundamentalism Martin Marty agrees: "not all fundamentalists were to be pretribulationist or dispensationalist or premillennialist, but all were inerrantist."[3]

Early scholars of the fundamentalist movement set the stage for this interpretation of fundamentalism as a movement which was based on an inerrantistic approach towards the Hebrew and Christian Scriptures. Norman Furniss, for example, underscored the foundational nature of the Bible within fundamentalism: "To the Fundamentalists, religious beliefs formed a pyramid, each tenet resting on the one below, with the infallible Bible as the broad foundation; to reshape one block, to remove another, would send the whole structure crashing to the ground."[4]

When Ernest Sandeen published his revisionist history of fundamentalism in 1970, he corrected many of the caricatures of the early scholars such as Furniss and Cole; but he retained this emphasis upon the centrality of the Bible within fundamentalist thought: "What made the fundamentalist theology of biblical authority so critical in the development of the Fundamentalist-Modernist controversy was the fundamentalist insistence upon this doctrine as the foundation of all Christian faith."[5] So crucial for fundamentalists was this emphasis on the centrality of an inerrant Bible that, along with a premillennial interpretation of eschatology, it constituted, in Sandeen's view, *the* definition of fundamentalism:

> A firm trust and belief in every word of the Bible in an age when scepticism was the rule and not the exception—this has been both the pride and the scandal of Fundamentalism. Faith in an inerrant Bible as much as an expectation of the second advent of Christ has been the hallmark of the fundamentalist.[6]

While these two fundamental characteristics of premillenialism and inerrantism existed in symbiotic relationship, in the last analysis, it was the inerrantism of fundamentalism which formed "the central question of fundamentalist historiography."[7]

Fundamentalist and evangelical scholars of the present have also depicted biblical inerrantism as one, if not the primary, definition of fundamentalism. Jerry Falwell counted twenty-seven articles in *The Fundamentals* dealing with the Bible, nine with apologetics, eight with the person of Christ, and only three with the Second Coming of Christ. Thus, J. I. Packer affirmed that "Jesus Christ constituted Christianity a religion of biblical authority."[8] James Barr summarizes what scholars, both those critical of fundamentalism and those supportive of it, feel was (and is) the central issue within fundamentalist thought: "For fundamentalists the Bible is more than the source of veracity for their religion, more than the essential source or textbook. It is part of the religion itself, indeed it is practically the center of the religion, the essential nuclear point from which lines of light radiate into every practical aspect."[9]

The Early Shields and the Bible: 1894-1918

This chapter on Thomas Todhunter Shields, one of the pre-eminent fundamentalist leaders of the 1920s,[10] attempts to show that the claim that the Bible was central to the thought of the *early* Shields is incorrect. More accurate, in this respect, would be Carl Henry's observation that: "The older apologetic was less hesitant to begin with Christ—not because it sought to detach Christology from bibliology, but because it sensed the danger that biblicism might seem to ascribe superiority to some principle other than the Christological."[11] A careful reading of the extant Shields material at the Jarvis Street Baptist Church in Toronto makes it clear that the person and work of Christ dominate his theology until the start of his

Jarvis Street ministry in 1910 or, more probably, until the end of World War I. This early Christological stress means that the common fundamentalist assumption concerning the stability of the doctrine which leading fundamentalists such as Shields expounded can, in this one case at least, no longer be supported. It underscores the important need for this chapter. If the person of Christ, rather than an inerrant Bible, formed the core of Shields's faith in his early years, when did inerrantism become central in his thinking; and what shape did it take?

To deny an inerrantist approach to the Bible in his pre-Jarvis Street years of ministry is not, however, to claim that Shields ever held to any theory of inspiration other than a conservative one. Shields himself, during the war years when his theology hardened and a form of "puritanism"[12] began to dominate, confessed: "once a pauper—was liberal enough, now a child of God I find myself getting more conservative all the time."[13] There is, however, no evidence of such liberalism and certainly no evidence of it with regard to his view of scriptural authority and interpretation. An 1898 sermon serves as an example of his conservatism. After noting that the Bible was written by human beings, Shields continued: "But God told these men just exactly what words to write.... Do you think God would ever tell a lie? No, the Bible says He 'cannot lie.' Then if God cannot lie and the Bible be His word, every word in the Bible must be true."[14]

This conservative approach, while containing the seeds of a full-blown inerrantism, was held in check, however, during his early ministry by the centrality of the person of Christ. While commenting on the Bible's relationship to modern scientific discoveries, Shields asserted in 1899:

> The Bible is God's word concerning sin and salvation. It is not so much His word concerning the sun and the moon and the stars, and this earth of ours, in their relation to each. This Book will ever be found to be in harmony with the true philosophy of things, and will never be at variance with science save that which is "falsely so-called," *but, notwithstanding, it is not to be regarded as a textbook on these things but solely as a textbook treating of sin and salvation* (emphasis added).[15]

Although Shields understood that God had written three books—i.e., nature, providence, and the Bible—the Bible "is the best book of the three; it is the best because it is the plainest and because it is the completest." It alone was God's "infallible revelation of His will."[16] But God's will was not that the Bible be the focal point of Christian faith and all human knowledge, rather that the person of Jesus the Christ form the focus of Christian faith.

In spite of his conservative interpretation of biblical inspiration, then, biblical revelation was secondary to the person and work of Christ in the pre-Jarvis Street years. The fact that the Bible should be treated only as a textbook on sin and salvation was one indication of the limits with which Shields approached the Scriptures. The other more important limit was that

the Bible merely witnessed to the salvation which could only be found in
the person and work of Jesus the Christ.

> Now my friends I cannot see what possible help the Bible can afford
> if you are "without Christ." Indeed if I were this moment without
> Christ, and if I had no hope that he could ever be mine, I think I
> should wish with all my heart that there be no Bible.... [W]ithout
> Christ the Bible is the most terrible book in the world.[17]

Two other closely connected factors which were influential in
tempering the "bibliolatry" of which fundamentalism is often accused
should also be noted. In the first instance, Shields distinguished between the
literal meaning of a given text and its spiritual significance. Such an
approach could have resulted in extravagant allegorizations except for the
fact that, according to Shields, the literal meaning and its spiritual
significance were not opposed to each other. "While it is a fact that the
narratives of the Old and New Testaments are literally true, they also have
a spiritual signification; and that while one may profit by the application of
its literal meaning, the deeper and more lasting benefits are ours when its
meaning is spiritually applied."[18]

This distinction between the literal meaning and the spiritual
significance was in harmony with the second factor: Shields used a
typological approach to interpret the Old Testament. "In contrast to the
Hellenistic or Alexandrian variety of allegorical exegesis, biblical typology
seeks to disclose genuinely historical patterns within the scriptural
framework; there must be a real and intelligible correspondence between
type and antitype."[19] Typological interpretation appeared early in Shields's
preaching. In an 1897 sermon on Canticles, a book of which he was
particularly fond, he wrote: "In the text under the figure of a shepherd girl
seeking her beloved, who also is a shepherd, there is most beautifully set
for the mutual attraction of Christ and His Church, that is to say the mutual
love of Christ and the believer."[20]

Such an approach coupled with a willingness to differentiate between
the literal meaning and the spiritual significance helped (in spite of Shields's
adherence to a conservative interpretation of the inspiration of Scripture) to
maintain a Christological centrality rather than a biblical centrality within
Shields's early theology.

As Shields was drawn deeper and deeper into theological controversy
as the 20th century unfolded, however, the role of the Bible began to
dominate over that of the person of Christ. In a 1905 sermon, he
acknowledged that the Bible was a "natural" book but insisted that it
contained a supernaturalism as well: "And so this Book is very natural. It
was written by men of flesh and blood as we are, by men who were born
as we are, who lived and died as we shall die. *And yet this book glows with
a supernatural fire*" (emphasis added).[21]

This emphasis on the supernatural was never absent from Shields's outlook on Christian faith. During his years at Adelaide Street Baptist Church in London, Ontario, however, it began to be a key factor in his preaching and teaching as he moved steadily and surely in a more conservative theological direction.

Nonetheless, it was not his experience at Adelaide Street but the impact of World War I which confirmed Shields in his conservatism and propelled him in the direction of a full-blown inerrantism. With respect to German biblical criticism, the war provided Shields with a ready-made opportunity to link German biblical scholarship with German militarism:

> I am bound to confess that I have long believed that German critics of the Bible were not intellectually honest, that their antagonism towards the written word was dictated by motives similar to those which inspired the Pharisees to conspire to crucify the Word Incarnate; they were moved by a natural bias against the principles which Christ exemplified, and which the Bible proclaims.[22]

It was this revelation of the true motives behind German biblical criticism which caused Shields to adopt a very positive stance towards the lessons which he hoped that the war would teach the Canadian people. One of those lessons, and increasingly the most important, was the supposed effect that the war would have in stemming what Shields saw to be a growing loss of confidence in the biblical text. It was Shields's firm belief, during the early part of the war, that the war experience would not only put a halt to this disillusionment with the Bible but would also undergird the importance of the Bible as a universal text which transcended and judged all races and all nationalities. In a 1915 sermon, he affirmed his confidence in the triumph of the Bible in terms which would also serve as his self-perception when he waged his own war against modernism in the 1920s:

> And in the sphere of human activity, this Book will be restored to its place. And men will return from their speculations to the life of faith, and from their philosophical vagaries to the verities of revelation. And the army of the Lord will go forth to battle armed with the weapon tried and true; and where human pride would fain have ruled, this Sceptre of Truth shall prevail.[23]

In spite of centring on the Bible as *the weapon* for use against the enemies of spiritual truth, though, Shields still spoke in 1915 in terms which, on the surface, managed to keep the Bible in a secondary and supportive role with centrality continuing to be accorded to the person of Christ: "After all that men have said and written against it [i.e., the Bible] it is still the one Book which is worth reading at such a time as this. *And it is all because it enshrines the Person of the Universal Man, who is also the Universal King*" (emphasis added).[24]

The Later Shields and the Bible

The new prominence which the Bible received within Shields's theology following World War I was clearly evident in the sermons which he preached and in the addresses which he delivered. In an address entitled "What Some Baptists Are Determined to Stand For," delivered in October 1922, Shields outlined some fundamental principles on which Baptist believers had to make their stand. Revealingly, the first principle was the inspiration and authority of the Scriptures, and it was only in the second instance that there came an insistence upon the essential deity of Jesus.[25]

This secondary role for Christ, as compared to a primary role for the scriptures, was accompanied by a growing tendency to speak about the Bible as if it were a living being: "This Book clearly makes a distinction between those who believe and those who do not believe. This book clearly tells us that there is salvation in Christ; and that apart from Christ there is no salvation."[26]

It was, apparently, the Bible rather than the risen Christ which was seen by Shields to be the living word of God. In a personal declaration of war against the enemies of orthodox faith, Shields cried out in February 1922: "To me this Bible is the word of God which liveth and abideth forever. I have ceased to be diplomatic with those who endeavour to undermine men's faith in the book. I count them the enemies of the souls of men."[27] Similarly, he affirmed nearly four years later:

> If it were possible to gather every single copy of this Book and make one great bonfire of it so that there should not be left anywhere upon earth a solitary copy of the Word of God, God could produce it again the next morning without one jot or tittle omitted, for He has a copy which He keeps Himself: "Forever, O Lord, thy word is settled in heaven."[28]

His spirited testimony concerning the centrality of the Scriptures continued to coexist with language which affirmed the centrality of Christ. It was, however, a centrality which functioned, increasingly, on only a theoretical and abstract level. The war with modernism was waged around the issue of biblical interpretation; and this meant that while the centrality of Christ was still affirmed, this affirmation was so clearly secondary to the focus on the Scriptures that as early as March 1923, while speaking to the student body of Gordon College in Boston, Shields had to remind them of the priority of the person of Christ: "Where then is our spiritual morn—our magnetic pole—our pole star, our morning sun? The Bible? Primarily, No! Are you surprised! Our standard is the God-Man Jesus Christ. *What I know of Him I know through the Bible.*"[29]

This screening function of the Scriptures, this insistence that what is known about Christ is known only through the Scriptures, along with an emphasis on the essential deity of Christ, distanced Christ from his people. As Shields asked rhetorically: "What do you know about Christ? Nothing apart from the Book. What do you know about the will of God? Nothing apart form the Book. What do you know about the divine pattern, what God wants you to be? Nothing apart from the Book."[30]

Shields's inconsistency with respect to natural revelation, which at times he affirmed and which at other times he seemed to deny, may be explained by this elevation of the Bible as the pre-eminent medium of revelation. Christ became more and more hidden behind the written word, more and more distanced from humanity; and so the voice of the risen Christ who testifies to the heart of believer and non-believer alike was largely muzzled. Christ was, in effect, imprisoned within the Scriptures.

Of course, he would not have explained it in this fashion. To him there was a dynamic, complementary interchange between Christ and the Scriptures. Christ was the theme of the Scriptures from beginning to end:

> This book from Genesis to Revelation has but one theme—properly understood, the Bible speaks only of Jesus Christ.... Every matter of which the Bible treats is related to the Person and Work of our Lord Jesus Christ.... Every word spoken before the advent of our Lord was a preparation for His coming, and everything recorded in this Book subsequent to His appearance amongst men is an explanation of that appearance.[31]

Thus, the circular justification of authority which Shields adhered to was that the Bible testified to and, thereby, authenticated Christ who testified to and, in turn, authenticated the Bible:

> Thus, as to motive, it comes to this: that our relationship to the Author of the Book will determine our relationship to the Book itself. It is inevitable: if we are rightly related to the Author we shall be rightly related to the Book; if we love the Author we shall love the Book; if we understand the Author in some measure we shall understand the Book; and understanding the Book we shall understand Him better.[32]

This circular argumentation concerning Christ and the Bible, it should be emphasized, occurred often within Shields's post-1918 sermons. Another instance of it was in his book of sermons on the trial of Jesus:

> You cannot consider the questions relating to the Person of Christ,—whence He came, who He is, wither He has gone, whether He is coming again,—without, at the same time, being forced to consider the bearing of their answer upon the Bible. All these questions are directly related to the Bible. On the other hand, you cannot consider any question in respect to the trustworthiness of the Scriptures, or in respect to anything of which it speaks, you cannot consider the Bible from any aspect without, by that consideration, being at last driven to ponder this question, Is Jesus the Christ?[33]

Closely related to this reciprocal relationship was the accompanying insistence that if one aspect of the biblical witness was shown to be untrue, then the whole edifice of biblical inspiration and, therefore, of Christian faith crumbled: "Well then, if it be true, it is a Book of divine origin, for it claims that for itself. It is either all that it claims to be, or else it is utterly valueless; and if it be divinely inspired, then this Bible is in a class by itself."[34]

In light of the intimate connection between Christ and the Scriptures, a connection in which Christ, while ostensibly being primary was practically relegated to a secondary position, as well as the assertion that if even one "error" was detected in the biblical text then the text was utterly valueless, it is little wonder that Shields fought with such vigour against modernist teachings. In his analysis, modernism undermined Christ indirectly by undermining the Scriptures directly:

> The cardinal principle of modernism is that it denies the divine inspiration and authority of the Word of God, the Bible. You may seek to evade it as much as you will, but that is the foundation of the whole matter: modernism denies that the Scriptures are divinely inspired, that they are the Word of God.[35]

Shields's description of the "Bible" (always capitalized) as the "Word of God" (also always capitalized) is curious in light of the Bible's own testimony to Christ as the Word of God and in light of Luther's distinction between the living Word contained within the written Bible. Karl Barth has popularized this distinction in contemporary theology by his differentiation between the living Word, the written word, and the preached word. Unlike some modern conservative-evangelical scholars who recognize Christ as the Word but who refuse to allow any cognitive dissonance between the living Word and the written word,[36] Shields always spoke in his post-1918 sermons of the Bible as the Word of God. As God's Word to humanity, it was completely true in all aspects: "This is my confession of faith: I believe the Bible to be the Word of God; I believe it to be so completely God's Word, that it is not only without error in respect to its spiritual message but that in matters of science and history, and of everything of which it treats it is the truth."[37]

As God's Word, the Bible was identified so closely with Christ in Shields's theology following the First World War that the two could be spoken of as if they were one, spoken of interchangeably:

> My Brethren, let us take courage! As there was no sepulchre which could hold the Incarnate Word, so there are no means by which this Bible can be destroyed. The original is kept where the alleged "assured results" of the critics have no weight: forever God's Word is settled in heaven! And when heaven shall be opened, and the Rider of the White Horse shall come down [from] the skies, He shall be

clothed in a vesture dipped in blood: and His name is called the Word of God.[38]

This conflation, this imprisonment, this displacement of the living Word by the written word meant that, for Shields after World War I, the Bible became the mediator between God and humanity, rather than Christ. As Shields put it in January 1933: "Fundamental to everything is this principle: *I approach the discussion as one who believes, without any reservations in the divine inspiration, infallibility and supreme authority, of the Bible as being the very Word of the living God. To me, this Book is the* supreme authority."[39]

In its displacement of Christ as the supreme authority within Christian faith, the Bible also was treated in a docetic fashion in much the same way as the person of Christ had been previously depicted. Shields's tendency to approach the Bible with docetic presumptions was directly based, then, on his treatment of the person of Christ. In his view, any kenotic element within Christ led inevitably to "open unitarianism." With all talk of Christ's kenosis being declared heretical, however, it was unavoidable that Christ's humanity would be viewed as a mere cloak which the essential Deity only assumed in a functionalistic manner.[40]

Writing about the supernaturalism of the Scriptures, Shields fell into the same trap. He meant to defend the humanity of the Scriptures.

> Now, divine inspiration does not destroy the peculiar characteristics of the personality through whom it speaks. As for instance, let us suppose there are different colours in these windows; there may be blue and purple and violet and yellow and red; and the morning sun streams through these coloured glasses. It is all sunlight, but it is coloured by the medium through which it shines.[41]

But the humanity of the Scriptures, like the humanity of Christ, was overwhelmed by Shields's stress on the supernaturalism of the Bible. In spite of the example of the coloured glass which presumably could not only change the colours of the sun but also, through defects in the glass, block the sunlight, in the last analysis, the Bible was seen by Shields as a "supernatural Book from beginning to end." Indeed, the Bible was so absolutely unique that it "could not be more utterly unlike every other book had it *literally dropped from the skies*" (emphasis added).[42]

An Assessment

"Irony" is the term with which Martin Marty characterizes modern American religion. Basing his analysis on Reinhold Niebuhr's influential use of irony to describe American history, the current dean of American church historians depicts the events in the religious history of the United

States between 1893 and 1919 as fitting the *Oxford English Dictionary* definition: "a condition of affairs or events as if in mockery of the promise and fitness of things."[43]

This concept is particularly applicable when considering Shields's Christology and its impact on his view of the Bible. It is supremely ironic that Shields, motivated by a strong desire to uphold the centrality of Christ against modernist reductions, ended up displacing Christ with the Bible. This, of course, was not unique to Shields, although he certainly was a leader in this movement and, as such, responsible for lending some credence to the charge of "bibliolatry" with which fundamentalism has been so often accused. John Dozois attempts to defend Shields from this charge of bibliolatry:

> One thing is certain. He possessed deep affection for the Bible, and believed its teachings were meant to be taken seriously. This accounts, to great extent, for his militant opposition to those he felt were undermining its message and authority. But to charge him with Bibliolatry is to misunderstand the nature of the love he had for "the Book." What concerned him was that the Modernists seemed to be reducing "the Book" to the level of all other books. Today we can see that his fears were not without foundation.[44]

Dozois has understated the high place of the Bible within Shields's theology in the years following World War I. Nonetheless, he is correct in rejecting the charge of bibliolatry. That has been the charge attached to various Protestants from the Reformation onward. The slogan "the bible and the bible only is the religion of Protestants"[45] has led many to conclude that certain elements within Protestantism, if not all of it, fell into an unhealthy veneration and use of the Scriptures. It is an accusation which has been levelled more recently against the fundamentalists. With its pejorative usage over the years, it is not a particularly helpful term for trying to understand and evaluate Shields's attitude toward the Bible.

That is not to say that Shields did not, at times, veer close to treating the Bible as some sort of paper god. It has been shown how, following World War I, the Bible began to displace Christ as the authority within Shields's theology. Moreover, the fact that Shields treated Christ's humanity in monophysitic and docetic terms meant that when the Bible supplanted Christ, it also took on a supernatural character which, in effect, negated any human element in the Christian Scriptures. This, of course, did not bother Shields and was, in fact, what attracted him to the Bible as the weapon of warfare against what he took to be modernistic reductionism and denial of the essential deity of Christ.

Shields's treatment of the Bible, however, should be of great concern; for it is essentially a mistreatment. Otto Weber delineates what happens to the Bible within fundamentalism in this way:

Just as in the Roman Church and theology the Word as event is subsumed into the Word of the Church, this happens in the Protestant realm with the Bible. The result is that the Bible is made the object of a similar apotheosis as that of the Church in the Roman world. This tendency can be seen anew and in a more extreme form in modern Fundamentalism; faith in God in Christ becomes faith in the infallibility of the Bible (naturally, the two are identified but the latter absorbs the former in practice).[46]

T. F. Torrance addressed this absorption or supplanting of Christ by the Scriptures in his 1981 Payton Lectures delivered at the Fuller Theological Seminary. In his analysis:

Fundamentalism stumbles, not so much at the consubstantial relation between Jesus Christ and God the Father, at least so far as his person is concerned, but at the consubstantial relation between the free continuous act of God's self-communication and the living content of what he communicates, especially when this is applied to divine revelation in and through the Holy Scriptures.[47]

According to Torrance, then, fundamentalism operates within a dualistic and static framework which:

cuts off the revelation of God in the Bible from God himself and his continuous selfgiving through Christ and in the Spirit, so that the Bible is treated as a self-contained corpus of divine truths in propositional form endowed with an infallibility of statement which produces the justification felt to be needed for the rigid framework of belief within which fundamentalism barricades itself.[48]

This means that "the living reality of God's self-revelation through Jesus Christ and in the Spirit is in point of fact made secondary to the Scriptures."[49]

Torrance's critique is confirmed by the movement of Shields's thought from a stress on the person of Christ to a stress on the Bible. What has clearly been shown, however, is that simply to shift a greater emphasis back to the person and work of Christ will not solve the conundrum which fundamentalism creates. That is to say, not only must the displacement of Christ by the Bible be corrected, but the fundamentalist tendency towards docetism and monophysitism must also be changed, since it was this monophysitic, docetic view of the person of Christ which, in Shields's theology at least, was the key element in his interpretation of the Scriptures.

An analysis of the thought of T. T. Shields leads to the important insight that, although fundamentalists and evangelicals must re-evaluate static, propositional views of divine revelation, they must also, and perhaps more importantly, re-evaluate what it means to claim that Jesus Christ was simultaneously God and Man if the centrality of the living Christ is to be authentically restored to conservative Christianity.

It should be unnecessary to comment that this is mystery that can never be fully understood. Nonetheless, it is possible to correct misunderstandings of the orthodox Christology of Chalcedon and to affirm the centrality of the person of Christ within all valid expressions of Christian faith. All evangelical beliefs should "point away from themselves to Jesus Christ alone as their truth and thereby acknowledge their own inadequacy and deficiency before him."[50]

Shields's evangelical beliefs failed to point away from themselves to the person of Jesus Christ because he moved from a Trinitarian to a Christomonistic position in which Christ was defined in monophysitic and docetic terms. This so distanced the Redeemer from humanity that Christ's mediatorial role (which is one of the essential truths preserved by the stress on Christ as very God and very Man) was lost and a vacuum was left into which Shields placed the Scriptures, which were treated in the same manner as he once had treated the person of Christ. It seems inevitable, then, that when Christ is torn apart and treated either as God alone (Shields's "essential deity") or as the supreme example of man (the pitfall of much of liberal Christology), in time, he no longer is the central truth of faith beyond which, as Jacques Ellul put it, "there is nothing—nothing but lies."[51]

Notes

NB: A version of this chapter appears under the same title in *Fides et Historia* 26 (Fall 1994): 42-57.

[1] C. H. Pinnock, "Biblical Authority, Past and Present, in the Believers' Church Tradition," in *The Believers' Church in Canada*, ed. J. K. Zeman and Walter Klaassen (Brantford, ON: Baptist Federation of Canada, and Winnipeg: Mennonite Central Committee, 1979), 84.

[2] Morris Ashcraft, "The Theology of Fundamentalism," *Review and Expositor* 79 (Winter 1982): 39.

[3] Martin E. Marty, *The Irony of It All: 1893-1919*, Modern American Religion, vol. 1 (Chicago: University of Chicago Press, 1986), 237.

[4] Norman F. Furniss, *The Fundamentalist Controversy, 1918-1931* (Hamden, CT: Archon Books, 1963), 15.

[5] Ernest Sandeen, "The Problem of Authority in American Fundamentalism," *Review and Expositor* 95 (Spring 1978): 211.

[6] Ernest Sandeen, *The Roots of Fundamentalism: British and American Millenarianism, 1800-1930* (Chicago: University of Chicago Press, 1970), 103.

[7] Sandeen, *Roots of Fundamentalism*, 107.

[8] J. I. Packer, *"Fundamentalism" and the Word of God* (Grand Rapids, MI: Wm. B. Eerdmans, 1958), 21; and Jerry Falwell, ed., *The Fundamentalist Phenomenon: The Resurgence of Conservative Christianity* (Garden City, NY: Doubleday, 1981), 3.

[9] James Barr, *Fundamentalism* (London: SCM Press, 1977), 36.

[10] For a popular (and hagiographical) biography, see Leslie Tarr, *Shields of Canada* (Grand Rapids, MI: Baker Book House, 1967); for a more scholarly work, see C. A. Russell, "Thomas Todhunter Shields, Canadian Fundamentalist," *Ontario History* 70 (December 1978): 263-80; reprinted in *Foundations* 24 (January 81): 15-31. Cf. David R. Elliott, "Three Faces of Baptist Fundamentalism in Canada: Aberhart, Maxwell, and Shields," chap. 12 in this volume.

[11] Carl F. H. Henry, *Evangelical Responsibility in Contemporary Theology* (Grand Rapids, MI: Wm. B. Eerdmans, 1957), 39.

[12] On a theological level, classical Puritanism expressed itself in a strong emphasis on biblical theology as a way to halt the advance of the Roman Catholic Church. This also describes the theology of Shields; he emphasized "biblical theology" as a way to halt the advance of modernism. Shields's revivalistic (i.e., pietistic) emphasis contrasts with his doctrinal (i.e., puritanistic) emphasis. J. J. Davis has criticized the revivalistic strain within the American tradition for bringing about the downfall of evangelicalism in the 1920s because it "tended to emphasize personal religious experience rather than rigorous theological reflection" (John Jefferson Davis, *Foundations of Evangelical Theology* [Grand Rapids, MI: Baker Book House, 1984], 34). In my analysis, the "downfall" of T. T. Shields came about precisely because instead of exploring the richness of a personal relationship with Christ he resorted to doctrine in the form of biblical inerrancy as his tool for combating modernism.

[13] Shields, sermon, "No Temple Therein," Rev. 21.22, 29 October 1916, Jarvis Street Baptist Church Archives, Toronto, ON (JSBCA).

[14] Shields, sermon, "Jesus Called a Child," Matt. 18.2, 13 January 1898, JSBCA.

[15] Shields, sermon, "Goodness of God," Rom. 2.4, 27 August 1899, JSBCA.

[16] Shields, sermon, "Christ's Sovereignty," 1 Cor. 15.25, 4 March 1900, JSBCA; Shields, sermon, "Jesus's Stripes," Isa. 53.5, 4 June 1899, JSBCA.

[17] Shields, sermon, "Without Christ," Eph. 2.12, 15 June 1902, JSBCA.

[18] Shields, sermon, "Take Ye Away the Stone," John 11.39, 17 March 1895, JSBCA.

[19] Alan Richardson, "The Rise of Modern Biblical Scholarship and Recent Discussion of the Authority of the Bible," in *The West from the Reformation to the Present Day*, ed. S. L. Greenslade, The Cambridge History of the Bible, vol. 3 (London: Oxford University Press, 1963), 335.

[20] Shields, sermon, "Christ Our Beloved," Cant. 1.7, 15 August 1897, JSBCA.

[21] Shields, sermon, "Fire on the Altar," Lev. 6.13, 30 April 1905, JSBCA.

[22] Shields, *Revelations of the War* (Toronto: Standard Publishing, n.d.), 82 (sermons of 1915).

[23] Shields, *Revelations of the War*, 100.

[24] Shields, *Revelations of the War*, 99.

[25] Shields, address, "What Some Baptists Are Determined to Stand For," Jude 1.3, 22 October 1922, JSBCA.

[26] Shields, sermon, "Wilt Thou Be Made Whole?" John 5.6, 1 October 1922, JSBCA.

[27] Shields, sermon, "The Second Coming of Christ" [no text], 13 February 1922, JSBCA.

[28] Shields, "The Virgin Birth," *The Gospel Witness*, 27 December 1925, 3.

[29] Shields, address delivered at Gordon College, Boston, MA, 29 March 1923, JSBCA.

[30] Shields, *The Doctrines of Grace* (Toronto: Gospel Witness, n.d.), 193 (lectures delivered in 1931).

[31] Shields, *Christ in the Old Testament* (Toronto: Gospel Witness, 1972), 13-14.

[32] Shields, *Christ in the Old Testament*, 11-12.

[33] Shields, *The Most Famous Trial in History*, 52 (printed without publication attributed), JSBCA.

[34] Shields, *Christ in the Old Testament*, 4.

[35] Shields, "Is There Any Modernism in Heaven?," *Gospel Witness*, 17 September 1925, 3.

[36] See, for instance, the 1978 "Chicago Statement on Biblical Inerrancy," *Journal of the Evangelical Theological Society* 21 (December 1978): 289-96; reprinted in J. I. Packer, *God Has Spoken*, rev. ed. (London: Hodder and Stoughton, 1979), 139-55.

[37] Shields, *Most Famous Trial*, 50.

[38] Shields, "The Cross and Its Critics" (an address delivered at the North American Pre-Convention Conference, Des Moines, IA, 21 June 1921) in *Baptist Doctrines* (Toronto: Standard Publishing, 1921), 83-84.

[39] Shields, *The Oxford Group Movement Analyzed* (Toronto: Gospel Witness, 1933). Cf. Shields, "The Finality of Christ," (an address to the British Isles Regional Conference of the International Council of Christian Churches, Edinburgh, [25 July 1952]), 5-6.

[40] Shields, "The Necessity of Declaring War on Modernism" (an address to the Baptist Fundamental League of Greater New York, Calvary Baptist Church, New York [12 April 1923]), 2. Cf. Mark Noll, *Between Faith and Criticism* (Grand Rapids, MI: Baker Book House, 1991), 165: "In the past, however, evangelical scholars have not entirely broken free form a docetic approach to Scripture…which treats the Bible as a magical book largely unrelated to the normal worship of the natural world."

[41] Shields, *Christ in the Old Testament*, 18-19.

[42] Shields, sermon, "Abraham Believed God," Rom. 4.3, 13 August 1922, JSBCA; Shields, sermon, "The Most Excellent Knowledge," 18 September 1930, reprinted *Gospel Witness*, 10 September 1987, 9.

[43] Marty, *Irony of It All*, 3.

[44] John Dozois, "Dr. Thomas Todhunter Shields (1873-1955) in the Stream of Fundamentalism" (BD thesis, McMaster Divinity College, Hamilton, ON, 1963), 128.

[45] Coined by William Chillingsworth (1602-44) as a defence of the rights of reason to investigate doctrinal matters in opposition to Roman Catholic ecclesiasticism.

[46] Otto Weber, *Foundations of Dogmatics* (Grand Rapids,MI: Wm. B. Eerdmans, 1981), 1:183.

[47] T. F. Torrance, *Reality and Evangelical Theology* (Philadelphia: Westminster Press, 1982), 16.

[48] Torrance, *Reality and Evangelical Theology*, 17.

[49] Torrance, *Reality and Evangelical Theology*, 18.

[50] Torrance, *Reality and Evangelical Theology*, 19.

[51] Jacques Ellul, *The Meaning of the City* (Grand Rapids, MI: Wm. B. Eerdmans, 1970), 130.

Chapter 14

D. R. Sharpe and A. A. Shaw:
Progressive Social Christianity
in Western Canada

J. Brian Scott

The formation of the Baptist Convention of Western Canada in 1907 ushered in a new era of Baptist cooperation and involvement in the domain of social service and social reform. The next annual meeting, at which it renamed itself "Baptist Union of Western Canada" (BUWC), might accurately serve as a beginning point from which to explore a Baptist response to the "social crisis" around the turn of the present century. Among the many administrators, organizers, pastors, and activists who played prominent roles in the fledgling organization, a large number brought with them a social awareness and a social conscience developed under the tutelage of Walter Rauschenbusch, the acclaimed American "Prophet of Social Christianity."

Social Christianity refers to the type of social and religious thought that borrowed heavily from a Ritschlian worldview as introduced to North America by Horace Bushnell and best exemplified in the writings of Walter Rauschenbusch and Shailer Mathews. This chapter uses the currently accepted terminology for this phenomenon in North American religious history. Social Christianity is defined as the concerted response of Canadian and American Protestant churches and individuals to the social crisis of the last two decades of the 19th century and the first three decades of the 20th century. This response "involved a criticism of conventional Protestantism, a progressive theology and a social philosophy, and an active program of propagandism and reform."[1] It profoundly influenced liberal theological education, ethnic and city mission endeavours, reform politics, and, to a lesser degree, medical services, research, and liberal arts education.

"Liberal" means a "point of view...which denotes both a certain generosity or charitableness toward divergent opinion and a desire for intellectual 'liberty'" and which places "a strong emphasis on ethical preaching and moral education...[in accordance] with the liberal view" of human nature.[2] The term "evangelical" refers to that impulse within Canadian and American Protantism that responds to the necessity to carry the Christian message of spiritual and social salvation to people without regard to social or racial status. In North American Social Christianity, it also refers to the reliance for spiritual and social guidance upon the ethical and social teachings of Jesus. Social Gospel, that peculiar episode within the larger history of Canadian and American Social Christianity, is more specifically defined as a gospel or code of ethics "resting on the premise that Christianity [is] a social religion, concerned with the quality of human relations on this earth" and is "a call for men to find the meaning of their lives in seeking to realize the Kingdom of God in the very fabric of society."[3]

The Rauschenbusch Influence

D. R. Sharpe and A. A. Shaw were two of the more prominent Rochester Theological Seminary graduates serving in western Canada during the first quarter of the 20th century. Along with J. Austin Huntley, H. R. McGill, H. F. Waring, M. L. Orchard, and others, they ministered in a variety of social service roles. Sharpe became for many western Baptists the social conscience of the BUWC. His further contribution to American Social Gospel initiatives has been the subject of American Baptist historiography. Shaw also contributed to Social Gospel initiatives in both Canada and the United States. An analysis of several lectures and addresses by these two Rauschenbusch-trained pastors will provide a model of western Baptist social Christianity as well as identify the western Baptist response to, and awareness of, the social crisis of the period.[4]

D. R. Sharpe was born in Pembroke, New Brunswick, and educated at the University of New Brunswick. He continued his studies at Rochester Theological Seminary and pursued post-graduate courses at the University of Chicago. While at Rochester, he was the student secretary of Walter Rauschenbusch.[5] His career was marked by a commitment to social reform within the denomination and outside the boundaries of church agencies.

Ordained by the United Baptist Convention of the Maritimes in 1908, he moved west to pastor Baptist churches in Edmonton, Calgary, and Moose Jaw. From serving First Baptist, Moose Jaw, Sharpe was appointed superintendent of the Baptist churches in Saskatchewan. He was active in the labour movement during the years 1912 to 1925 and was a prominent leader in interdenominational and civic movements while serving also as the chairman of the Sunday School Board of the BUWC and Sunday School superintendent for the Saskatchewan Convention. He left western Canada in 1925 and began an illustrious career in Baptist, community, and ecumenical work in Cleveland, Ohio. He wrote the official biography of

Walter Rauschenbusch and three other books: *The Light of Liberty*, *The Triumph of Religious Liberty*, and *The Call to Christian Action*.[6]

J. Austin Huntley was born in Nova Scotia in 1876 and educated at Horton Academy and Acadia University, graduating with a BA in 1900. After training at Rochester Theological Seminary, where he studied under Rauschenbusch, he pastored First Baptist Church in Brooklyn, New York, before coming to First Baptist Church in Calgary, Alberta, from 1915 to 1918. Later pastorates included churches in New York, New Brunswick, and Hamilton, Ontario. While at First Baptist, Calgary, Huntley became active in Baptist Union social service and social advocacy, particularly in the Inter-church Forward Movement.[7]

H. R. McGill, another student of Rauschenbusch, pastored Strathcona Baptist, Edmonton, from 1912-1917. While there, he was the leading force in the establishment of a Christian Education Centre. Resigning from the Baptist ministry, McGill served a Presbyterian church in Kamloops, British Columbia, and later Marpole United Church in Vancouver, British Columbia. Although McGill was affiliated with the BUWC for only five years, he participated actively in its social service activities.[8]

A. A. Shaw was yet another Rauschenbusch-trained pastor who left his social service imprint upon the BUWC. Educated at Acadia University and Rochester Theological Seminary, he pastored Baptist churches in Nova Scotia, Manitoba, Massachusetts, New York, and Ohio. While at First Baptist, Winnipeg, Shaw took an active part in the Baptist Union's Social Service Committee activity; and his address to the assembly in 1908 was a clarion call to social action. He promoted the social message of his mentor Rauschenbusch as a pastor and activist and later as the president of Denison University, Granville, Ohio.[9] Shaw, McGill, Huntley, and Sharpe are representative in type and calibre of the Rochester graduates who served at various times in western Canada.

A. A. Shaw: The Social Ministry of the Church

A. A. Shaw, a Rauschenbusch-trained pastor, can be given a great deal of credit for raising the "social consciousness" of western Baptists. His series of addresses to the BUWC in November of 1908 urged western Baptists to vigorous moral and social action. In the three lectures, he identified with "a growing conviction in the hearts of the leaders of Christian thought and life, that the Church has a definite social ministry to perform, and that it has too largely failed to perform that ministry."[10]

In his first address, Shaw identifies five areas of concern: the industrial crisis; corruption in public life; social vices; the plight of new immigrants; and the challenge of the city. Responding to the industrial crisis, he provides a searing critique of capitalism's (and the Church's) neglect of the working poor and the unemployed:

> I think, for instance,...of the two great warring industrial classes; the one, great in numbers and in power of productive labor, the other, few in numbers but great in influence...in open conflict, now working in sullen distrust, never nearer together than a state of armed neutrality. I think of our immense resources, of our vast accumulation of capital, and at the same time of the great army of the poor and of the able bodies unemployed. I think of the terrible loss of human life through the greed of great corporations who are unwilling to pay the necessary price of human safety. I think of the lightning rate in the increase of corporate wealth and the snail like pace in the improvement of the lot of the 99 per cent of those who produce that wealth. I become aware of the comparatively small number of trades union men in our churches and of the increasing feeling on their part that their interests do not have a due share of the thought and the sympathy of the church.

The Church, in his view, has chosen also to ignore political corruption, social vices, and the immigrant "problem." In regard to the latter, he calls upon the Baptists to give the new immigrants "a more just and adequate idea of the church as we know it" (118).

The city, in turn, confronts the Church with the challenge to create and implement a program to combat the social evils that flourish in the rapidly expanding urban areas. He calls attention to those individuals or groups that are "as much in love with the person and the purpose of Jesus Christ as we are, [but] who no longer associate themselves with the church because they believe that they can realize His ideals outside the church." (120). He points out how easy it is to criticize the remedies proposed by "the socialist agitator" but admonishes Baptists: "the church that shares Christ's spirit and Christ's passion will [not] fail of brotherly kindness and social ministry." Jesus enunciated the "Kingdom of God" in terms that those around him understood; now Canada's Baptists must answer the question: "What signs are you showing of the Kingdom's approach?" (121).

The Church, however, seems indifferent and unwilling to act in a prophetic manner. The underlying problem is that

> the church [has] turned its back upon the real facts of life.... Thirty years ago she turned her back upon the prophets of a new science,... and the result was that she lost the leadership of thought among intelligent men. Today she turns her back in precisely the same way upon the new scholarship which devotes itself to the investigation of religion...and the result is that...intelligent men prefer to do their own thinking upon religion without any guidance from the church. But worse than all, she has lost the knowledge of her own mission (122).

"The only and the adequate response is to live the life and do the works Christ expects of us... His call must be immediately obeyed" (123).

Shaw's second address is directed toward the Church's responsibility to conquer the hostility and indifference that it confronts in society in order to realize "Christ's vision of a Kingdom of Righteousness, Truth and Love" (124). He outlines a plan which would enable the Church to reclaim its former role of reformer of man and society. He concedes that the Church's primary function is the regeneration of human character but insists she must go further and realize a greater aim, that of organizing and directing the regenerated life for social betterment.

The first duty of the Church is "to see the actual" (124). "It is easy to see only what we wish to see, and to view the unlovely through the rosy glasses of a superficial optimism", to be blinded by self-interest or comfortable living; "but to be Christian in any true sense is to see with the eyes of Christ; and that means to see things as they are, and to look behind the facts that produce them." The second duty is social repentance, "to confess the social sins with which [one] is inevitably connected and to repent of them." The third duty calls for a vision of Christ's ideal: Christ won individuals in order to establish his Kingdom. In the words of Shailer Mathews: "The gospel of the Risen Christ is also the gospel of regenerate men building the eternal life into a fraternity that must some day include all social relations" (125).

Shaw's blueprint to heroically and deliberately achieve Christ's social ideal is for the Church to become a Kingdom of God in miniature. "All of the church's activities and the lives of its members [must be] in harmony with the ethics of Christ." This means that the church must "see to it that none of its members derives revenue from any property that is a source of vice and social misery" and that "the church manifests the spirit of love among its members", removing "all distinctions and barriers between its members until they become a true Christian brotherhood" (126). To this end, the pulpit must become a "centre of social evangelism;" and social regeneration—e.g., following Rauschenbusch, slum renovation, play-grounds, and old age pensions—must be a common pulpit topic (127).

It is not enough, Shaw asserts, for pastors to attack social abuses; they must attempt to show the relation of the gospel's truth to the causes of social misery. He advocates a campaign of education in all departments of the church which would constantly emphasize that the gospel of Christ is to be directly applied to all phases of human life (128). There must also be an outlet for the individual's social energies:

> The church should keep a wise and regulative hand on all the social activities of its members. It should lead the new life along well defined and carefully considered channels.... Every church in a city or town should have a life saving station right in the place where the wreckage multiplies. Then she must have a care for the diseased body, must relieve the hungry, clothe the naked, aid the out of work, in all ways to seek to remedy the results of wrongs.... There must be

set on foot influences to improve the public health, to improve the
wage-earner's lot, to improve home conditions, to supply uplifting
recreations, to shut off the cause of crime (128).

Shaw's third address emphasized the cross of Christ as the focal point
for a social dynamic in Christian social evangelism. In a passionate plea for
Christian sacrifice in the arena of social service, he calls for a new
dedication to the Great Commission:

> We have looked on the heroism of the slum worker, of the home
> missionary, of the apostle to the jungle tribes of Africa or to the
> cannibals of the South Seas with an easy complacency, as though that
> were a peculiar brand of consecration not to be expected of the
> Church as a whole. But it is the sheerest self deception to think for
> a moment that Christ can be satisfied or the work of the Church
> accomplished with anything less than the absolute and complete
> surrender of our lives on the altar of sacrifice (133).

Shaw's comprehensive challenge to the assembled delegates in
Vancouver in the inaugural year of the BUWC serves as a symbolic "call
to arms" for a Baptist initiative against social vices, particularly that of
intemperance. The importance of his series of lectures was not immediately
apparent, but the substance of his critique would be an irritant in Western
Baptist endeavour for years to come. The call to action would be repeated
by other social Christians of the period; but none would phrase it in such
powerful, eloquent, and passionate language as had A. A. Shaw.

D. R. Sharpe: Baptist Social Reform for the 1920s

D. R. Sharpe, the superintendent for the Baptist Convention of
Saskatchewan, focused his report to the annual meeting of Saskatchewan
Baptist churches in 1920 on the social mission of the Christian Church.
Sharpe, also Rauschenbusch-trained and the Baptist Union's most tireless
social activist, laid out in crystal clear terms the overwhelming urgency for
a far-reaching program of social initiatives among the Baptists of
Saskatchewan. In the preamble, he calls Baptists to action:

> We meet as Christians, as those convinced that the Kingdom of God
> on earth is deeply involved in what we say and do in this Convention,
> and that a just and biding reordering of the entire human family is the
> chief enterprise, not only of the Church but of every individual
> Christian. From this basic conviction we waged war upon fraud and
> oppression. In the contest we felt the orientation of a spiritual glow
> because we fought for life's unalterable good.... The abolition of evils
> that menace nations, labor, capital, classes, is a sacred duty
> incumbent upon society at large and a duty which will not wait on the
> whims of false prudence or the designs of calculating and sordid
> selfishness.[11]

Pointing to Jesus as a prototype for societal change, he argues for a model of social reform based upon the militancy of Christ's response to the status quo:

> He had dared to oppose the forces of reaction, the money-changers, the ecclesiastical and commercial autocrats. He made His appeal and dedicated His life to the despised, the lowly, the outcast, and the oppressed. He refused to gain the comfort and security of one who stands by the ruling class. He dared to stand out against the "rulers in high places." He chose "men of low degree" for His companions and apostles. He was the Founder of a New Kingdom, the Herald of a New Day and the Champion of a New Order—in which justice would supplant greed, brotherhood displace class privilege, and love conquer selfishness (64).

Sharpe questions whether the Christian Church still follows his example and teaching:

> The answer is an array of appalling facts. A blood-stained world of famine and starvation on the one hand and colossal self-indulgence on the other, with God's human family torn and separated by international suspicion, class hatred, political partisanship and industrial conflict. Nine-tenths of the wealth of the United Kingdom is possessed by less than one-tenth of the people, and nine-tenths of the people possess only one-tenth of the wealth, a system which cannot be defended for one single moment, and for the reason that the greatest Founder of Social Institutions the world has ever seen laid it down two thousand years ago, "Thou shalt love thy neighbor as thyself" (64).

Sharpe moves from lament to outline the future task of the Church if it is to become a relevant force in post-WWI Canada: "God grant that it may not be too late before the whole church, in pulpit, pew and practice, shall...be prepared to make the sacrifices involved in acting frankly and fully upon the principles of brotherhood and of equal value of every human life" (65).

Avarice, selfishness, "mammon and grinding competition" are "strongholds of evil" that "work havoc over the broad spaces of human life." He calls for a "strenuous reaffirmation of the principles of justice, mercy and brotherhood as sovereign over every department of human life" (65). To do so the Church must accept and respond to three challenges. The first is "the challenge of intelligence," i.e., the Church must be intelligent enough to deal with social problems of great magnitude and complexity. The second is "the challenge of foreign missions."

> If we believe Christianity is adapted to the whole human race, if it can solve the perplexities, meet the needs and promote the welfare of all nations, now is the opportunity of its adherents as never before to prove this and to win their way among all peoples.... The foreign missionary is...the representative not only of the religion of Jesus

> Christ, but of international good-will; the creator not only of Christian churches, but of all international civilization; not a sectarian ecclesiastic, but an ambassador of all communions and a world statesman (66).

The third is "the challenge of character" in the preachers, physicians, and teachers sent to other nations and serving at home (66).

Sharpe proposes that the Church has a twofold duty to the world. It must promote the "great principles of Jesus" and it must "make clear that the values of the world are in human lives."

> All are entitled to a fair share of the goods of life.... The civilization that sacrifices personalities to things, or the welfare of the many to the greed of the few, is unchristian and is not worthy to live. Moreover, human welfare is achieved not by each individual, each family, each class and each nation seeking its own welfare, but in all seeking the welfare of all. The problems of society, national and international, are solved by the Golden Rule intelligently applied. They can be solved in no other way. The duty of the hour is the acceptance of the law of love as the principle of action, as individuals, families, classes, churches, nations (67).

The Church's central task in establishing the new order is not

> to create or lead political parties...to settle strikes, or to champion economic programs...to negotiate, conduct law courts or to appoint ambassadors. Its business, jointly with the family, and the school, is to produce the men and the women who with clear vision, high purpose, and trained ability, will do all of these things, and doing them will save the nation and the world (68).

Christians in their homes, their schools, their business enterprises, and their governments must employ Christian principles; they must be "men and women who will look at the world as Jesus saw it, and find their joy not in exploiting it, but in promoting its highest welfare" (68).

The pastor is the keystone of any program of home mission work; and to succeed:

> He should be more than a preacher depending mainly upon public assemblies for his opportunities and results. He should carry his message of salvation into the homes of the people, and face the careless, the scornful, the neglected, and even the hostile, with the claims and the blessings of the Gospel, and so extend his ministry, persistently and consistently, unto all the homes of his parish and into the unchurched settlements, and communities that they may be contiguous thereto.... He should be an expert "personal worker," while never losing sight of his opportunities as a preacher of the Gospel and as a minister to the social needs of the community (71).

The next year, Sharpe continued his blueprint for social reform in another address to Saskatchewan Baptists. He began in eschatological terms:

Four or five times in human history has there been such a time as this
and this is the greatest of them all. A thousand years of human history stretch out before us and we are privileged to live and make our
contribution of life and substance on the threshold of the most significant era in human history.... Thoughtful men are persuaded now as
perhaps they never were before that religion alone can conserve the
true values and promote the highest interests of society, and that
religion is an indispensable factor in the reconstruction of the world
and in the restoration of social harmony.[12]

He identifies the "Baptist heritage" as being particularly suited to the social
reconstruction and the "social fellowship of the races" (82). Recounting the
names and the contributions of such Baptist luminaries as Balthasar
Hubmaier, Alexander Carson, William Carey, Adoniram Judson, John
Bunyan, and Roger Williams, Sharpe applauds their special brand of
"Baptist independence" which allowed them to arrive at a "unanimity of
essential convictions" that set them apart from other religious individuals.
Using these revered figures as models, he calls for a new evangelism to
spread the message of the new order and the coming Kingdom (83).

Sharpe argues that although it had raised the moral tone of society, the
Church had failed to identify with the teachings of Jesus, especially in the
social sphere: "A church which is not strikingly and indisputably better than
the world cannot convince the world of sin" (84).

The Church must uncompromisingly proclaim the deadly peril of
riches. She must substitute cooperation for the absolutely and
incurably unchristian principle of competition. The dominant aim of
commerce and industry must come to be, not profits, but service. The
sacred task of government must be lifted from its present level, too
often marked by sordidness and immorality. The Church must, in
short, do in regard to the business and political immorality of our day
what she did in regard to slavery and intemperance—she must create
a new conscience (85).

Young people, especially, are ready to commit themselves to this task; and
the Baptists of Saskatchewan need to fully accept the evangelical nature of
the whole Christian gospel:

The Church has only to realize that her surrender must be complete;
that the implications of Christian discipleship must be followed to the
end; that the whole man in all his network of relations, family, civic,
economic, must be dominated by the leavening influences of the Gospel of Christ, and the divine stream, now choked and dammed, will
carry its fertilizing waters into the moral deserts of the world. T h e
secret of a mighty and irresistible evangelism is a full-orbed gospel.
The evangel must be as definitely, fervidly, aggressively personal as
ever of old. At the same time, her evangel must gather into itself that
new divine passion for fighting disease, and abolishing poverty and
crime, and saving the child life, and making cities clean and healthy

and beautiful—a passion which is, perhaps, the special gift of the
Holy Spirit of our age (85-86).

To this end, religious education must be a first consideration of the
Church. Sharpe, long-time superintendent of Sunday schools in Saskatchewan, understood the importance of religious training both in the home and
in the church:

> A better knowledge of childhood, better standards for training, a
> more adequate organization and equipment in the church school, a
> keener sense of community interests and the recognition of the
> necessity of closer cooperation of all forces serving the welfare of the
> child are the first steps to an improvement of conditions (86).

Sharpe, like Shaw, is representative of a small but influential group
of Rauschenbusch-trained pastors who brought their reformist approach to
the moral and social crisis based on the liberal evangelical ideal of the
"Kingdom of God." Their critique of the Church's performance in the
social sphere and the subsequent call to action with a suggested plan of
attack reached a large number of the Baptist Union's constituency.

Conclusion

Moral and social reform issues received a disproportionate amount of
attention in Baptist circles over the course of the first fifteen years of the
BUWC. The social service committees, boards of moral and social reform,
and the various resolution committees attempted to grapple with diverse and
complex social problems of local, regional, and international proportions.
Almost always reformist and progressive in their rhetoric, Baptist leaders
of the period were calling for the establishment of far-reaching reforms to
check the spreading tide of moral and social decay.

Using a seemingly Marxist critique of a society experiencing
disintegrating moral and social values, the various Baptist speakers,
organizers, and activists advocated a radical blueprint for societal
reformation based on a well-defined Kingdom of God ideal. Calling for the
establishment of a new social order predicated upon the principles of liberal
social democracy and located in the social teachings of Jesus of Nazareth,
some key Union Baptists, in the fashion of other Protestant denominations
in western Canada, attempted to respond constructively to the social crisis
of the first part of the 20th century.

In the minds of most western Baptists, the control or, better yet, the
total prohibition of "demon rum" would be a panacea for all social ills and
vices of the day. Gambling, political and civic corruption, vices of all
kinds, the "white slave traffic," venereal disease, and the like, all flowed
from the use and abuse of alcohol. Other social problems—unemployment,

poverty, atrocious working conditions, inadequate housing, and militarism, among others—although of grave concern, were relegated to a lesser status behind the alcohol problem.

The sermons, lectures, and addresses so prominently displayed in the BUWC yearbooks reflected a comprehension of the much wider societal malaise. With a pronounced emphasis upon national and international programs for social and moral reform and a familiarity with the important relevant literature of the period, Shaw and Sharpe spoke the language of American social Christianity. Trained by the leading Social Gospel figure in America, Walter Rauschenbusch, they articulated liberal evangelical solutions to society's ills. Their optimistic message was that an immanent deity, acting at a particular moment in history through the words and deeds of Christian men and women, would finally usher in the long-awaited "Kingdom of God" in a very real and practical manner on earth.

A. A. Shaw and D. R. Sharpe, with H. F. Waring, J. Austin Huntley, H. R. McGill, and M. L. Orchard, Rauschenbusch-trained and -motivated pastors and activists throughout western Canada, saw themselves and the Baptist Union as catalysts for the realization of the Kingdom. So they threw their idealism and energy into the work of the many social service and social reform committees and boards of the BUWC and its member conventions. Though the task remains incomplete, their vision remains to challenge Baptists on the threshold of the 21st century.

Notes

[1] Charles Howard Hopkins, *The Rise of the Social Gospel in American Protestantism: 1895-1915* (New Haven, CT: Yale University Press, 1940, 1967), 3.

[2] Sydney E. Ahlstrom, *A Religious History of the American People* (New Haven, CT: Yale University Press, 1972), 779.

[3] Richard Allen, "The Social Gospel and the Reform Tradition in Canada, 1890-1928," *The Canadian Historical Review* 69 (December 1968): 381-82.

[4] For further discussion of Canadian Social Christianity, see Phyllis D. Airhart, "The Eclipse of Revivalist Spirituality: The Transformation of Canadian Methodist Piety, 1884-1925" (PhD diss., University of Chicago, 1985); Richard Allen, *The Social Passion: Religion and Social Reform in Canada, 1914-1928* (Toronto: University of Toronto Press, 1971); Alan Artibise, *Winnipeg: A Social History of Urban Growth, 1874-1914* (Montreal: McGill-Queens University Press, 1975); Stewart Crysdale, *The Industrial Struggle and the Protestant Churches in Canada* (Toronto: Ryerson Press, 1967); Brian J. Fraser, *The Social Uplifters: Presbyterian Progressives and the Social Gospel in Canada, 1875-1915* (Waterloo, ON: Wilfrid Laurier University Press, 1988); Michael Horn, *The League for Social Reconstruction: Intellectual Origins of the Democratic Left in Canada* (Toronto: University of Toronto Press, 1980); J. A. Irving, *The Social Credit Movement in Alberta* (Toronto: University of Toronto Press, 1959); S. M. Lipsett, *Agrarian Socialism: The C.C.F. in Saskatchewan* (Berkeley, CA: University of California Press, 1950); W. L. Morton, *The Progressive Party in Canada* (Toronto: University of Toronto Press, 1950); Edward Pulkar, *We Stand on Their Shoulders: The Growth of Social Concern in Canadian*

Anglicanism (Toronto: Anglican Book Centre, 1986); J. Brian Scott, "'Responding to the Social Crisis': The Baptist Union of Western Canada and Social Christianity, 1908-1922" (PhD diss., University of Ottawa, 1988); and Margaret Van Die, "Nathaniel Burwash: A Study in Revivalism and Canadian Culture, 1839-1918" (PhD diss., University of Western Ontario, London, 1987).

[5] For an introduction to Rauschenbusch at Rochester, see Robert T. Handy, *The Social Gospel in America, 1870-1920: Gladden, Ely, and Rauschenbusch* (New York: Oxford University Press, 1966), 252-63. Also, Ahlstrom, *RHAP*, 800-802; Kenneth Cauthen, *The Impact of American Religious Liberalism* (New York: Harper and Row, 1962), 105-107; Martin Marty, *Righteous Empire: The Protestant Experience in America* (New York: Dial Press, 1970), 204-14; and Ronald C. White, Jr., and Charles Howard Hopkins, eds., *The Social Gospel* (Philadelphia: Temple University Press, 1976), 36-48.

[6] "Dr. Sharpe, A Biography" (manuscript in Canadian Baptist Archives, McMaster Divinity College, Hamilton, ON); W. J. N. Stephen, *Souvenirs of the Fiftieth Anniversary, 1883-1933: A History of First Baptist Church, Moose Jaw* (Moose Jaw, SK: First Baptist Church, 1933), 8-10; *Who's Who in America*, vol. 32 (1962-63), 2822; and C. C. McLaurin, *Pioneering in Western Canada* (Calgary, AB: by the author, 1939), 323.

[7] *Hamilton Spectator*, 4 April 1936; *Canadian Baptist*, 9 April 1936; Lucy Lowe Bagnell, *At the Sixtieth Milestone: The Story of First Baptist Church, Calgary, Alberta* (Calgary, AB: Jubilee Committee, First Baptist Church, 1949), 25-26; and McLaurin, *Pioneering*, 198-99.

[8] *Strathcona Baptist Church Story: Seventy-Five Years* (Edmonton, AB: Strathcona Baptist Church, 1970), 13-14.

[9] *First Baptist Church, Winnipeg: Fiftieth Anniversary, 1875-1925* (Winnipeg, MB: First Baptist Church, 1925), 12; McLaurin, *Pioneering*, 182; and A. A. Shaw biographical file, CBA.

[10] A. A. Shaw, "The Social Ministry of the Church: 1. The Challenge of the Social Need; 2. The Quest; 3. The Altar Fire," BUWC, *Year Book* (1908), 117. To alleviate extensive footnoting, the page numbers for the numerous quotations from Shaw's three addresses are indicated parenthetically in the text.

[11] BUWC, *Year Book* (1920), 64. Subsequently, the location of quotations from this report are identified in parentheses in the text.

[12] "To the Baptists of Saskatchewan: A Statement and A Challenge," BUWC, *Year Book* (1921), 81. Page numbers for this address appear in parentheses in the text.

Index